Mobility and Employment
in Urban Southeast Asia

Date Due

About the Book and Authors

Although the literature on rapid urbanization in the Third World is considerable, the role of intermediate-sized cities in this process is not well documented. In this comparative study, the contributors examine urbanization and development in five intermediate-sized cities in Indonesia and the Philippines. Their focus on population movements (both permanent and temporary) and patterns of employment illuminates how the complex relationships between the two phenomena influence the growth of cities. Some of the specific variables analyzed include characteristics, problems, and perceptions of migrants, nonmigrants, and circulators; the role of the formal and informal sectors; labor creation; and the alleviation of poverty.

Michael A. Costello is deputy director of the Research Institute of Mindanao Culture, Xavier University, Cagayan de Oro City, the Philippines. **Thomas R. Leinbach** is professor of geography and international affairs at the University of Kentucky, where **Richard Ulack** is professor of geography. **Marilou Palabrica-Costello** is a research associate at the Research Institute of Mindanao Culture, Xavier University, where she is also a member of the sociology faculty. **Bambang Suwarno** is a member of the economics faculty at the Institute Keguruan dan Ilmu Pendidikan, Bandung, Indonesia.

Mobility and Employment in Urban Southeast Asia

Examples from Indonesia and the Philippines

Michael A. Costello,
Thomas R. Leinbach, and Richard Ulack

with Marilou Palabrica-Costello
and Bambang Suwarno

Westview Press / Boulder and London

International Studies in Migration

Copyright © 1987 by Westview Press, Inc.

Published in 1987 in the United States of America by Westview Press, Inc.; Frederick A. Praeger, Publisher; 5500 Central Avenue, Boulder, Colorado 80301

Library of Congress Cataloging-in-Publication Data
Mobility and employment in urban Southeast Asia.
   (International studies in migration)
   Bibliography: p.
   Includes index.
   1. Rural-urban migration—Indonesia—Case studies.
2. Rural-urban migration—Philippines—Case studies.
3. Labor supply—Indonesia—Case studies.   4. Labor
supply—Philippines—Case studies.   5. Urbanization—
Indonesia—Case studies.   6. Urbanization—Philippines—
Case studies.   I. Costello, Michael A.   II. Leinbach,
Thomas R., 1941–   .   III. Ulack, Richard, 1942–
IV. Series.
HB2107.M62   1987   307.2   87-10649
ISBN 0-8133-7352-2

Composition for this book originated with conversion of the authors' word-processor disks.
This book was produced without formal editing by the publisher.

Printed and bound in the United States of America

Contents

Figures and Tables

Foreword

For the past four decades, unbridled expansion and growth of primate and capital cities in Southeast Asia have preoccupied the attention of policy-makers and researchers alike. Although these cities have witnessed unprecedented prosperity, acute social and administrative problems associated with the attendant highly skewed distribution of incomes, deteriorating urban services, and limited productive employment have called into question the wisdom of continued growth. Alternative regional and urban development strategies must be examined.

This study represents a new generation of inquiry that attempts to gain a better understanding of smaller urban places in the remote and frontier regions in Southeast Asia. A set of intriguing hypotheses attempting to unravel the complicated relationships between population movements and employment opportunities as they relate to the growth of certain urban places and the rural hinterland have been posited. The study is aimed at illuminating the processes of urbanization and development in North Sumatra Province of Indonesia and the Central Visayas and Northern Mindanao regions of the Philippines. The roles of the informal sector, labor creation, and poverty alleviation are some of the subjects brought into relief in the investigation. Empirical findings of the five-city study—Medan, Pematang Siantar, and Tebing Tinggi in Indonesia, and Cebu and Cagayan de Oro in the Philippines—are a major contribution to the literature of urbanization in Southeast Asia and to urban policy formulation in the two countries.

One of the strengths of this project lies in its carefully designed comparative methodology and the richness of data yielded by the questionnaires. To my understanding, only the salient results are reported in this volume. Comparative research across nations and cultures is an invaluable but highly complex undertaking. This project entailing the cooperation of researchers and administrators of four universities in Southeast Asia and those of the University of Kentucky was indeed challenging and demanding from every point of view. It is a fine example of comparative research at the highest level of international collaboration and good will. The researchers are to be congratulated for initiating and completing a joint research enterprise that will be remembered not only for its bountiful findings but for the manner in which the researchers worked together toward their common objectives.

At a more personal level, I find it a great satisfaction to see this project completed and appearing in printed form. While on the staff of the International Development Research Centre in Ottawa, I had the singular fortune of being associated with the project from beginning to end. I was much impressed with the professionalism shown by all researchers toward their project, an important factor that greatly aided my work in the administration of the research grant to the two universities in Indonesia and the Philippines. In my field visits to the study areas in 1983, I was struck by the thoroughness with which the field surveys were being planned and the questionnaires designed and perfected. In all, I feel privileged in having played a small part in facilitating this study.

This volume appears at a time when we are not a great deal wiser about intermediate and small cities in Asia, in particular about their bridging roles between rural development and the growth of large cities. While we are yet to understand more fully the links between urbanization and the growth of varying-sized cities, it is hoped that this study will advance our understanding of regional development and policy-making in relation to urbanization in Asia.

Yue-man Yeung
The Chinese University of Hong Kong

Acknowledgments

This monograph reflects our combined interests in population issues and development questions within the Southeast Asian region and is in many ways a product of our research experience over the last fifteen years in Indonesia and the Philippines. We also feel that a work such as this reflects the nature and quality of our graduate training in geography at the Pennsylvania State University, and in sociology at the University of Chicago and the University of Kentucky. We wish to record our appreciation to advisors and faculty at those institutions.

Debts of gratitude for a comparative work such as this are indeed too numerous to enable us to acknowledge in the limited space available the many individuals who shared ideas, provided information, and offered encouragement or other support. We do wish to record, however, our gratitude to several sources. In Indonesia, permission to carry out the research was provided by the Indonesian Institute of Sciences (LIPI) and at the provincial level by the office of the Governor of North Sumatra. We are grateful to the many officials in the urban areas of Medan, Pematang Siantar, and Tebing Tinggi who assisted us. Special thanks go to Ir. Karnold Pohan, the manager of the Medan Urban Development Project.

Assistance for this research was also provided by the faculty and students at the University of North Sumatra, particularly Dean O. K. Harmaini of the Faculty of Economics, Ir. Meneth Ginting of the Faculty of Agriculture, Robinson Tarigan of the Economic Research Institute, and field supervisors Yasona Sidauruk, Iskandar Syarief, Friston Siregar, Haida Yasin, Arnita Zainuddin, and Adja Syafinat, all of whom are faculty members in agriculture or economics. In addition, appreciation is extended for support provided by Rector M. N. Somantri and Institut Keguruan dan Ilmu Pendidikan (IKIP), Bandung.

In metropolitan Cebu special thanks go to Fr. Theodore Murnane of the Office of Research at the University of San Carlos. Also at the University of San Carlos Fr. Wilhelm Flieger of the Office of Population Studies and Fr. Herman van Engelen of the Water Resources Center provided considerable support. Thanks must also go to the regional office of the National Economic Development Authority for generously allowing use of air photos which greatly facilitated detailed mapping of the survey areas in metropolitan Cebu.

The field supervisors for the Cebu portion of the study were Nat Anzano, Bernie Canizares, and Gina Poloyapoy, and the secretary was Maphlinda Oyangoren. Without the hard work of these individuals and the more than twenty interviewers the study could not of course have been carried out.

In Cagayan de Oro the data were collected under the auspices of the Research Institute for Mindanao Culture, Xavier University. We would especially like to thank Rev. Francis C. Madigan, S.J., Director of the Institute, for his cooperation and encouragement. Special thanks also go to Marilou Tabor, Magadalena Cabaraban, Vickie Regidor, Nora Langajed, and Regina Estoquia for their help in carrying out the project. Finally, without the generous support and assistance of various officials in both Cebu and Cagayan de Oro, this research could not have been carried out.

We wish also to gratefully acknowledge the generous financial support provided for our project by the National Geographic Society, National Science Foundation (INT-8203890-A-B), and the International Development Research Centre (3-P-82-0038-02). In addition, Professor Leinbach gratefully acknowledges assistance by the Department of Geography and the Centre for Advanced Studies at the National University of Singapore during a Fulbright-Hays Research Award period in 1985–86. Manuscript preparation was capably handled by Wendy Schloss, Jymemia Hamilton, and Sylvia Henderson in the Department of Geography at the University of Kentucky. Special thanks go to Gyula Pauer, director of the Cartographic Laboratory at the University of Kentucky for his map designs and cartographic work.

All of the people and organizations cited above should of course be absolved of any responsibility for the interpretations and conclusions that follow.

Our hope is that in some small way this monograph will be useful to academics, planners, and policy-makers in Indonesia and the Philippines as well as throughout the Southeast Asian region by providing information and new insights on migration to and employment in the intermediate-sized city. In the last analysis, works such as this are often most useful for the new research questions which they pose, thus giving direction to future investigations. If our interpretations and related questions do indeed provoke new inquiry our considerable efforts in carrying out this study will have been worthwhile.

Michael A. Costello
Thomas R. Leinbach
Richard Ulack

1

Introduction

It has been recognized for some time that rapid urban growth in Southeast Asia as well as elsewhere in the Third World poses a major threat to the achievement of social and economic goals. Recent evidence suggests that the problems of urban development and management in the future are likely to increase considerably from the present situation as cities continue to grow (Linn, 1983). The problems are compounded when we recognize that rural populations are also increasing and that poverty levels are high in both rural and urban areas. As a result many nations have initiated efforts to control population growth. However, until recently many governments have failed to give adequate attention to the importance of the urbanization process in national development (Friedmann, 1973). The stimulus which has provoked action is the revelation that the critical problems of cities reflect the even more serious problems in rural areas. Further it is also now accepted that corrective strategies must recognize the close interrelationship between rural and urban growth so that efforts to solve the problems of one do not lead to exacerbation of the difficulties of the other (Goldstein, 1978; Todaro and Stilkind, 1981).

Urbanization issues in national development have been the focus of considerable study. A large amount of literature has developed from the investigations of levels and rates of urbanization, components of urban growth, and the problem of urban primacy where overly rapid growth in massive metropolitan areas, for example Jakarta and Manila, has resulted in a number of associated problems such as those related to service provision, congestion, and pollution. Given the concentration of facilities and investments in these cities various corrective strategies have emerged. For example, decentralization policies and growth center strategies have emerged which aim at reducing regional disparities and developing resource frontier regions (Lo and Salih, 1978). These efforts, however, have been shown to have considerable limitations and the feeling, on the part of some, is that urban-based investment strategies frequently serve only as more efficient devices for channeling wealth to larger urban centers. Derived in part from these insights, new ideas have been marshalled in an attempt to provide successful intervention measures. The most noteworthy of these are the notions of 'agropolitan development' (Friedmann and Douglass, 1978; Friedmann, 1985), which advocates growth by embedding the key elements of urbanism in dense rural areas, and 'diffuse urbanization' (Hackenberg, 1980), where the productivity mechanism is assigned to rural service centers which are capable of facilitating industrial growth in rural areas.

Within Southeast Asia the rapid but parallel growth of both rural and urban populations has prevented the attainment of a significant level of urbanization. But a small number of cities have attained substantial size and economic diversity. For example, in the southern Mindanao region of the Philippines there has occurred a distortion in the emerging urban hierarchy as manifested by "size class jumping." A variant of the diffuse urbanization theme may be working here where the distribution of urban services to rural populations may take place from a small number of large cities by relying on modern transport and communications to bypass the need for intervening lower-order urban places (Hackenberg, 1983).

In addition to these aspects of urbanization research, two other related and intertwined problems have received attention. While natural increase is acknowledged as the major contributor to the growth of most Third World cities, rural to urban migration remains as a considerable force as well. Indeed, in some cases net migration has surpassed natural increase as the primary growth component (Renaud, 1981). Along with the consideration of migration, there has also been a growing interest in and recognition of the importance of temporary movements, or circulation, to the city. Recent research on these topics have ranged from empirical migration and circulation studies to the advancement of conceptual approaches to rural-urban mobility and the migrant's decision processes (e.g., Pryor, 1979; De Jong and Gardner, eds., 1981; Prothero and Chapman, 1985). Coupled with these has been the evolution of writings on 'urban dualism' which refers to the existence of a limited 'formal sector' represented by industry and western style commerce alongside an 'informal sector' that is composed of largely traditional oc-cupations, such as petty trading and other marginal activities (Geertz, 1963; McGee, 1978, 1979; Santos, 1979).

While some very useful and penetrating observations have resulted from these efforts, much more research is needed which examines the interrelated aspects of these elements. In addition, while it is clear that primate and very large cities account for a major portion of the urban population and represent severe problems, there is a growing feeling that empirical research has perhaps overemphasized these nodes while too often the real and potential role of intermediate and small cities in the development process has been overlooked.[1] Assuming there is some validity to the 'diffuse urbanization' hypothesis, then it is imperative to begin the systematic examination of these intermediate-sized or secondary centers because future development may hinge on a viable system of settlements that intervene between the primate city and the rural village (Hackenberg, 1980).

A major reason for examining the role of the intermediate city in development is in connection with their labor creation and poverty alleviation potential. Given the imbalances in economic structure which lead to problems of labor absorption through the formal sector, the informal sector is now seen as a vital and dynamic sector which can provide opportunities for urban bound movers. Improvement in labor earnings can be effected by improving the balance between the growth of labor supply and demand. Several policy positions have emerged regarding the development of the informal sector as a strategy to alleviate urban poverty (e.g., McGee, 1978). In addition an array of policy steps can be taken at the city level to help increase the earnings of the poor. These include improvements in local administration, regulation, and taxation. Public service investment can also improve the operations of small scale enterprises (Linn, 1983). While research has, of course, recognized the important role of the informal sector, the relationships between this sector and migration and migrant characteristics as well as circulation and circulator characteristics have not been thoroughly explored and are in need of further empirical verification and elaboration.

Finally, it has been noted recently that a major void in urban research, especially in the developing countries is the paucity of comparative analyses especially in Asia (Walton, 1979; London, 1983). It has been impossible to make cross-national statements about the viability of different sized communities for promoting employment and social mobility. Clearly there is a need to know whether common patterns and structures surrounding movement and employment appear in settings whose cultural origins, economic activities, and government impress may be quite different. In addition, the effects of urban bias are much more complex than is revealed by differences in the dispersion of public expenditures (Lipton, 1976). The choice of policy instruments to solve urban problems is difficult unless all the processes and structures which may influence development are properly understood (Salih, 1982). Hopefully, the comparative framework will aid the more efficient search for solutions.

The major purpose of this research monograph is to compare and contrast the population movement and employment characteristics associated with a set of secondary cities in Southeast Asia: Indonesia's fourth largest city, Medan, and the Philippines' second largest metropolitan area, Cebu, along with the smaller cities of Pematang Siantar and Tebing Tinggi in Sumatra and the Philippine city of Cagayan de Oro. All of these cities are considered intermediate in size since their total populations fit into the range conventionally defined as secondary: between 100,000 and 2.5 million persons (Rondinelli, 1983, 48). In addition, all of the cities are important nodes in their respective regions: North Sumatra Province of Indonesia and the Central Visayas and Northern Mindanao Regions of the Philippines. Finally all of the cities have experienced steady population growth in recent years. Since research on intermediate-sized cities is so limited and because little has been accomplished in the way of comparative urban research, this research is viewed as a beginning toward building a body of knowledge about the mobility and employment characteristics and problems in such sized cities in one Third World region.

More specifically there are several basic issues and empirical questions which we seek to address in this monograph. First, how do the institutional facilities (economic, health, educational, transport) available differ among the five cities? Are there significant differences and structures involved which may relate to differences in and impact upon mobility and employment? Second, how do migrant and nonmigrant households sampled within the five cities differ in terms of age-sex contrasts, education, income, employment, house type, and possessions? Third, how do the migrant characteristics and migrant adjustment processes differ? Particular attention is given here to the year of movement, the origin of the move, age at migration, and number of moves. In addition to the basic profiles of the migrants we examine the reasons for migration and the importance of economic versus non-economic motives. Of considerable interest is the adjustment process which includes pre-move contacts with the destination, ties to origin, and status changes.

A major consideration is the employment patterns of the migrants. A detailed examination of the occupational patterns is carried out. Coupled with these we seek to learn of differences in information quality and sources, the length of job search, formal versus informal sector employment, and recent occupational changes. Throughout we compare characteristics of the job holders and their situations. Of increasing interest too in employment research is the nature and importance of secondary jobs. This issue will be examined in and compared among the study sites.

In addition, we feel that too little attention has been given to the perceptions and motivations of both migrants and nonmigrants and the decision making process in a cross cultural context. In this light we therefore examine and compare the locational preferences and perceptions of both migrant and nonmigrant household heads. Included here are residential and employment preferences and future intentions, perceptions of qualities associated with various sizes of cities and contact with the respective primate cities, Jakarta and Manila. Finally, motivational research on migration has found a value-expectancy model to have considerable utility in viewing and analyzing migration behavior (De Jong and Gardner, 1981, 13–58). The value-expectancy approach is explained and explored here as a tool which may yield further understanding of the migration decision process in differing city sizes and cultural contexts.

Along with the analysis of migrants and their characteristics, we feel that circulation behavior must also be examined since little research has considered such mobility within the context of the intermediate city. A basic goal therefore is to learn of the importance of circulation in our three largest cities (Medan, Cebu, and Cagayan de Oro) and to examine the characteristics of those identified as circulators.

While the direct concern of our analysis is the data gathered on the above topics in five specific cities, we realize the importance of planning and policy issues in general. To this end it is vital that a broader statement be provided which addresses the complex issue of the intermediate-sized city's future in the development pattern. The final chapter of the monograph will highlight some of the many policy implications which may be derived from these studies.

Such implications may in part deal with the question of feasible options for influencing pre-existing population distribution and population mobility patterns. For example, the perceptual data collected in the several cities will be of great help in assessing how members of the general public in the two national settings feel about life in differently-sized communities. In turn, these perceptions will influence the potential of such communities to attract migrants, and thus the viability of plans to establish them as truly functional centers with growth potential within the urban hierarchy (Hansen, 1979; Rondinelli, 1983).

Particular concern has been taken in the five cities to measure participation within the informal employment sector, as well as to see how these activities are related to migrant, circulator, and mobility characteristics. This information will no doubt prove invaluable for assessing government policies in this area. Some city and national-level policies in Indonesia and the Philippines have been designed to eliminate certain informal sector activities, such as scavenging and sidewalk-vending, that are seen as incompatible with the operation of a "modern" urban community. Possible detrimental effects of these policies upon the urban poor, rural-to-urban migrants, and villagers dependent upon remittances from such movers have frequently been cited but only rarely measured empirically.

Another point of relevance concerns the possible impact upon migration of an expanding transport system, both roads and vehicles (Hugo, 1981; Leinbach, 1983; Leinbach, 1986b). In a related arena possible changes in urban transport policies, such as proposals to phase out jeepneys and trishaws or pedicabs from crowded urban streets have important implications for current and potential migrants. Further knowledge of the possible impact of government mobility plans will aid greatly in evaluating the practicality of such approaches.

A final objective of the monograph is to include a review of past and current government policies toward urbanization in Indonesia and the Philippines. Of particular interest are those policies and programs which address secondary urban centers. Ultimately we deal with the specific question of cityward migration for employment purposes. Should it be encouraged and if so what forms of movement and employment might be encouraged?

A Further Review of the Literature

Our introduction has provided a general overview of the basic literature which surrounds this research. The intent here is to provide some additional background which will assist the reader in grasping the importance of and need for our own and additional work. The individual chapters will further relate relevant research to the specific topics under consideration.

As mentioned previously there is now a growing body of literature on urbanization and national development. Indeed, within the past five years at least three major treatments of this topic have appeared (Renaud, 1981; Gilbert and Gugler, 1982; Linn, 1983). In part these new treatments derive from the spatial planning concerns of Friedmann (1966; 1973). There has been, however, little emphasis in these general treatments and elsewhere on the role of small and intermediate-sized cities in development. A recent book by Rondinelli (1983) and two international symposia in Bangkok and Nagoya have served to widen exposure of the topic. Papers are beginning to emerge from the former (e.g., Banerjee and Schenk, 1984) and a published volume was produced from the latter (Mathur, 1982). Earlier important works will now also be sought out and given new interest and focus (e.g., Osborn, 1974; Ulack, 1975). The essential argument underlying these works is that secondary cities can and should make an important contribution to development. Deconcentrating urbanization, reducing regional inequities, increasing administrative capacity, reducing urban poverty, and stimulating rural economies are among the most important of these contributions (Rondinelli, 1983, 9–46).

The literature on cityward migration, with impact assessments at both the rural and urban ends, is huge and is nearly impossible and indeed inappropriate to survey here. Within Southeast Asia, the work by Pryor (1979), Sternstein (1976), and Douglass (1983), reveal good summaries of the nature and extent of the research. The topic of mobility and the urban labor market has attracted a significant amount of research. One of the best known early studies in this area is that of Todaro (1969). A recent volume perhaps portrays better than any other the most recent findings in this area of investigation (Sabot, 1982). One major finding from this work challenges the accepted view of the impact of out-migration on rural productivity and income distribution. That is, incomes of nonmigrants will not necessarily increase nor will the standard of living between the source and receiving areas of migrant labor narrow. Indeed, it is suggested that in some circumstances out-migration may perpetuate and widen existing income gaps. In addition, it is suggested that the consequences of migration may vary dramatically with the structure of the labor market within which migrants are moving. For example, high wage jobs tend to go to migrants able to finance a lengthy period of search (Sabot, 1982, 232). In addition to this work, a more recent volume focuses upon urbanization and migration including some aspects of employment within the broad Southeast Asian region (Hauser, Suits, and Ogawa, eds., 1985).

Dealing with the search for employment through migration ultimately brings us to the topic of the structure of the labor market. The conceptual distinction between 'formal' and 'informal' sectors was pointed out above and has attracted a great deal of attention from researchers. The work of the geographer, McGee (1971; 1973) and the anthropologist, Geertz (1963), in Southeast Asia pointed to this distinction as a fertile ground for research. These earliest pieces have stimulated additional efforts given the critical importance of the employment issue in development. Among these are a major study of hawkers in Southeast Asian cities (McGee and Yeung, 1977), an investigation of urban development and employment in Jakarta (Sethuraman, 1976) and an assessment of the impact of migration upon informal sector earnings in Manila and secondary cities (Koo and Smith, 1983). Nearly all of these studies have focused on the largest city in the nation chosen for study. Two major exceptions to this generalization apply to works on the trishaw or pedicab operators in Ujung Pandang, Sulawesi, Indonesia (Forbes, 1981a; 1981b) and the impact of agropolitan development on Davao City, Mindanao, Philippines (Hackenberg, 1983).

Survey Methodology

Selection of particular study sites was conditioned in part by the experiences and backgrounds of the researchers, as well as by the relative population sizes and locations of the places to be studied. Another important consideration was that the selected cities had high population growth rates during the 1970s. In four of the five study cities (Pematang Siantar being the lone exception) population growth rates were higher than national averages (Table 1.1). Indeed, population growth rates in two of our study cities, Tebing Tinggi and Cagayan de Oro, were even more rapid than those of the primate cities of each nation, Jakarta and Manila. Such high rates of population growth, of course, imply a pattern of heavy in-migration. As such, our study populations include a large share of migrants and circulators as well as nonmigrants. A final criterion for study site selection was that cities from different size categories were to be included. This strategy

Table 1.1

POPULATION GROWTH IN
INDONESIA AND THE PHILIPPINES,
1970 OR 1971 TO 1980

Place	Population 1970 or 1971	Population 1980	Percent Growth 1970 or 1971 to 1980	Avg. Annual
Indonesia	119,208,229	147,490,298	23.7	2.4
Jakarta	4,579,303	6,503,449	42.0	3.9
Medan	1,000,741	1,373,747	37.3	3.4
*Baru	122,587	147,879	20.6	2.1
*Barat	130,137	154,967	19.1	1.9
*Kota	214,579	230,609	7.5	0.8
*Timur	166,889	200,358	20.1	2.0
Deli	27,397	79,507	190.2	11.8
Sunggal	72,434	147,769	104.0	7.9
Denai	98,474	158,473	60.9	5.3
Tuntungan	16,739	27,332	63.3	5.4
Johor	50,378	73,759	46.4	4.2
Labuhun	40,258	71,929	78.7	6.7
Belawan	60,869	81,165	33.3	3.3
Pematang Siantar	129,232	150,149	16.2	1.6
Tebing Tinggi[a]	30,314	92,087	203.8	12.4
Philippines	36,684,486	48,098,460	31.1	2.7
Manila	3,966,695	5,925,804	49.0	4.0
Metro Cebu	450,417	664,679	47.6	3.9
*Cebu City	317,175	442,281	39.4	3.3
Mandaue City	54,849	105,077	91.6	6.5
Lapu-Lapu City	26,589	43,015	61.8	4.8
Consolacion	8,752	12,526	43.1	3.6
Talisay	43,052	61,780	43.5	3.6
Cagayan de Oro	128,319	227,312	77.1	5.3

*Core areas of city and the defined urban boundary in 1971.

[a]1971 and 1980 figures for Tebing Tinggi are not entirely
comparable as there was some territorial expansion during the
1970s. In this respect the Medan urban boundary also was
enlarged by seven kecamatan between the two census years.
For further details on this annexation see Leinbach (1987).

Source: Indonesian national censuses, 1971 and 1980; Philippine
national censuses, 1970 and 1980.

allowed us to compare and contrast the mobility and employment characteristics of different-sized places, ranging from smaller urban centers to cities which were ranked as the second and fourth largest within the national urban hierarchy.

The cities included in the study are Medan, Pematang Siantar, and Tebing Tinggi, all located in North Sumatra Province, Indonesia (Fig. 1.1); and metropolitan Cebu and Cagayan de Oro City, located in Cebu and Misamis Oriental Provinces, the Philippines, respectively (Fig. 1.2). Medan and Cebu are the largest of the five cities. As we define the metropolitan areas here, Medan probably included over one million persons in 1980 and Cebu's metropolitan area numbered about two-thirds of a million. The 1980 metropolitan area populations of Cagayan de Oro, Pematang Siantar, and Tebing Tinggi were approximately 120,000, 80,000, and 40,000, respectively. (Population figures given in Table 1.1 for Cagayan de Oro, Pematang Siantar, and Tebing Tinggi are for the entire political areas which include also areas that are rural in character; figures given for Medan and Cebu reflect the metropolitan population only). As explained below, we have attempted to limit our study population to the actual urban area population. Because each nation has its own definition of "urban" and because nations have widely-varying levels and scales of urbanization, it is neither possible nor necessary to arrive at a standard definition of an intermediate-sized city (Bose, 1982). As stated above, those who generalize often use the figures 100,000 to 2.5 million in population as describing the size class for such cities. Size ranges, however, may vary considerably depending upon the nation's definition of an urban area and it's absolute size.

Sampling Procedures

Upon beginning the project, a thorough reconnaissance of each of the cities was carried out (Leinbach and Suwarno in Medan, Pemantang Siantar, and Tebing Tinggi; Ulack in Cebu; and Costello and Palabrica-Costello in Cagayan de Oro). Provincial and city officials were contacted in order to obtain maps, data, reports, and other materials, and to elicit help in gaining the confidence of local leaders and residents in the selected survey areas. Field reconnaissance and analysis of the secondary materials allowed the principal investigators at each site to determine its metropolitan area boundary and also to determine those areas of each study city which were growing quickly and populated mainly by persons of lower socioeconomic status. An early decision was made to oversample such rapid growth, low income areas.

In the three Indonesian cities the areas to be surveyed were randomly selected from among those administrative units in each of the cities. In Indonesia, each of the major administrative units (provinces) is subdivided

Figure 1.1 North Sumatra Province

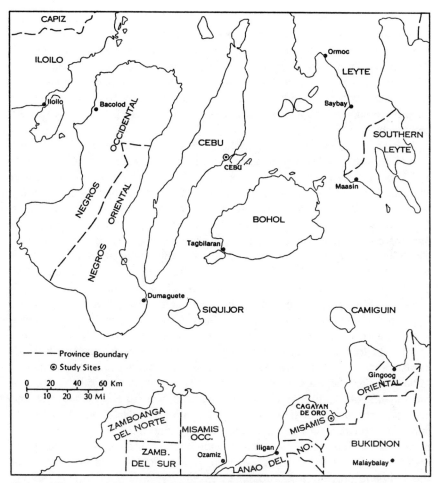

Figure 1.2 Central Visayas and Northern Mindanao

into districts (*kabupaten*) which are in turn divided into sub-districts (*kecamatan*). Each sub-district or *kecamatan* is divided into a series of individual villages called *desa* or *kelurahan,* which are the smallest administrative units in Indonesia. The first phase of the selection process was to select *desa* randomly and the second phase of the sampling operation was to select a random sample of *rukun tetangga* in each *desa*. A *rukun tetangga* is what may be thought of as a "neighborhood" and each is usually comprised of from thirty to fifty households. By law, each *desa* register contains information pertaining to all *rukun tetanggas*. It was thus possible to use this list to enumerate all such neighborhoods in each selected *desa*. Having done this, *rukun tetanggas* were then selected randomly. The third stage of the random selection process was to select individual households from the list of households secured for each of the selected neighborhoods. In cases where a dwelling unit was occupied by more than one household, the random grid procedure was utilized. That is, each household in the dwelling unit had an equal chance for selection. The number of households selected in each neighborhood was based upon the population size of the neighborhood, i.e., population-proportionate-to-size (PPS) procedures were employed.

In *Kotamadya* Medan, for example, there are 11 *kecamatan* and 116 *desa* (Fig. 1.3); similarly Pematang Siantar consists of 4 *kecamatan* and 29 *desa* and Tebing Tinggi consists of 3 *kecamatan* and 21 *desa*. In order to make the sample as representative as possible of Medan's metropolitan population, we excluded two *kecamatan*. One was rural in character and the other, Belawan, was in reality a separate, port city. From the remaining nine *kecamatan* 12 *desa*, were selected for interviewing (Table 1.2; Fig. 1.3). Neighborhoods lying within these *desa* were then selected randomly, from which 1,100 individual households were ultimately chosen for interview. Similar procedures were followed in Pematang Siantar and in Tebing Tinggi.

In the Philippines major administrative units are provinces, of which Cebu and Misamis Oriental are two. Provinces are subdivided into towns (municipalities) and cities (chartered cities), each of which are in turn subdivided into *barangays* (or villages; formerly *barrios*), the smallest administrative unit. An early task was to define the metropolitan areas for Cebu and Cagayan de Oro, both chartered cities. In the case of Cebu, that meant eliminating that part of the city that was rural in character and adding portions of contiguous chartered cities (Mandaue and Lapu-Lapu) and municipalities (Consolacion and Talisay) that were in reality a part of metropolitan Cebu (Fig. 1.4).[2] This yielded 95 (of 173) *barangays* for Cebu and 47 (of 80) in the case of Cagayan de Oro. In Cebu, the first stage of the sampling procedure was to select 12 *barangays* at random from among the 95 that comprised the urban area (Fig. 1.4). Each of the 95 *barangays* were assigned a sequence of numbers proportionate to the size of their populations; thus, the larger the *barangay*, the greater its chance for selection. The second stage of the sampling procedure was the random selection of individual households, which was carried out in the following manner. First, it was found that large scale (1:2,500 and 1:10,000) recent maps and air photos (1980) were available that provided coverage of most of the urban portion of Cebu. With the aid of three supervisors and one mapper, detailed maps were made of all structures in each of the selected *barangays*. Next, all *barangay* maps were carefully field checked to determine which structures were not dwelling units and to add those structures too new to appear on the photos. Once accomplished, all dwelling units were numbered on the maps. Using a table of random numbers, a sample of dwelling units was

13

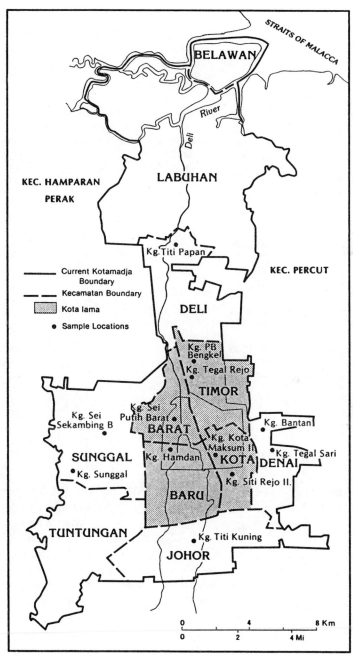

Figure 1.3   Medan Urban Area: Political Subdivisions and Interview
Locations

Table 1.2

AREAS SAMPLED[a]

Place	1980 Population	Total Desa or Barangays (number)	Desa or Barangays Sampled (number)	Households Sampled (number)
Medan	1,220,653	106	12	1,100
Baru	147,879	15	1	37
Barat	154,967	10	1	113
Kota	230,609	22	2	142
Timur	200,358	12	2	164
Deli	79,507	5	1	78
Sunggal	147,769	12	2	123
Denai	158,473	9	2	396
Tuntungan	27,332	11	0	0
Johor	73,759	10	1	37
Pematang Siantar	80,295	15	4	250
Siantar Barat	37,477	8	2	135
Siantar Utara	42,818	7	2	115
Tebing Tinggi				
Padang Hulu	36,791	8	2	150
Metro Cebu	664,679	95	12	1,000
Cebu City	442,281	49	7	747
Mandaue City	105,077	22	3	158
Lapu-Lapu City	43,015	6	1	54
Consolacion	12,526	5	0	0
Talisay	61,780	13	1	41
Cagayan de Oro	122,251	47	14	800

[a]Total city populations given here may differ from those shown in Table 1.1 due to exclusion of districts not lying within the city's metropolitan (in the case of Medan) or urban (for Pematang Siantar, Tebing Tinggi, and Cagayan de Oro) area.

Source: See Table 1.1 and Sample Survey Data.

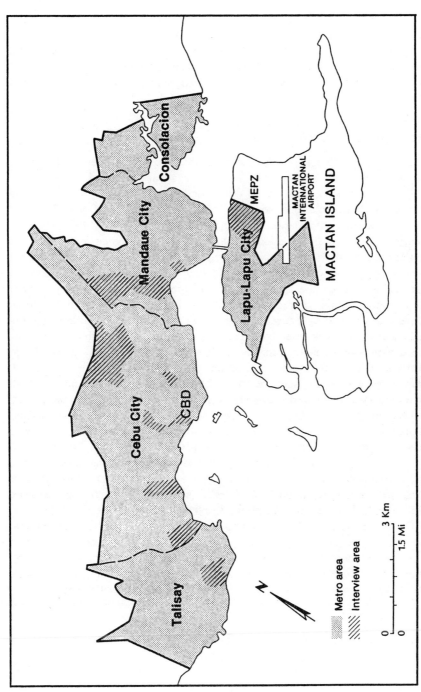

Figure 1.4 Metropolitan Cebu: Political Subdivisions and Interview Areas

then selected within each *barangay.* The number to be selected was proportionate to the *barangay's* population size. As in Indonesia, if a dwelling unit had more than one household a random selection process was used to select the household to be interviewed. A similar procedure was employed in Cagayan de Oro except that all selected *barangays* were field mapped since air photos were not available.

The Questionnaire

The primary data were gathered through the use of similar questionnaire surveys. The core instrument for these surveys was developed in September, 1982, during a joint meeting of the principal investigators in Cagayan de Oro. Each household questionnaire consisted of five sections. The first section asked for information from the head of household, while the second was directed towards the spouse. Information was gathered from the head and spouse on their migration and employment histories, as well as about their socioeconomic and demographic characteristics. Detailed data were also gathered from the spouse about all other household members, about ethnic and cultural characteristics of the household, about the material possessions owned by household members, and about commuting patterns (e.g., journey-to-work, medical facilities, and market). The third section of the questionnaire sought information from all persons fifteen years of age or older who were currently visiting (i.e., temporarily) the household. Conversely, the fourth section asked the spouse for information about all members aged fifteen and above who were temporarily away. Such temporary visitors or persons temporarily elsewhere may be classified as circular migrants. The final section of the questionnaire asked the head or spouse questions about their perceptions.[3] The findings reported in Chapters 2–6 of this monograph are based largely on the sections for the head, spouse, and perceptions. Results on circulatory behavior and the characteristics of circulators are reported on in Chapter 7 (see also Leinbach and Suwarno, 1985; Ulack, Costello, and Palabrica-Costello, 1985).

On the average, about one hour was needed to administer the questionnaire. Interviewers were carefully selected and trained from among college students or recent graduates who applied in each of the three largest cities. The University of North Sumatra (Medan), the University of San Carlos (Cebu), and Xavier University (Cagayan de Oro) provided nearly all the supervisors and interviewers used in the study. Almost every worker had had prior experience in conducting social science survey research, and all underwent an intensive training on the survey instrument and the purposes of the study.

In Medan, questionnaires were administered between December 1, 1982 and January 31, 1983 and in Pematang Siantar and Tebing Tinggi questionnaires were administered during the period from February, 1983 to March 15, 1983. In all, 1,100 households were included from Medan, 250 were completed in Pematang Siantar, and 150 were administered in Tebing Tinggi. In Cebu, 1,000 households were interviewed between June 18, 1983 and August 20, 1983 and in Cagayan de Oro 800 interviews were completed, also during 1983 (Table 1.2). All interviews were conducted in the appropriate language: Bahasa Indonesia for the northern Sumatra study sites and Visayan in Cebu and Cagayan de Oro. By and large cooperation from the respondents was excellent. For example, in Cebu there were only 26 refusals among potential respondents and in Medan there were 86. In the case of refusals, standardized procedures were invoked to select alternate households.

All questionnaires were coded at the respective field sites by trained coders. Open-ended or unstructured questions, like reasons for migration, were coded on the basis of what the respondent emphasized in his or her answer. After the coding, data were keypunched in Indonesia or, in the case of the Philippine data at the University of Kentucky, and transferred onto magnetic tape for analysis utilizing the SPSSX package. The five principal investigators spent the Summer of 1984 at the University of Kentucky where they developed the outline for this monograph and began analyzing the data.

Notes

1. The terms secondary and intermediate-sized city are used interchangeably throughout the monograph. For further information on definitions see Rondinelli (1983, 47–83), Mathur (1982), and Bose (1982).

2. Thanks are due to Fr. Wilhelm Flieger of the University of San Carlos Population Institute for providing us with a definition of the urban area of metropolitan Cebu. Similarly, Cagayan de Oro's urban area is that defined by the Research Institute for Mindanao Culture, Xavier University.

3. In the Indonesian sample, a head or spouse were administered the perception section in every household included in the sample. In the Philippines a perception section was administered in every other household in the sample. Thus there were 1,500 perception sections completed in Indonesia and 900 in the two Philippine cities. The number of heads and spouses who completed the perception section were approximately equal since a head was the respondent in every other household.

2

The Study Areas

It is our aim in this chapter to provide information about the setting and conditions which have affected the migration and employment characteristics of the five study cities. In order to accomplish this we must first discuss the national and regional contexts in which the study areas are located.

The population of both Indonesia and the Philippines, as is so for all Third World nations, is still predominantly rural. Nearly four-fifths of the Indonesian population and two-thirds of that in the Philippines now live in rural areas (Population Reference Bureau, 1985). There are striking contrasts between the rural and urban populations of these nations, not the least of which are the inequalities that exist between the city and the countryside. For example, the inhabitants of urban areas, and especially those of the very largest cities, have on average much higher incomes and educational levels. For Indonesia the most recent reliable assessment of this question has come from a World Bank study which demonstrated that the greatest increases in average monthly household consumption expenditure between 1970 and 1976 were in the urban areas, especially those of Java (World Bank, 1980). In 1970 rural consumption levels were estimated to be 60 and 83 percent of the urban levels in Java and the Outer Islands respectively; for 1976 these figures were 47 and 72 percent. More recent data, for 1980, indicate that these levels are 51 and 75 percent, respectively. Even allowing for the problem of underreported income in higher income households it is clear that central government policies have resulted in a significant reduction in regional income inequality in Indonesia. Overall distribution policies between regions have been successful. Nonetheless these data also suggest that urban-rural differences in consumption within regions are far more significant than regional differences. While urban-rural differences are less pronounced in Sumatra than in Java, it is evident that the urban areas of Indonesia continue to be characterized by considerably higher consumption levels than rural areas (World Bank, 1984). Examination of a similar time period in the Philippines also reveals a large gap between urban and rural areas. Unlike Indonesia, though, this gap seems to have narrowed somewhat. Analysis of average family expenditures reveals that in the Philippines rural expenditure levels were 50 percent of those in urban areas in 1961. In 1965 the figure was 46 percent; in 1971 it was 51 percent and in 1975, 63 percent (NEDA, 1982, 566). Still, given the large gap between rural and urban income levels in both Indonesia and the Philippines, and especially the gap that exists between rural areas and the primate cities, it is little wonder that so many have migrated from the countryside to the cities.

The existence of such inequalities is not surprising given the emphasis upon development in urban areas, and especially in the primate cities. These patterns have their origin during the Dutch colonial period in Indonesia and the Spanish and American colonial periods in the Philippines. Jakarta and Manila became the administrative capitals and the focal points of commerce, cultural activities, educational opportunities, and what little manufacturing there existed. The cities were the collecting, processing, and export points for the primary commodities produced in the peripheral rural hinterlands. Since political independence in 1947 for Indonesia and 1946 in the Philippines this situation has by and large been maintained with the two countries continuing to provide mostly primary commodities in international trade.

A recent major explanation offered for the spatial inequalities, lack of industrialization, large rural populations, and economic dependence on primary commodities that characterize Third World economies is dependency theory (Frank, 1967; Dos Santos, 1970). While there may be disagreement about the importance of this theory as an explanation for poverty in the Third World today, it is certainly true, despite recent improvements,[1] that the conditions it describes do portray the situation in Indonesia and the Philippines. The mobility and employment characteristics under discussion here can only be understood in the context of these national conditions.

The Regional Settings: Economic Characteristics

As discussed earlier Indonesia is politically divided into 26 provinces (Fig. 2.1). While the primary political subdivisions in the Philippines are also called provinces, such areas (there are 74) are much smaller than those in Indonesia. However, for census purposes the Philippine government has also divided the nation into 13 administrative regions (Fig. 2.2). Because these regions are more comparable to Indonesia's provinces in population and areal size, subsequent discussion about the regions in which the study cities are located will compare Indonesia's provinces and the Philippines' "regions."

The three Indonesian study cities are all located in North Sumatra Province. In 1980 North Sumatra had a total population of 8,360,894, or 5.7 percent of the national population. Medan, Indonesia's fourth largest

Table 2.1

DISTRIBUTION AND AVERAGE ANNUAL GROWTH RATE OF
GROSS DOMESTIC PRODUCT (PERCENT)

Sector	Indonesia		Philippines	
	1982 Distribution	1970-82 Annual Rate	1982 Distribution	1970-82 Annual Rate
Agriculture	26	3.8	22	4.8
Industry	39	10.7	36	8.0
Manufacturing[a]	(13)	(13.4)	(24)	(6.6)
Services	35	9.3	42	5.2

[a]Manufacturing is a part of the industrial sector, but its share
of GDP is shown separately because it typically is the most
dynamic part of the industrial sector. In addition to
manufacturing, the industrial sector includes mining,
construction, electricity, water, and gas.

Source: World Bank, 1984, 220-223.

city, is the provincial capital. Pematang Siantar and Tebing Tinggi are the
second and third largest urban places in this province. Both of these cities
are service centers for their sizable agricultural hinterlands. Cebu is located
in the central Visayas region. It is the regional capital and the second largest
city in the country. The city is located on the island (and province) of
Cebu. With a total land area of only slightly more than 5,000 square
kilometers, the island is relatively small. In 1980, the population of the
Central Visayas was 3,787,374, or nearly 8 percent of the national total.
Cagayan de Oro City is located on the much larger (97,880 square kilometers)
island of Mindanao. It is the capital of Misamis Oriental Province and the
largest city in the Northern Mindanao region, which comprises seven
provinces with a total population of 2,758,985, or 5.7 percent of the nation's
population. Medan, Cebu, and Cagayan de Oro are each the dominant cities
of their respective provinces and regions and are the major collecting and
processing points for the products of their rural hinterlands.

The economic structures of the two nations are typical of those found
in developing nations. Both have been classified as "lower middle-income"
by the World Bank. The sectoral distribution of their gross domestic products
is also very similar except that manufacturing is relatively more important
in the Philippines (Table 2.1). In 1982 manufacturing accounted for 24
percent of the GDP in the Philippines and only 13 percent in Indonesia.

Table 2.2

REGIONAL GROSS DOMESTIC PRODUCT
NORTH SUMATRA, CENTRAL VISAYAS, AND NORTHERN MINDANAO,
1980 (PERCENT)

Sector	North Sumatra	Central Visayas	Northern Mindanao
Agriculture	35.8	19.4	37.9
Industry	27.9	34.1	26.2
Manufacturing[a]	(7.0)	(16.1)	(14.4)
Services	35.9	46.5	35.9

[a]See note in Table 2.1.

Source: Ginting and Daroesman, 1982, 57; VIHDA, 1983, 4.

However, the manufacturing sector in Indonesia grew much more rapidly during the 1970 to 1982 period than that of the Philippines, 13.4 percent compared to only 6.6 percent.

These national figures are reflected in the regional economies of our study areas and are important to consider because they help in understanding the occupational structure and mobility characteristics of the study cities. There are some significant differences in the GDP of North Sumatra as compared to that of the two Philippine regions (Table 2.2). Although the bulk of the labor force in all three regions was employed in farming pursuits, agriculture in North Sumatra contributed a much greater share (36 percent) of the GDP because the region is well-known for its plantation crops. Estate crops accounted for about 12 percent of the total GDP of the region. Like the entire large island of which it is part, North Sumatra Province is in a sense a "resource frontier" because population densities in rural areas are still not very high and opportunities for employment are available on the oil palm and rubber estates that were begun during the Dutch colonial era. Agricultural land in estate crops accounted for about one-half of all farmland in the province, while rubber and oil palm comprised nearly one-half the estate total of 379,000 hectares in 1973.[2] North Sumatra accounted for 87 percent of the nation's area in oil palm, 46 percent of the land planted to rubber, 15 percent of the total land area in tea estates, and 13 percent of the total in cocoa. The major traditional crop was paddy rice, which accounted for two-thirds of the agricultural land area in non-estate crops. In addition to agriculture there is oil, gas, timber, and minerals and extraction of such resources have considerable impact on services, manufacturing, and trade, especially in the provincial capital, Medan, and its major port outlet, Belawan.

In both the Philippine regions, and most especially in the central Visayas, rural densities are very high affording little opportunity in agriculture. At the same time, subsistence agricultural pursuits are more commonly found than are those of a more commercial nature. For this reason the share of GDP from this sector is significantly less than in North Sumatra. The central Visayas region is more aptly described as a "lagging" region because there are so few opportunities in rural areas. Northern Mindanao is generally similar, although the agricultural potential of this region is greater, given the fact that rural population densities are lower and soil exhaustion less common. Corn is the major subsistence crop grown in both regions because the area is too hilly or too dry to yield much rice. In the central Visayas the area in corn production is about four times that in rice whereas nationally the area in rice production is about ten percent greater than that in corn. In northern Mindanao the area in corn is about one-half times as large as that in rice. Coconuts and fruits are also of some commercial importance in Northern Mindanao. The Del Monte plantation, located near Cagayan de Oro in Bukidnon Province, produces pineapples that are canned and exported to the world market. The canning factory represents the city's major manufacturing establishment. Indeed, over two-thirds of the pineapple production of the Philippines comes from northern Mindanao. Sugar cane is of some importance in the central Visayas and has recently been introduced on a fairly large scale in northern Mindanao. Commercial agricultural commodities are processed in manufacturing establishments in the cities of both regions. In addition to the pineapples canned in Cagayan de Oro, coconuts, copra, oil palm, and rubber are the bases for major agro-industries in Cebu or Medan.

Other primary commodities of importance to the regions include those produced through mining and logging activities. The first of these two categories is reflected in the industry sector of Tables 2.1 and 2.2. In Indonesia and North Sumatra mining accounts for a large share of the GDP because of the doubling of oil production between 1975 and 1980, as accompanied by a tripling of export prices during this same period. The mining contribution to North Sumatra's regional income in 1980 was 15 percent and growth occurred at an annual rate of nearly 20 percent from 1975 to 1980. Both of these figures with respect to mining exceed the contribution and growth of mining at the national level (Ginting and Daroesman, 1982, 56–57). The only mineral of major importance in the two Philippine regions is copper, which is produced in Cebu Province. The central Visayas accounted for nearly 23 percent of Philippine mineral output by value. The greatest share of this was derived from copper; Cebu Province produces over two-fifths of the nation's copper. Mining activities are of less importance in northern Mindanao, but the region is one of the major logging and wood-processing centers of the nation.

As was so for the nations, manufacturing is considerably more important in the two Philippine regions than it is in North Sumatra (Table 2.2). In North Sumatra manufacturing even lags behind the national share. As is so for the nation, however, this sector has shown strong growth in recent years. The average annual growth rate in manufacturing was over 16 percent in North Sumatra from 1975 to 1980 (Ginting and Daroesman, 1982). Despite this encouraging figure, the fact remains that there were in 1980 a total of 385 large and medium industries in the region employing only 36,207 workers. There were also very few small and cottage industries. Together these manufacturing industries accounted for only one percent of the labor force.[3] Thus, although there has been some growth in wood products and consumer goods there is very little modern industry apart from agricultural processing. The above growth rate may in fact be attributable to the Asahan dam and industrial complex and to factories which are just starting up.

In the two Philippine regions manufacturing accounted for a significantly greater share of the GDP. Growth rates in this sector appear to be higher during the early 1970s for these two regions than for the nation as a whole. In the central Visayas employment in manufacturing increased by 12.5 percent between 1972 and 1975, as compared to 3.9 percent in northern Mindanao. The average intercensal increase for the Philippines was 3.8 percent for this same period (Pernia, *et al*, 1983, 132). In terms of value added the central Visayas increased its manufacturing output by 22.3 percent during this period, while that for northern Mindanao went up by 21.8 percent. The comparative figure for the nation as a whole was only 13.9 percent (Pernia, *et al*, 1983, 136).

A more recent time period, 1975 to 1978, shows remarkable growth in manufacturing employment for the nation as a whole, 154 percent (from about 730,000 to over 1.8 million). Nearly all of this increase occurred in metropolitan Manila which in 1978 contained two-thirds of the nation's manufacturing employment. Employment in manufacturing also increased in the central Visayas during this period, though the rate of growth (29 percent) was less rapid. Total manufacturing employment in northern Mindanao increased by nearly 80 percent (NEDA, 1982, 471–472). Much of this has been connected to the establishment of a new industrial estate on the outskirts of Cagayan de Oro. The city's location is attractive to industry due to the presence of cheap electrical power (a large hydroelectric power station is located nearby).

The vast majority of this manufacturing employment is of course located in the region's major cities, Medan in North Sumatra, Cebu in the central Visayas, and Cagayan de Oro and Iligan in northern Mindanao. Iligan, second in size to Cagayan de Oro in northern Mindanao, experienced major industrialization beginning in the early 1960s (Ulack, 1975).[4] As pointed out later, Pematang Siantar and Tebing Tinggi in North Sumatra account for just over 6,000 employees in large and medium scale industries.

The share of the gross domestic product in the service sector, which includes transportation, communications, finance, and trade, is similar between the two nations and among the three regions. In all cases the service sector accounted for between 35 and 45 percent of the GDP (Tables 2.1 and 2.2).

The Regional Settings: Population and Migration

As we have already noted, the intermediate-sized cities under study have, with one exception, all experienced very rapid population growth during the 1970s (Table 1.1). Regional growth has also been significant during this period in at least two of the three study regions, though less so for their major cities. North Sumatra's population increased from 6.6 million in 1971 to nearly 8.4 million in 1980 for an increase of 26.3 percent for the period. While this increase is of course less than the 35.7 percent experienced in Medan, it is still more rapid than the 23.7 percent for the nation. Even excluding Medan, North Sumatra's population grew more rapidly than that of the country as a whole. The implication is thus that the entire province experienced net in-migration during the 1970s. Similarly, the northern Mindanao region grew more rapidly than the Philippine national average during the 1970s (41.2 percent compared to 31.1 percent). This suggests a pattern of fairly large net inmigration. In northern Mindanao, the inmigration affected the region's cities and also some of its interior rural areas such as those in Bukidnon and Agusan del Sur provinces. Even though coastal northern Mindanao has long been densely populated, the more interior portion of this region is still a "pioneer frontier" (Ulack, 1977). In the present decade population growth in some interior rural areas, however, has slowed because of the insurgency that is affecting the region.

Whereas these two regions have been growing more rapidly than their corresponding national averages, the central Visayas has long been experiencing net outmigration. Between 1970 and 1980 the region's population increased by only 24.9 percent. If metropolitan Cebu is excluded this figure falls to only 20.9 percent, as compared to the national average of 31.1 percent. During the 1970s people have been leaving the rural portions of the region, either for metropolitan Cebu or for elsewhere in the Philippines. Rural outmigration has been a characteristic of the central Visayas, and especially Cebu Province, during the past four decades. Prior to the present century the region experienced very rapid population growth as a result of its advantageous situation and the absence of malaria (Vandermeer, 1967). As such, it became over-populated. The employment of traditional farming techniques in hilly areas of the region (only 13 percent of the region's land area is less than 18 percent slope) quickly led to soil depletion. Declining yields resulted for the region's major crops, corn and coconuts. It is today estimated that over 80 percent of the region's total land area suffers moderate to severe soil erosion (NEDA, 1979, 18). Certainly such "push" factors in the rural areas are a major explanation for the heavy outmigration in this lagging region. Many of the outmigrants from the central Visayas migrated to nearby northern Mindanao. For this reason the predominant ethno-linguistic group in that region is Visayan. The traditional farming practices that were used in places like Cebu have also been transplanted to Mindanao, thus resulting in the appearance of similar problems to those found in rural Cebu.

With regard to migration, it is clear that during the 1960s and the first half of the 1970s, northern Mindanao had one of the highest rates of net inmigration in the Philippines. During the 1960s only the southern Mindanao and the National Capital Region had a higher net migration rate and during the 1970-1975 intercensal period no other region had a higher net migration rate (Pernia, et al, 1983, 60-61). Southern Mindanao includes Mindanao's largest city, Davao, as well as a frontier agricultural region which has attracted thousands of migrants from all over the Philippines during most of the twentieth century. On the other hand, the central Visayas region ranked thirteenth and twelfth among the nation's 13 regions in terms of its net migration rate for the 1960-1970 and 1970-1975 periods. A regression analysis of the interregional migration patterns for both Philippine census periods revealed that employment opportunities at the destination, kinship and ethnicity (as measured by common language at origin and destination), and farm density at origin were the most important explanatory variables for these patterns (Pernia, et al, 1983, 62).

As noted above, many of the migrants to northern Mindanao came from the central Visayas. This statement is supported by the fact that during the 1970 to 1975 period nearly 25 percent of the 81,935 inmigrants to northern Mindanao came from the central Visayas. The next three leading source regions were southern, eastern, and western Mindanao with 18.2, 16.9, and 16.1 percent, respectively (NEDA, 1981, xiii). Examination of a map of the Philippine regions clearly reveals distance to be an important explanation for these migration patterns. Those 51,081 persons who arrived in the central Visayas during the 1970-1975 period came predominantly from northern Mindanao (18.2 percent), southern Mindanao (15.9 percent), and the National Capital Region (14.8 percent). Such patterns suggest the importance of historic streams (between Mindanao and the Visayas) as well as ties between the nation's two principal cities. Those 89,787 persons who left the central Visayas went principally to northern Mindanao (22.6 percent), the National Capital Region (21.3 percent), and southern Mindanao (20.1 percent) again demonstrating these same ties.

According to the 1980 census and World Bank estimates, North Sumatra ranked fourth lowest among Indonesia's 26 provinces in net migration. Only Central Java, West Sumatra, and South Sulawesi had lower rates. However, in the 1970 census only the provinces of Lampung in southern Sumatra, Jakarta, and Jambi and Riau in east central Sumatra had higher net migration rates. Inmigration has been very significant in North Sumatra for decades. During colonial times the stream from Java to the province dominated all other interprovincial migration streams (Hugo, 1979). North Sumatra still has nearly ten percent of its population comprised of persons who have lived in another province. However, at least 63 percent of all inmigrants in the province had lived there for more than ten years while recent years, as suggested above, have also seen a significant pattern of outmigration. This indicates that inmigration is becoming a less important factor in the province's population growth (ESCAP, 1981, 83–84). By far the dominant source provinces for North Sumatra have been Central Java and East Java Provinces with nearby West-Sumatra and Aceh Provinces secondary source areas. The dominant destinations have been Jakarta and Central Java with nearby Aceh, West Sumatra, and Riau also attracting North Sumatra's outmigrants. As was the case with the Philippine migration streams there is evidence of the importance of distance, the attractiveness of the primate city, and the stream-counterstream flows in this case.

While interregional migration has been quite significant in both settings, intraprovincial (i.e., short-distance) moves have of course accounted for a much greater number of migrants. In Indonesia such moves accounted for at least five to six times the number of migrants as measured in terms of interprovincial moves (ESCAP, 1981, 81). As will become evident below the bulk of migrants to our study cities have come from other parts of their respective provinces, particularly from rural areas. This seems to be attributable to a number of factors, chief of which are the great differences that exist between rural and urban areas in terms of infrastructure, services, and income (Booth and Sundrum, 1981, 202–205), as well as the increasing pressures on the land as rural populations continue to grow, causing declines in average farm size and resource depletion.

The Study Cities

The populations of the study cities, with the exception of Pematang Siantar, grew more rapidly than their corresponding national averages during the 1970s (Table 1.1). While urban growth rates in Third World primate cities are invariably high, such is not always the case for intermediate and secondary cities. It is thus important to consider the conditions and

Table 2.3

FOREIGN TRADE FOR THE PORTS OF BELAWAN, CEBU, AND CAGAYAN DE ORO,
1978, F.O.B. VALUE IN MILLION DOLLARS

Port	Imports Dollars (millions)	Imports Percent of National Total	Exports Dollars (millions)	Exports Percent of National Total
Belawan	426.5	6.4	646.0	5.5
Cebu	124.7	2.6	247.6	7.2
Cagayan de Oro	105.3	2.2	215.5	6.3

Source: Biro Pusat Statistik, 1979; NEDA, 1982.

characteristics within the study cities which have brought about their
generally high rates of population growth.

As the dominant manufacturing, trade, and transportation center in the
region, Medan has a critical role to play in regional development (Leinbach,
1987). Manufacturing in the city is based in large part upon the petroleum,
rubber, and oil palm produced in the city's economic hinterland; the most
important industries are the manufacture of chemical products, petroleum,
rubber, plastics, and food and beverage processing. In 1980, total international
exports from Belawan, the seaport that serves Medan, amounted to nearly
1.2 million tons while imports were in excess of one million tons. By value,
export and import levels were higher than anywhere in Sumatra except for
Riau, where oil shipments predominate. Imports accounted for 6.4 percent
of national imports and exports accounted for 5.5 percent of the total (Table
2.3). Because of its import-export function, Medan also has a significant
role to play in the provision of wholesaling and transportation functions,
as are needed for the collection and distribution of goods.

A significant concentration of industry is also present. This consists
mainly of the processing of primary exports and is thus linked closely to
the regional resource base. By value the leading exports from Medan in
1980 were rubber, oil palm, and coffee, all primary agricultural commodities.
There is some reason to believe that the city will be a future center of the
chemical industry.

In recognition of this primary economic function, several major transportation investments are being planned or carried out for Medan. These
include a major expansion of Belawan port, a limited access highway (the

Belmera), a railroad upgrading project, and expansion of the city's airport. To better serve the rural hinterland northern Sumatra's 11,600 kilometers of roads, 45 percent of which are now paved, will also be improved. Included in these improvements is the Trans-Sumatra Highway which runs from the southern tip of the island through Medan (and also Pematang Siantar and Tebing Tinggi) to Banda Aceh in the extreme north (Fig. 1.1). Such improvements in transportation will greatly facilitate the movement of goods and people and further affect the growth and urban form of Medan.

As is true of Third World cities everywhere, the major area of employment in Medan is the broadly defined service sector; only about 13 percent of the labor force was engaged in industry and handicrafts in 1978. Data from 1980 show that 47 percent of the large and medium industry enterprises in North Sumatra Province were located in Medan. The total employment associated with these was 15,880 workers for an average of 88 workers per firm (Statistics Office, 1981). Also typical of Medan's role as a Third World city is the large share of its workers found in the informal sector. This topic will be discussed in detail in Chapter 5.

Like North Sumatra Province, Medan experienced fairly high rates of economic growth during the 1969–1973 period. Investments were made in rehabilitating and increasing its capacities in both economic and social infrastructure. Private sector expansion in processing, manufacturing, trade, finance, and other services stimulated the economy. There are unfortunately no reliable estimates of gross domestic product for the city, but analysis of various key measures suggests that the rate of growth and income has slowed considerably. A very rough estimate of Medan's gross domestic product in 1978 is approximately Rp 320,000 million, or some 27 percent of the provincial RGDP.

As befits any large regional center, the largest share of banks, health facilities, motor vehicles, telephones, radio stations, and the like are located in Medan. In early 1979, for example, there were a total of 105 banks operating in North Sumatra of which over 40 had their offices in Medan. Some 26 hospitals with 2,609 beds, 62 maternity clinics, 81 dental clinics, and 42 family planning clinics were also operating in the city at this time.

Motor vehicle growth was quite high during the five-year period preceding the study; passenger cars increased by 8 percent and trucks and buses by over 10 percent for this same period. As of 1981, nine bus companies with a total of 417 buses serve an estimated 145,000 persons daily. The city bus system, however, does not play an important role in public transportation. The operating routes are restricted to a few main roads. All lines depart from the Central Market area in the central business district. Some 460 taxis were registered in Medan but these also do not form a major component of the public transport system of the city. The major forms of transportation are the *bemo* (four-wheeled minibus) and the ubiquitous *becak*. In 1981 there were some 3,350 *bemos* operating on 19 routes. There were 13,000 registered *becaks* and probably several thousand more which were unre-gistered. Additionally there were some 2,150 motorized *becaks*. *Becak* drivers hire their vehicles from owners on a daily basis; average daily earnings for a *becak* driver are Rp 1,500. Since the vast majority of the population does not own vehicles, public transportation is crucial to local mobility. Public transportation is also a major employer in cities like Medan; many are employed as drivers, both in the formal sector (e.g., bus drivers) and the informal sector (*becak* drivers).

Pematang Siantar, while considerably smaller than Medan has the status of *kotamadya* and is the second largest urban place in North Sumatra Province. Pematang Siantar is the capital city of the *Kabupaten* of Simalungun. The city is situated on the main Trans-Sumatra highway approximately 130 kilometers, or three hours, southeast of Medan. It is the major service center of the most important commercial agricultural region in the province (Fig. 1.1).

In 1981 the city's 129 small industries included rice milling, cooking oil, lumber, food, ice, and beverage firms. The 23 medium and large scale industries included six cigarette manufacture, four plastics, four printing, two textile, two match, and two farm tool firms. The total employment in these larger industries was approximately 4,542 workers. Because the city is an agricultural center, small stores, markets, and individual selling stands (*balerong*) are commonly found. This is typical of most such cities and provides considerable employment in the large informal sector.

The transportation sector is also important to the city; Pematang Siantar had 110 inter-city buses, 155 city buses and *oplets* (mini-vans), 472 motorized *becaks*, and 93 *becak dayung* (unmotorized pedicabs). Facilities in the city include four movie theaters, five pharmacies, six banks, thirteen hotels (with 248 rooms), and 4,610 telephones. These data combine to give the impression that Pematang Siantar is a secondary city and is far lower in the functional hierarchy than is Medan.

Even further down the urban hierarchy is Tebing Tinggi, the third of the north Sumatran study cities. Whereas the population is given as 92,000 for the entire city, only about one-half of these are actually residing in the urban portion of the city. Nonetheless, and even considering the territorial expansion of Tebing Tinggi, the city's population has increased dramatically in recent years (Table 1.1). The city, like Medan and Pematang Siantar, has the official and autonomous status of *kotamadya*. Tebing Tinggi is located about 80 kilometers, or one and one-half hours, from Medan on the major north-south trunk road (Fig. 1.1); the function of the city is primarily that of a service center for a large estate-oriented agricultural hinterland which extends to Sumatra's east coast. While the city has no large industries, there were 15 medium-sized industries in 1981 with 480 permanent and

1,230 semi-permanent employees. There were also numerous small manufacturing enterprises including 49 food-related industries with 581 workers. As of 1981, Tebing Tinggi had only three banks, two movie theaters, two pharmacies, six hotels, and 588 telephones. Clearly, the city is considerably below Pematang Siantar in the functional hierarchy. Its population, however, is growing considerably faster.

The two intermediate-sized cities selected in the Philippines, metropolitan Cebu and Cagayan de Oro, ranked second and seventh in population size among all Philippine metropolitan areas (Pernia, *et al*, 1983, 179). As we have already noted, Cebu is some ten times smaller than Manila and Cagayan de Oro is about one-quarter the size of metropolitan Cebu. Just as was the case for Medan, both cities are the primary trade and transportation centers for their respective regions. Both are also provincial capitals.

Cebu and nearby Mactan Island, which is connected to Cebu by a toll bridge, were the first places contacted by the Europeans (Ferdinand Magellan was killed on Mactan in 1521). This fact, along with the city's central location in the Philippine archipelago and its excellent harbor have facilitated Cebu's emergence as a major metropolis. The city has become the focal point for transportation in the central and southern Philippines and only Manila can claim a larger share of the nation's international and internal trade and passengers. Nearly 16 percent (2.4 million metric tons) of the nation's interisland trade was accounted for by the port of Cebu, along with nearly 30 percent of the Nation's interisland ship passengers. Indeed, Cebu's port accounted for more interisland passengers than did even Manila. This of course is due partly to the fact that Cebu's only transportation links with other major centers are by sea or air, whereas Manila has extensive land connections. Cebu accounted for about four percent of the nation's total foreign trade in 1978, consisting of two percent of its imports and over seven percent of total exports. These percentages are comparable to those for Belawan (Medan's outport), though their total value is only about one-third as large (Table 2.3). The primate cities of both countries, of course, still account for a disproportionate share of foreign trade, over 92 percent in the case of the Philippines (NEDA, 1982, 701). In addition to the city's importance as a seaport, Cebu has the nation's second largest air facility, an international airport located on Mactan Island.

By value the major export from the port of Cebu in 1980 was the coconut oil processed in the city. Rattan from Mindanao and *buri* provide the materials for the labor intensive local furniture industry. The city has become internationally known for its rattan furniture and *buri* products, which are, respectively, the second and third ranked exports from Cebu. Indeed, rattan had replaced coconut oil as the top export from Cebu by 1983. Shellcrafts and seashells represent the fourth leading export category from the port of Cebu. These are also labor intensive (and very low wage) industries, thus providing considerable employment. Food and beverage processing and the apparel industries are also important to the city's economy. Another manufacturing employer is the Mactan Export Processing Zone (MEPZ), opened in 1980 adjacent to the international airport on Mactan Island. The industries located in the zone provide jobs for over 1,500 workers who produce watches (Timex), garments, television cable, and electronic goods.

The future importance of manufacturing in Cebu is indicated by the fact that the national government's development strategy for the central Visayas is presently centered around a rapid labor intensive industrialization directed partly toward international markets. Metropolitan Cebu is at the core of this strategy since it has a reasonably diverse industrial base, a high degree of agglomerative economies, a rapidly growing labor force with relatively well-developed skills, and a tradition of entrepreneurial ability (mostly Chinese), along with a lack of other employment opportunities in the region (NEDA, 1979, 15). Clearly, the emphasis on manufacturing and on jobs in the formal employment sector is greater in Cebu than in any of the Indonesian study cities.

As is the case with its population size, the city ranks second in the Philippines in virtually every other urban functional category. Thus metropolitan Cebu ranks second in the nation in the number of AM and FM radio stations (nineteen), the number of television stations and daily newspapers (four in each category), the number of banking facilities (about 75 in all categories), and the number of manufacturing establishments (1,676 in all size categories). The city, however, is not the center for land transportation that one might at first expect, given its size. This, of course, is because Cebu Island is small and contains no other large urban center. Thus, land transportation serves only the small towns and rural communities located on the island. Nevertheless, the 464 city-based public transport firms reported a total of 4,980 units including 200 public utility buses (PUBs), 1,145 public utility jeepneys (PUJs), 1,332 taxis, and 1,460 small public utility (PUs) cars (NEDA, 1979, 140). For this reason we may conclude that land transportation and especially sea transportation, as discussed above, provide considerable employment for the city's labor force.

As we have already noted, Cagayan de Oro with a 1980 urban population of about 120,000, experienced very rapid growth during the 1970s (Table 1.1). In addition to being the major trade and transportation center for northern Mindanao, Cagayan de Oro is an important food processing and industrial growth center, and a regional center for higher education. In addition to the major pineapple canning plant, which employs over 5,000 workers, a large industrial estate has recently been developed near the city. This estate is located in Tagaloan, a municipality some 24 kilometers from Cagayan de Oro's central business district. This route is via the new National Highway, which is in excellent condition, thereby facilitating commuting to the estate from Cagayan de Oro. At present, the major industry in the estate is the Kawasaki steel sintering complex but other multinational corporations have also opened. The presence of these and smaller industries in and near Cagayan de Oro has provided many members of the local labor force with an opportunity for formal sector employment, while also stimulating growth of informal sector and service type jobs.

Cagayan de Oro accounted for 584,000 metric tons of domestic cargo in 1980, about four percent of the nation's total. Whereas this total was considerably less than that from Cebu, the value of Cagayan de Oro's total foreign trade was nearly equal to that of Cebu (Table 2.3). In fact the total tonnage exported from the port was greater than that from any Mindanao or Visayan port and accounted for nearly six percent of the nation's total export tonnage. Much of this total represented lumber exports from Mindanao's interior areas. The port ranked sixth nationally in interisland ship passengers in 1980, with nearly half a million persons landing in or departing from the city.

Cagayan de Oro, centered on the northern Mindanao coast astride the National Highway, is also a focal point for land transportation. Some 1,300 PUJs serve the city and nearby areas and over 250 buses, belonging to 12 buslines, are based in the city. These carry passengers to and from nearby towns as well as to more distant cities in Mindanao, such as Butuan, Iligan, and Davao. Approximately forty banking establishments are located in the city, as well as nine AM and FM radio stations, and two television stations. There are no daily newspapers. The city is clearly below Cebu in the Philippine urban hierarchy but functionally is a larger urban place than either Pematang Siantar or Tebing Tinggi.

Finally, it is perhaps useful here to synthesize the historical and, especially, the economic changes that underly the growth of the two largest cities in our city. It is, of course, the implications of these changes for mobility and employment which are ultimately sought.

Rapid growth in Medan's population between 1930 and 1961 was fueled largely by the commercial agricultural sector, especially tobacco, rubber, and oil palm. In addition, by the 1960s a small manufacturing base which emphasized textiles had been created. While Medan's dramatic early growth slowed during the 1960s, this was also a decade of considerable inmigration and one in which the earlier expansion of manufacturing was reversed. Industrial data for Medan in the early 1970s reflect an economic recovery charted by the Soeharto government in an attempt to recoup the industrial stagnation brought on by the political turbulence of the mid-1960s. The dominant industrial sectors at this point were textiles and machinery, especially repair firms. Unlike Semarang, Bandung, and Jogjakarta, there was considerable industrial balance in Medan (Leinbach, 1987). This diversity was derived largely from the city's situation on the edge of a resource frontier. Promising future industrial expansion and growth was heralded.

By the early 1980s distinct shifts occured in the distribution of manufacturing firms and employment. Traditional industries, especially food-related, accounted for fewer but larger firms and a lower share of employment than a decade earlier. The textile industries' share of employment also dropped as a result of strong Javanese competition and a weak technological transition. Conversely, the rubber and plastics sector has been strengthened under the import substitution strategy. Other structural changes in industry elsewhere in Indonesia are only partly mirrored by changes in the Medan economy as a result of the particular resource base, technological lags, and weaker market strength in the region. In fact, the lack of stronger growth in industry in the urban area may in part also be attributed to the decentralized nature of processing industries in the region. Industrial development in Medan is depressed as a result of the recent international recession. But in addition infrastructure inadequacy and the lack of sound urban services subvert attempts to generate new secondary activity. Even more important, appropriate policies and an economic climate to induce new investment are not present. New entrants into the labor market are faced largely with the choice of government service activities that generate income through service provision.

As in Medan, the early growth of manufacturing in Cebu may be traced to the local and regional resource base. Historically the city has been the major center for the assembly and processing of various primary products from the surrounding region, most notably copper, coconut products, and forest products. While the structural change in the industrial economy of Medan reveals a strong loss in the employment proportion of textiles, this did not occur in Cebu. Just over 25 percent of manufacturing employment in Cebu in 1980 was attributed to textiles in contrast to only seven percent in Medan. This suggests that Cebu has not had strong extra-regional competition in this sector. Wood and wood products employment dominate the manufacturing employment distribution in Cebu whereas rubber and plastics do likewise in Medan. This distinction reflects differences in the available and worked resource base as well as political and technological factors. Timbering efforts in North Sumatra are dispersed around the province although wood products account for seven percent of manufacturing employment in Medan, a proportion equivalent to that in textiles. Machinery and repair firms account for a more substantial component of manufacturing employment in Medan than in Cebu. Basically, service firms and the tertiary sector must be viewed as the primary source of employment for new entrants to the labor force in Cebu. Overall however it is clear that the manufacturing sector in Cebu is more dominant than that in Medan. The major problems affecting small firms as well as to some extent large firms in Cebu are the lack of technology, defective financial management, inadequate working capital, and physical infrastructure. Given the differences, however, in the industrial (especially manufacturing) component between Cebu and Medan, we might speculate that an industrial policy and strategy are better established in the former node. Clearly a closer more detailed comparison is required to fully justify such a conclusion. In any case, manufacturing employment in both urban areas should not be viewed as a major absorption factor for the burgeoning labor force.

The Study Populations

It is the aim of this final section to compare and contrast some of the major characteristics of the sampled populations. The basic question to be addressed deals with the comparative socioeconomic and mobility char- acteristics of the household heads in the five study cities.

Socioeconomic and Demographic Characteristics

Table 2.4 provides a general overview of some basic characteristics of the study populations. The data give information for household heads as a whole; breakdowns by migration status and employment categories will be provided in succeeding chapters. The differences that exist among the five cities are not surprising given national and city size differences. For example, educational levels are higher in the two Philippine cities although differences along these lines are not profound. The modal category for all five cities is six to eight years of completed schooling (Table 2.4). Interestingly, the smaller cities of Pematang Siantar and Cagayan de Oro have higher average educational levels than Medan or Cebu, respectively. In Cagayan de Oro at least, part of the reason for this is that household heads in this setting are significantly younger than in Cebu (37 vs. 44 years on the average). Among adult Filipinos an inverse relationship exists between age and educational level.

In the Philippines there is a greater emphasis on education as is indicated by the fact that nationwide only 10 percent of the adult male population and 12 percent of the adult female population is considered to be illiterate. By comparison similar figures for Indonesia are 22 percent and 42 percent, respectively (Population Reference Bureau, 1982). The considerable educa- tional difference between the sexes in Indonesia is partly a function of the lesser emphasis placed on female education in Moslem societies. In the Philippines, the importance of education greatly increased during the colonial period with the introduction of the American educational system (Doeppers, 1984). As is so throughout the Third World, educational levels in the study cities are greater than those found in nearby rural areas. One indication of

Table 2.4

SELECTED SOCIOECONOMIC AND DEMOGRAPHIC CHARACTERISTICS,
NONMIGRANT AND MIGRANT HEADS OF HOUSEHOLD,
FIVE STUDY CITIES

Characteristic	Medan (N=1100)	Pematang Siantar (N=244)	Tebing Tinggi (N=140)	Cebu (N=1000)	Cagayan de Oro (N=800)
Percent school years completed					
None	4.9	5.5	2.2	2.9	0.3
1-5 years	18.4	11.8	25.2	16.3	10.7
6-8 years	31.4	32.8	41.0	29.1	30.1
9-11 years	19.1	23.9	15.1	23.9	29.2
12-15 years	23.0	22.7	14.4	25.8	29.8
Over 15	3.2	3.4	2.2	1.9	--
Mean school years completed	7.8	8.2	6.9	8.7	9.3
Mean income (dollars)	113	106	85	125	109
Percent female	6.8	9.8	2.2	11.6	12.1
Mean age (years)	41.9	41.9	40.2	44.1	37.4
Percent unmarried	8.3	9.9	4.3	13.8	10.1
Mean age at marriage (years)	24.9	24.8	24.2	24.9	24.1

Source: Sample Survey Data.

this can be gleaned from the results of surveys that were completed in selected rural villages located in the same provinces as the study cities. For example, the mean number of school years completed by among a sample of heads of household in 200 randomly-selected households in two rural *barangays* located in Cebu Province was only 4.5 years. Such differences are important to consider because it is the rural population that comprises a major portion of those who migrate to cities.

Overall income levels were similar among all the study cities, at least in terms of absolute values. Utilizing the dollar conversion rates in effect at the time when the surveys were undertaken (675 Indonesian rupiahs or

10 Philippine pesos to the dollar) it was found that househeads earned approximately $109 monthly in Indonesia and $119 in the Philippine cities. Differences by city size were as expected, i.e., the larger the city, the higher the income. Although absolute differences were not great, comparisons between the Indonesian and Philippine cities on the income dimension should only be made with care, since national-level statistics show per capita incomes to be some 50 percent higher in the Philippines than in Indonesia (Population Reference Bureau, 1983). On the other hand, North Sumatra's per capita income is higher than the Indonesian average by 60 percent whereas average family income is more than 10 and 35 percent, respectively, below that of the overall figure for the Philippines in the central Visayas and northern Mindanao. Of course, wide variations exist between the urban and rural portions of these regions. Again, relying on income data gathered in rural households it was found that the household heads surveyed in rural areas of Cebu Province had average incomes about 40 percent that of heads in the city. Given such extreme differences (which also existed in Misamis Oriental and North Sumatra Provinces) it is little wonder that so many migrate from the rural areas to the cities.

Other characteristics of household heads were generally quite similar among the study cities. Household heads were almost always male and married, the average age of household heads was about 40 to 45 years except in Cagayan de Oro where it was 37, and the average age at marriage was 24 to 25 years of age.

One of our major purposes in this monograph is to compare and contrast the importance of employment as a motive for mobility to the cities under study. In the chapters that follow we provide information for spouses (both migrants and nonmigrants). Our focus, however, is upon heads of household since these are nearly always the principal breadwinners of the family. The majority of spouses and other household members were not gainfully employed in any of the study cities, particularly for those in North Sumatra. In Medan, for example, of the 1,022 spouses interviewed, only eight percent were employed. In Cebu employment of spouses was much more significant, with the comparative figure in this case being slightly over 40 percent. We do not want to minimize the significance of female employment, or of labor force participation among other household members, but our primary unit of analysis will be the migrant head of household. As we have already noted there are a small number of females among household heads. These, of course, are included in our analyses.

In addition to the educational factor, another important difference between the Indonesian and Philippine study cities lies in the area of employment. As shown in Table 2.5, a larger share of the household heads in Indonesia are employed in the informal sector than is the case for the Philippines. In all three Indonesian study cities between two-thirds and three-quarters

Table 2.5

FORMAL AND INFORMAL SECTOR EMPLOYMENT,
NONMIGRANT AND MIGRANT HEADS OF HOUSEHOLD,
FIVE STUDY CITIES (PERCENT)

Sector	Medan (N=1092)	Pematang Siantar (N=239)	Tebing Tinggi (N=138)	Cebu (N=862)	Cagayan de Oro (N=709)
Formal	34	35	26	59	47
Informal	66	65	74	41	53

Source: Sample Survey Data.

of the heads of household were employed in the informal sector. In contrast, about 60 percent of the heads in metropolitan Cebu were employed in the formal sector, along with almost one-half of all heads in Cagayan de Oro. This finding fits with the previously-noted pattern of a greater emphasis on formal manufacturing activities in the two Philippine cities, especially in Cebu.

Migration Characteristics

Our definition of a migrant is one who lived somewhere other than his present city of residence at age 15. Thus, anyone in the three north Sumatran cities who lived in a *kotamadya* or *kabupaten* other than their present city of residence, or anyone in the two Philippine cities who lived in a chartered city or municipality other than those that comprise metropolitan Cebu or Cagayan de Oro, was considered a migrant. We have chosen to compare present place of residence at age 15 (rather than place of birth) because reasons for moves before age 15 are almost always family-related. Based upon this definition 30 percent (325) of the household heads in Medan, 20 percent (48) of the heads in Pematang Siantar, 26 percent (36) of those in Tebing Tinggi, 39 percent (386) of the household heads in Cebu, and 70 percent (561) of those in Cagayan de Oro, were migrants. The much higher percentage of migrant househeads in Cagayan de Oro is to be expected given that the city has grown more rapidly than the two larger study cities (Table 1.1). Moreover, migrants who have arrived in Cagayan de Oro have done so more recently than those who arrived in either Medan or Cebu (Table 2.6). Among the three largest study cities, migration to Medan has tended to concentrate more in the less recent past. Of the migrants sampled

Table 2.6

YEAR OF MIGRATION TO MAJOR STUDY CITIES,
MIGRANT HEADS OF HOUSEHOLD (PERCENT)[a]

Year of Move	Medan (N=241)	Cebu (N=374)	Cagayan de Oro (N=556)
1978-1983	4	16	28
1973-1977	10	16	28
1968-1972	11	14	17
1963-1967	15	12	11
1958-1962	16	10	7
1953-1957	20	10	4
1948-1952	14	8	4
<1948	11	14	1

[a]Pematang Siantar and Tebing Tinggi have been excluded from this table due to insufficient sample size.

Source: Sample Survey Data.

in Medan, only 14 percent moved to the city since 1973 whereas nearly one-third of those in Cebu and over one-half of migrant heads in Cagayan de Oro came during this period (Ulack and Leinbach, 1985).

Important differences exist with regard to migration origins among the study cities' household heads. One such difference can be noted from Table 2.7, wherein it is apparent that a much larger proportion of migrants to Medan came from other urban areas in Indonesia, whereas rural inmigrants far outnumbered those from urban places in the four other study cities. Not surprisingly, the majority of migrants to the two smaller Indonesian cities came from nearby rural origins, while over two-fifths of the migrants to Medan came from urban areas. In contrast, less than one-fifth (in Cebu) and one-quarter (in Cagayan de Oro) of migrants originated in urban areas. Certainly the lack of opportunities in the rural areas of both the central Visayas and northern Mindanao was a factor in "pushing" migrants to these cities. Although urban definitions vary between the two nations and therefore

Table 2.7

MIGRANT ORIGINS OF HOUSEHOLD HEADS,
FIVE STUDY CITIES (PERCENT)

Origin	Medan (N=325)	Pematang Siantar (N=48)	Tebing Tinggi (N=36)	Cebu (N=387)	Cagayan de Oro (N=561)
Rural	44	69	81	82	74
Urban	56	31	19	18	26
Same province or region	52	67	86	58	41
Other province or region	48	33	14	42	59

Source: Sample Survey Data.

findings are not precisely comparable, the contrast between these locales and Medan is large enough to suggest that a difference does in fact exist.

In Medan about one-half (52 percent) of migrant heads claimed their residence at age 15 to be North Sumatra Province whereas in Cebu 58 percent came from the areally much smaller, but fragmented, central Visayas region (Table 2.7). This implies that the distance a migrant to Medan travelled was considerably greater than that of a migrant to Cebu. That migration to Medan from other parts of North Sumatra is relatively more modest than that to Cebu from nearby areas is not surprising since, as discussed earlier, the region is a frontier area where rural population densities are still relatively low and economic opportunities still are in abundance. The central Visayas, because of the topography and history of settlement, has limited opportunities in rural areas. In Cagayan de Oro only 41 percent of migrant heads came from northern Mindanao but a further 25 percent came from the nearby central Visayas reflecting the historic migration stream discussed earlier.

The specific origins of those migrants who came from outside the province or regions under study generally consist of nearby locations (Table 2.8; Figs. 2.1 & 2.2). In Medan, one-half the migrants came from North Sumatra Province and a further 30 percent originated in the three contiguous provinces of West Sumatra, Aceh, and Riau. The great majority of migrants in the

Table 2.8

MIGRANT ORIGIN BY PROVINCE OR REGION,
HEADS OF HOUSEHOLD,
FIVE STUDY CITIES (PERCENT)

Region and Province of Origin	Medan (N=325)	Pematang Siantar (N=48)	Tebing Tinggi (N=36)
Sumatra			
North Sumatra	52	69	86
Aceh	10	13	6
Riau	4	4	6
West Sumatra	17	4	3
Jambi	2	-	-
South Sumatra	1	-	-
Bengkulu	*	-	-
Java and Madura			
West Java	3	-	-
Jakarta	2	4	-
Central Java	6	2	-
East Java	3	4	-
Yogyakarta	1	-	-
Madura	-	-	-
Kalimantan (4 provinces)	-	-	-
Bali and Nusa Tenggara (3 provinces)	-	-	-
Sulawesi, Other (6 provinces)	*	-	-

*Indicates less than .5% from province; - indicates zero.

Source: Sample Survey Data.

Table 2.8 (continued)

Region of Origin	Cebu (N=386)	Cagayan de Oro (N=561)
Central Visayas	58	25
Western Visayas	5	4
Eastern Visayas	10	6
Northern Mindanao	6	41
Western Mindanao	3	5
Central Mindanao	3	6
Southern Mindanao	5	5
Bicol	1	1
Southern Tagalog	1	2
Metro Manila	5	3
Central Luzon	1	1
Ilocos	2	1
Cagayan Valley	*	*

*Indicates less than .5% from region.

Source: Sample Survey Data.

smaller cities of Pematang Siantar and Tebing Tinggi originated in North Sumatra. The trend for Cebu and Cagayan de Oro was similar. In Cebu, 59 percent came from the central Visayas and a further 22 percent came from the nearby eastern and western Visayas and from northern Mindanao. In Cagayan de Oro, some 41 percent originated from other places in northern Mindanao and 25 percent came from the nearby central Visayas. In short, the well-known frictional effect of distance on migration intensity is clearly evident in all cases. In general, though, migration fields are wider for the larger cities. Comparison of the provinces and regions listed in Table 2.8 with their locations in Figures 2.1 and 2.2 clearly reveal these characteristics.

As might be expected, the primate cities of the two nations, Jakarta and Manila, did not contribute a large share of the migrants to any of the five study cities. It is noteworthy, however, that over five percent of the migrants to Cebu did come from the Philippines' largest metropolitan area, which suggests there is some movement "down" the urban hierarchy in this case.

Ethnically, both Indonesia and the Philippines are very diverse nations. For this reason one would expect that the larger cities, at least, would reflect this diversity of ethnic backgrounds among their inmigrant populations. In fact, Medan's inmigrants are ethnically diverse but those of the other cities are not. In the Medan sample the largest group of migrants were the

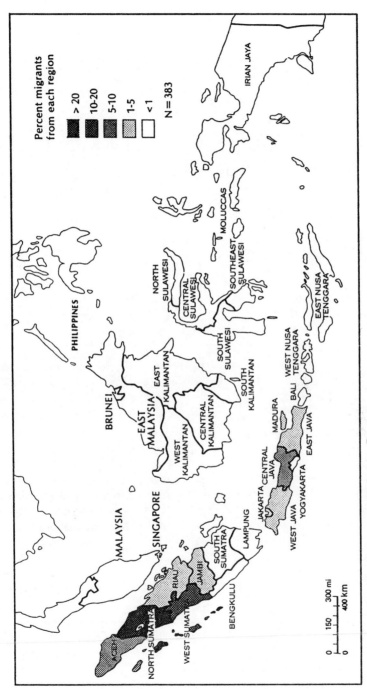

Figure 2.1   Origins of Migrants to Medan by Province

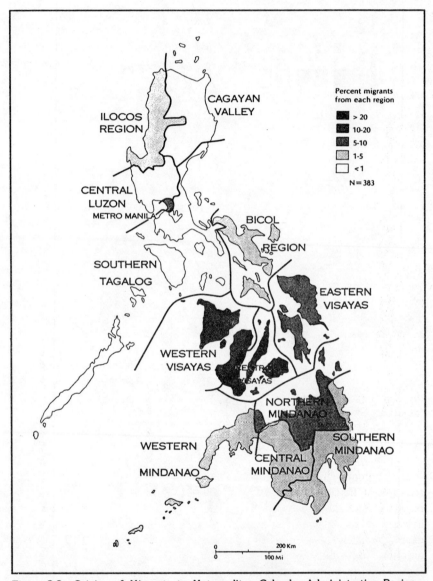

Figure 2.2   Origins of Migrants to Metropolitan Cebu by Administrative Region

Javanese (31 percent), as followed by the Minangkabau from West Sumatra (25 percent), the various Batak tribes from northern Sumatra (22 percent), the Melayu (8 percent), and the Acehnese (6 percent). The preponderance of Javanese among recent migrants is not particularly surprising since migration from Java to North Sumatra has dominated interprovincial migration since colonial times. Thus, the largest ethnic group among the nonmigrants of Medan were the Javanese who comprised 44 percent of this group. The proximity of the Minangkabau coupled with their peripatetic nature helps explain their importance in Medan, as well as elsewhere (Naim, 1973). Similarly, the Toba Batak are "culturally supportive of mobility" (Pryor, 1977, 74). In short ethnic groups are sometimes known for their propensity to migrate and thus ethnicity can be a factor in understanding reasons for mobility.

Certain Filipino ethnic groups are also well-known for their mobility. For example, large numbers of Ilocanos from northern Luzon have moved to other parts of the Philippines, as well as to international destinations like Hawaii. In Cebu and Cagayan de Oro, however, there is not the degree of ethnic heterogeneity as was found in Medan, at least if one uses the origin and primary language spoken as the basis for defining ethnicity among migrants. Among the migrant household heads, over 95 percent in both Cebu and Cagayan de Oro stated that they spoke Visayan. These differences may be accounted for by some of the factors noted in our preceding discussion. North Sumatra is a frontier area opened during colonial times which has attracted people from all over Indonesia. This is not unlike the Philippines' premier frontier area, southern and central Mindanao and its principal city, Davao (Ulack, 1977). Although recent population growth in Cebu and Cagayan de Oro, like Medan, has also been rapid, the growth of the two Philippine cities has come principally from their own ethnic reservoir rather than from other ethnic regions of the nation.

Summary

In summary, the socioeconomic, demographic, and migration characteristics of household heads in the five study cities are similar in many respects. Such differences that exist can be explained largely by the variations in national and regional settings, as well as by differences in city size. For example, differences in education can be attributed in large part to a greater emphasis on education in the Philippines. The larger share of the work force found in formal sector occupations in the two Philippine cities is due partly to the importance of manufacturing industries in these locales, especially in Cebu.

North Sumatra is still something of a frontier area. Some rural land is as yet available and employment in estate agriculture is possible. In addition, the province, like all of Sumatra, has been affected by oil production. Thus the cities of the region have benefited through agro-industrial and oil-related manufacturing establishments that have been recently opened. Such industries, and the employment opportunities perceived to exist have attracted migrants to Medan, from both urban and rural areas all over Indonesia. The region's smaller cities have also experienced considerable inmigration, but this has been predominantly from nearby rural areas.

Migration to both Cebu and Cagayan de Oro has been more recent than that to Medan and has been largely from rural areas, especially those in the densely populated Visayas. The central Visayas, as we have seen, is a region with few and declining opportunities in the overpopulated rural areas. For this reason many have moved to cities like Cebu and Cagayan de Oro. Both of these cities have experienced increased manufacturing activity and both, like Medan, are the most important centers of commerce and transportation within their respective regions. As is the case with Medan, employment opportunities are thus perceived to exist and, indeed, there is much that is true in this perception, especially in comparison to opportunities in rural areas. Both the formal and informal sectors provide jobs to migrants and nonmigrants alike. Certainly the migration can be expected to continue, at least for the short run.

What are the differences between migrants and nonmigrants? Why do migrants come to the cities? How do migrants adjust to life in the city and what types of employment do they find? Do migrants improve their economic situations once in the city? How do migrants and nonmigrants perceive the future? What are the characteristics of non-permanent movement with respect to the cities under consideration? These are some of the major questions we seek to answer in the chapters that follow.

Notes

1. It is important to qualify, in Indonesia at least, the incidence of and recent changes in poverty levels. Between 1970 and 1980 the proportion of people living in poverty, defined as the minimum food expenditure requirement to purchase 18 kilograms of rice per month per capita, declined from 57 to 40 percent. In addition, there was a rapid reduction in urban poverty over the same period. The latter of course contributes to the problem of rapid urbanization in Indonesia.

2. Indonesian agricultural statistics are taken from Biro Pusat Statistik (1979) and based upon the 1973 *Agricultural Census*, the most recent available. Philippine agricultural data are from NEDA (1982).

3. A 1978 National Labor Force Survey reports 2.9 million total employed in North Sumatra Province with 131,000 employed in manufacturing. Using these figures manufacturing accounts for 4.4 percent of the total provincial employment. The differences in manufacturing employment between the North Sumatran and national

reporting is undoubtedly due to the inclusion of agricultural processing labor on estates in the larger figure.

4. Strictly speaking, Iligan City is not located in the Northern Mindanao administrative region. This city, however, is located near to Cagayan de Oro and is actually situated near the geographic center of northern Mindanao. Since the data for the study were collected, the Philippines has experienced considerable economic and political turbulence. Negative economic growth rates were posted in both 1984 and 1985, with the manufacturing sector being expecially hard hit.

3

Social and Economic Characteristics
of Migrants and Nonmigrants

As was seen in the opening chapter, fairly strong theoretical support now exists for policies designed to promote movement to secondary urban centers. What seems to be less certain is the extent to which these ideas coincide with empirical realities in the Southeast Asian setting. That is, to what extent does migration into the smaller urban centers of the region actually serve to enhance national development?

One way of approaching this question is to examine ways in which migrants to such cities differ from urban natives, that is from nonmigrants. In cases where social and economic differences between these two groups are large, the migration process may clearly be expected to have a substantial impact upon the population composition of the receiving city. At times, the nature of these compositional changes could be adverse, as would be the case if cityward migrants tended to be poorly skilled and subject to high rates of unemployment. Additional knowledge is thus needed on this question, in order to further our understanding of the likely demographic consequences of programs designed to establish small and medium-sized cities as alternate growth centers.

Information on patterns of migrant selectivity may also be of help in forming mobility policies. To be effective, such policies must be based upon reliable information about the background and goals of cityward migrants, so that a set of meaningful mobility-related incentives and disincentives may be identified. For example, the provision of various urban amenities (housing, security, primary education) may be of relatively little importance to young and unmarried migrants who plan to stay with relatives soon after their arrival in the city.

Previous Studies

Previous analyses of migrant-nonmigrant differentials in the developing world are not of one accord. A number of authors have taken an essentially negative perspective on this question, choosing to emphasize the wretched living conditions of most city-bound migrants, their lack of training for the urban labor market, and the resulting patterns of social disorganization which are to be found in those neighborhoods where migrants congregate. Thus, Lerner (1967, 33) writes of the "suffering mass of humanity displaced from the rural areas to the filthy peripheries of the great cities," while La Greca (1977, 66) views rural-urban migrants in the developing world as living "in some of the worst slums imaginable" and as constituting "one of the major social problems of modern man." For his part, too, the human ecologist Amos Hawley (1971, 275) notes that

> in his transfer from rural to urban sectors of the economy, the migrant meets on a personal level one of the major problems of development. His manual skills, such as they may be, are scarcely appropriate to urban populations. . . . In the contemporary developing countries, and in the degree to which they have borrowed Western industrial and institutional lore, the technological gap between rural and urban occupations is too wide to be leaped by migrant peasants.

On the other hand, results from various demographic analyses would appear to cast the migration process in a more favorable light. In general, such studies have found rural-urban migrants to be of relatively high "quality." Thus, it is a virtually universal finding that rural-urban migrants are better educated than stayers (nonmigrants) in their source community (e.g., Simmons and Cardona, 1972; Speare, 1974; Connell, et al, 1976). Indeed, some studies have shown migrants to hold levels of educational and occupational attainment that are similar to or even higher than those found for nonmigrants in their city of *destination,* despite the relatively high levels of educational attainment to be found therein (e.g., Paydarfar, 1974; Ingram, Pachon, and Pineda, 1982). Unemployment rates, too, do not appear to be higher among migrants than among urban natives. The opposite, in fact, may frequently prove true (Udall and Sinclair, 1982). Overall, cityward migrants in the LDC's tend to see themselves as having gained economically from their move and do not plan on returning to their community of origin, even in cases where they are currently living in slum or squatter neighborhoods (Ulack, 1978).

What little is known about migration patterns in Indonesia and the Philippines does not appear to be in sharp disagreement with the above-noted results. Studies have shown that citybound migrants in both locales tend to be unmarried and concentrated in the young adult ages (e.g., Speare, 1976; Palabrica-Costello, 1980). Females predominate in streams toward all types of urban areas in the Philippines, but only among Jakarta-bound migrants in Indonesia (Speare, 1976; Hardjono, 1980; Engracia and Herrin, 1984).

Rural-urban migrants in Indonesia tend to come from higher status families than rural stayers, while educational levels among citybound migrants in this setting are higher than those found among nonmigrants in either the community of origin or of destination (Speare, 1976; Hardjono, 1980; Hugo, 1983). Such strong patterns of positive selectivity may be linked to the lower levels of geographic mobility and urbanization found in Indonesia. In the Philippines, where such types of movements are more common, the evidence for positive selectivity is correspondingly weaker. Among males, permanent migrants to the city tend to be slightly better educated and to hold higher status occupational positions than urban nonmigrants. The opposite, however, appears to be true for migrant women, although this group, too, seems to be better educated than female rural stayers (Palabrica-Costello, 1980; Engracia and Herrin, 1984).

One problem with studies of this sort is that they are frequently based upon survey results from a study conducted in the national primate city (e.g., Speare, 1976; Hardjono, 1980). In other cases, disaggregation of national-level data on citybound migrants into streams directed toward the primate city, as compared to those headed towards secondary urban centers, has not been carried out (e.g., Engracia and Herrin, 1984). Thus, relatively little is known as yet about the patterns of migrant selectivity which hold for small to medium-sized cities in Southeast Asia.

On the one hand, an argument could be made for the proposition that migrants to smaller urban areas will rank below natives of these cities in terms of their level of educational or occupational status. In general, migrant selectivity has been found to be greater in streams toward larger cities (Connell, *et al*, 1976). A reason for this lies in the fact that migrant selectivity is correlated positively with the length of the migration stream since streams toward the national capital city are typically longer (and from a greater variety of source areas) than those to secondary urban centers. Compared to the national primate city, small urban areas are also characterized by lower standards of living and less adequate provision of urban amenities and infrastructures (Castillo, 1979; McGee, 1982), thus making them less attractive to the more highly qualified migrants.

Theodore Fuller's recent analysis of population mobility in Thailand, however, provides a somewhat different perspective. According to this study, migrants to secondary urban centers are positively selected in comparison to nonmigrants in these cities. Migrants to smaller cities were also doing better economically than those who had chosen to go to the capital city of Bangkok (Fuller, 1981). The positive selectivity of migrants to small and middle-sized cities may be attributable to the fact that more highly qualified natives of these places have in turn been selected out in streams toward the national primate city. Various additional factors, which are associated with smaller urban centers but lacking from the national primate city, are also seen by Fuller as facilitating the process of upward social mobility among migrants.

Differences which exist *among* the five study cities, as well as between this group as a whole and the national capital city, might also be investigated by the present study. This type of analysis must be viewed as exploratory in nature, since the number of cases at each stage of the urban hierarchy is small and subject to unique historical and geographical forces. One hypothesis which bears looking into, however, concerns the relationship between the overall rate of population growth in a city and the patterns of educational and occupational selectivity which are found there. In general, studies have shown that migrant selectivity tends to decline as the volume of such movements increases (Lee, 1966; Browning and Feindt, 1969). For this reason, we might well expect selectivity to be lowest in the cities of Cagayan de Oro and Tebing Tinggi, which have experienced the most rapid rates of intercensal growth during the period immediately preceding the present survey.

That the present analysis is based upon representative samples of household heads and spouses must also be reiterated at this point. This strategy was chosen in order to focus upon those individuals who are most responsible for the welfare of their families and most involved with those issues (e.g., family planning, nutrition, education) which will be affecting the future course of national economic development. It is likely, however, that somewhat different patterns of migrant selectivity would emerge if our study population had been based upon a sample of all adult members of the household. This latter approach would have no doubt resulted in the identification of larger numbers of migrants who are young adults, unmarried persons and domestic servants. For this reason results from the present analysis will not be directly comparable with those from some earlier studies, which included data on persons other than household heads and spouses.

Findings

Data on the age, sex, and marital status composition of migrant household heads will first be discussed. Since we are interested in identifying the characteristics of migrants, it makes the most sense in this context to focus on age and marital status at the time of migration to the present community, rather than upon current age and marital status.[1] These results are shown in Table 3.1, along with comparable figures on the sex composition of migrants and nonmigrants in each of the five study sites.

The data show that a majority of migrant household heads in all study cities moved when they were in the young adult ages (less than 25 years of age) and unmarried. These results are by no means surprising, insofar

Table 3.1

SOCIO-DEMOGRAPHIC CHARACTERISTICS OF HOUSEHOLD HEADS,
BY MIGRANT STATUS AND STUDY CITY[a]

Migration Status	Medan	Pematang Siantar	Tebing Tinggi	Cebu	Cagayan de Oro
I. Sex (percent male)[b]					
Migrants	94.5	92.9	100.0	87.9	88.2
Nonmigrants	92.5	89.3	97.1	88.6	86.8
II. Age at time of move (percent aged 25 years or less)					
Migrants	84.6	84.0	77.8	69.8	56.5
III. Marital status at time of move (percent single)					
Migrants	71.4	68.6	65.4	74.6	59.0

[a]Sample sizes in all tables in Chapter 3 are, with minor fluctuations, for migrants: 347 in Medan, 56 in Pematang Siantar, 34 in Tebing Tinggi, 387 in Cebu, and 552 in Cagayan de Oro. Sample sizes for nonmigrants for these same cities are 745, 187, 104, 607, and 228, respectively.

[b]None of the five intracity differences in sex composition were found to be statistically significant.

Source: Sample Survey Data.

as most previous studies have shown a predominance of young adults and single persons among migrant populations.

The data also show a very large percentage of migrants to be males. This, of course, is chiefly attributable to our focus upon household heads, and should not be taken to imply that males are more likely than females to migrate. In any event, comparable figures for the nonmigrant group are equally high, with none of the ensuing differentials being statistically significant.

The proportion of male household heads, among both migrants and nonmigrants, is uniformly higher in the three Indonesian cities than in either Cebu or Cagayan de Oro. This can probably be explained in terms of cultural and religious differences between these two societies.

Table 3.2

MEAN NUMBER OF MOVES FOR MIGRANT HOUSEHOLD HEADS[a]

	Medan	Pematang Siantar	Tebing Tinggi	Cebu	Cagayan de Oro
Premarriage moves	0.50	0.36	0.33	0.79	1.57
Post-marriage moves	0.16	0.07	0.07	0.54	1.33
Ratio of pre- to post-marriage moves	3.12	5.14	4.71	1.46	1.18

[a]Unmarried household heads were excluded from this tabulation.

Source: Sample Survey Data.

Geographical mobility is more highly concentrated in the young adult ages among the Indonesian respondents than for those moving to Philippine cities. Despite this, no clear cross-cultural differences are apparent with regard to the proportion of migrants who moved while they were married, evidently because marriage takes place at earlier ages in Indonesia than in the Philippines.

Confirming evidence for these conclusions may be obtained from statistics on the average number of moves made by the respondents before and after their marriage. While Filipinos showed higher levels of migratory behavior at both periods in their life, this differential was especially large for the post-marital phase. Only about one of every eight Indonesian household heads claimed to have moved during this period, as compared to averages of 0.54 and 1.33 moves since marriage among the Cebu and Cagayan de Oro respondents (Table 3.2).

Table 3.3 presents our findings on the levels of education attained by migrants and nonmigrants in the five study cities. The proportion of Philippine household heads who have graduated from high school is about twice as high as is the case for the Indonesian respondents. This fits with the findings of previous studies, which have generally shown levels of educational attainment to be higher in the Philippines than in other countries of the developing world.

We might also expect that levels of educational attainment would be related positively to city size. No strong evidence to this effect is manifested in our data, though, except for the very low standing on this variable for

Table 3.3

HOUSEHOLD HEADS WITH A HIGH SCHOOL DEGREE OR HIGHER,
BY MIGRANT STATUS AND STUDY CITY (PERCENT)

Migration Status	Medan[a]	Pematang Siantar	Tebing Tinggi	Cebu	Cagayan de Oro
Migrants	32.3	26.3	21.8	49.1	49.6
Nonmigrants	24.1	26.9	15.2	45.6	56.8

[a]The difference between migrants and nonmigrants was statistically significant for this city (p<.01).

Source: Sample Survey Data.

Tebing Tinggi (the smallest study city). It is of some interest to note that the expected positive relationship between city size and educational levels is found somewhat more strongly for the subsample of migrants than among urban natives. This might be a reflection of Fuller's thesis that middle-sized cities like Cebu and Medan are themselves subject to a heavy attrition of their more skilled (native-born) populace, due to the selective outmigration of members of this group toward the primate city.

The most important conclusion to be drawn from Table 3.3 relates to the different levels of education attained by migrants and nonmigrants. In general, the data do not support the thesis that migrants to these secondary urban centers are more poorly trained than the native-born populace still residing there. In fact, migrants are better educated than nonmigrants in three of the five study cities, with one of these comparisons (for Medan) being statistically significant. In a fourth city (Pematang Siantar) the two groups are essentially equal, while only in Cagayan de Oro does the nonmigrant sample exhibit a higher level of educational attainiment, on the average, than do the migrants. This particular finding, though, may be due to the unusually high levels of in-migration which have been directed towards Cagayan de Oro during the past decade and is, in any event, statistically insignificant.[2]

Of equal importance for our investigation of migrant "quality" is the comparative level of occupational status. Since somewhat different coding schemes were used for the occupational variable in the Indonesian and Philippine studies, comparisons to this effect may only be made on a within-country basis. These data are shown in Tables 3.4 (for the Philippines) and Table 3.5 (for Indonesia).

Table 3.4

DISTRIBUTION OF MAJOR OCCUPATIONAL CATEGORIES,
HOUSEHOLD HEADS, BY MIGRANT STATUS, PHILIPPINE CITIES (PERCENT)

Category	Cebu		Cagayan de Oro	
	Migrant	Nonmigrant	Migrant	Nonmigrant
Professional	8.4	4.6	3.9	4.2
Administrative	4.5	3.4	5.1	3.7
Clerical	6.6	4.0	6.6	6.5
Sales	14.8	21.1	22.0	15.9
Farming	4.2	3.8	6.0	9.3
Transportation & Communication	17.2	15.4	17.7	24.8
Manufacturing & Construction	30.7	37.3	28.1	23.4
Services	13.6	10.5	10.5	12.1
Totals	100.0	100.1	99.9	99.9

Source: Sample Survey Data.

As shown in the first of these two tables, migrant heads in Cebu City are more heavily concentrated in the three groups of while collar occupations (professional, administrative, and clerical) than are nonmigrants. Migrants also show a slight predominance in services and in occupations devoted to transportation and communication, while they are underrepresented in sales, manufacturing and construction activities. These data provide little support for the stereotyped view of cityward migrants as clustering near the bottom of the occupational hierarchy and, indeed, would seem to provide some moderately strong evidence for the existence of an opposite pattern.

The occupational placement of migrants and nonmigrants in Cagayan de Oro differs somewhat from that in Cebu, though the overall conclusion that migrants are as least as well-off occupationally as nonmigrants persists. Despite their lower level of educational achievement, Cagayan migrants are slightly more likely than nonmigrants to hold a white collar position and a little less likely to be in a service occupation.

Table 3.5

DISTRIBUTION OF MAJOR OCCUPATIONAL CATEGORIES,
HOUSEHOLD HEADS, BY MIGRANT STATUS, INDONESIAN CITIES (PERCENT)

Category	Medan		Pematang Siantar		Tebing Tinggi	
	M	N	M	N	M	N
Government service	18.2	13.0	27.1	18.5	11.3	13.9
Private sector	17.9	14.4	12.6	10.5	0.3	6.8
Retail trade	16.7	17.6	11.0	13.7	18.7	11.4
Farmer	2.0	2.2	1.9	4.6	7.6	1.4
Manufacturing & construction	9.5	12.6	11.4	8.0	8.9	10.8
Transportation, service, self-employed	16.2	14.0	15.3	14.2	8.9	13.5
Daily workers	3.1	4.4	0.0	4.7	10.8	6.8
Temporary workers	16.4	21.7	20.7	25.9	33.4	35.4
Total	100.0	99.9	100.0	100.1	99.9	100.0

Source: Sample Survey Data.

Results for the two largest Indonesian cities provide confirming evidence for these patterns. In both Medan and Pematang Siantar it is migrants, rather than nonmigrants, who are concentrated in the more prestigious government and private sector (corporate) positions. Conversely, fewer migrants must suffer the insecurity of being only a "daily" or a "temporary" worker. Thus, it is only in Tebing Tinggi that migrants are not at an advantage over urban natives in terms of their occupational placement. Even here, however, the proportionate differences are not large, and based upon too small a sample size to warrant the conclusion that migrants hold a lower occupational status than nonmigrants.

When the various occupations are categorized as belonging to either the formal or informal labor sector, similar results are forthcoming.[3] Contrary

Table 3.6

HOUSEHOLD HEADS EMPLOYED IN FORMAL SECTOR,
BY MIGRANT STATUS (PERCENT)

Migrant Status	Medan[a]	Pematang Siantar	Tebing Tinggi	Cebu[a]	Cagayan de Oro
Migrant	38.6	40.0	22.2	65.8	54.2
Nonmigrant	31.4	32.8	28.4	54.2	53.0

[a]The differences between migrants and nonmigrants are
statistically significant for Medan ($p<.05$) and Cebu ($p<.01$).

Source: Sample Survey Data.

to the commonly-held view that cityward migrants flock to informal sector
jobs, our data show a larger proportion of migrants than of nonmigrants
to be formal sector workers in four of the five study cities, with Tebing
Tinggi again being the lone exception. In this case, two of these comparisons
(for Cebu and Medan) were large enough to attain statistical significance
(Table 3.6).

We have speculated earlier that migrant selectivity may be somewhat
less positive in those cities (Cagayan de Oro and Tebing Tinggi) which
have attracted the greater volume of inmigrants during recent years. In
general, our findings on educational and occupational selectivity do support
this speculation. This would seem to indicate that programs designed to
attract migrants to secondary urban centers will become counterproductive
if they result in very heavy rates of inmigration.

Comparisons were also made with respect to two other indicators of
economic activity. The first of these related to the spouse's employment
status. Other than the not unexpected fact that spouses from the Philippine
study cities were more likely to be in the labor force than were those from
Indonesia, differentials on this variable did not follow any particular pattern
and were uniformly too narrow to attain statistical significance. Overall,
42.5 percent of the spouses falling within our Philippine sample were counted
as being in the labor force, as compared to only 28.6 percent from Indonesia.
Efforts to more fully incorporate Indonesian women into the development
process appear called for, given this finding.

A second indicator of economic activities which is available from the
survey refers to the extent to which one or more members of the household
is operating some sort of family business. Inter-country comparisons on

Table 3.7

HOUSEHOLD MEMBERS ENGAGED IN A FAMILY
BUSINESS, MIGRANTS AND NONMIGRANTS (PERCENT)

Study City	Migrants	Nonmigrants
Cebu	24.5	25.5
Cagayan de Oro	32.2	31.3
Medan	17.6	15.6
Pematang Siantar	26.5	9.8
Tebing Tinggi	32.3	11.1

Source: Sample Survey Data.

this item parallel those obtained for the spouse's employment status, perhaps because many of the Philippine working women are engaged in some sort of small business, such as operating a small corner, or *sari-sari,* store (cf. Hackenberg and Barth, 1984). Overall, 28 percent of our Philippine respondents affirmed that someone in their family was operating a business, as compared to only 16 percent of those from the Indonesian study sites.

Based on his review of differential migration studies, Browning (1971) has hypothesized that migrants to cities in the developing world represent a select group of dynamic, risk-taking individuals. If this were indeed the case, we would expect to find that larger proportions of the households headed by migrants would have one or more members engaged in a family business. As shown by the figures in Table 3.7, our data do lend slight support to this thesis. In four of the five study cities migrants are over-represented in the family business category. Again, these differentials are not large enough, save for the case of Pematang Siantar, to allow for the conclusion that migrants are more likely than nonmigrants to engage in a family business but they do show members of this group to have at least reached parity on this variable with the native-born urbanites.

To this point in our analysis, then, we have been able to show that migrants to the five cities hold a consistent, though modestly-sized advantage over urban nonmigrants with regard to their position in the city's economy. They are somewhat better educated than nonmigrants, more likely to be found in a high status or formal sector occupation, and slightly more likely to be associated with a family business. Migrant spouses are also about equally likely as those who were born in the city to be working. Given these findings, we would therefore expect that the levels of living experienced

Table 3.8

MEAN NUMBER OF CONSUMER ITEMS OWNED,[a]
BY MIGRANT STATUS

Migrant Status	Medan[b]	Pematang Siantar	Tebing Tinggi	Cebu	Cagayan de Oro
Migrant	5.28	4.60	3.58	4.31	4.56
Nonmigrant	4.42	4.11	3.22	4.53	4.44

[a]The ownership scale includes nineteen items: car, motorcycle, bicycle, radio, black and white television, color television, sewing machine, phonograph, tape recorder, electric fan, wrist watch, telephone, clock, electric iron, gas or electric stove, electric rice cooker, refrigerator, air conditioner, and camera.

[b]The difference between migrants and nonmigrants for Medan was statistically significant (p <.01).

Source: Sample Survey Data.

by migrants would not be substantially lower than those found for urban natives; in fact, the opposite might well prove true.

In order to shed further light on this question, we constructed a simple additive scale of the respondent's ownership of consumer goods, as based on questions about nineteen such items, ranging from a camera to an automobile. Data were also available from the survey on the household head's income, but the ownership scale proved superior to this variable for a number of reasons. Foremost in this regard was the scale's presumed greater validity, insofar as responses about earnings are notoriously inaccurate in both settings. Secondly, the ownership scale gives a better indication of the economic status of the household as a whole, since it is affected by the economic contributions of the spouse, as well as those provided by the husband.

Table 3.8 presents our findings for this indicator. The results shown in this table are fully compatible with those given earlier. Differences between the migrant and nonmigrant groups on the ownership index are not large, but those which do exist tend to favor the migrant category. At the time of the survey, geographically mobile respondents were owning a greater number of consumer items in four of the five study cities, with this differential being large enough to attain statistical significance in Medan.

In order to see if migrant status has an independent influence upon ownership levels, statistical controls should be made for certain other associated variables which may be confounding this relationship. For example, it has been shown earlier that migrants to Medan are significantly better educated than non-migrants in this city. Since we would expect levels of living to be higher among better educated respondents, it might therefore be this variable, rather than migration status *per se,* which is the actual determinant in this case.

In order to take this possibility into account, a multiple regression model of consumer goods ownership was constructed and run independently for each of the five study cities. In addition to the migration status factor ("MIGSTAT"), four other variables have been entered as statistical controls in these models. These are the sex, age, level of educational attainment, and employment sector of the household head.

Findings from previous studies would lead us to expect that households headed by males, older persons, and the better educated would have higher levels of living than those not falling within these categories (Birdsall and McGreevey, 1978; Visaria, 1980). The relationship between employment sector and living standards is less immediately evident, however, since some authors have concluded that informal sector workers can earn as much, or nearly as much, as those in the formal sector (e.g., Lloyd, 1979; Koo and Smith, 1983).

As shown in Table 3.9, results from the regression analysis are approximately uniform across the five study cities. Weak positive relationships between migration status and consumer goods ownership are still in evidence for four of the five study sites, even with the other factors held constant. The statistically significant relationship which was found for Medan also remains in evidence.

The respondent's level of educational attainment was found in all study sites to be the strongest predictor of the household's level of living. As expected, relationships in this case were uniformly positive. Positive (and statistically significant) relationships were also found in all cases for the age variable, evidently reflecting the fact that households in the later stages of the family life cycle have had more time in which to acquire material possessions. Older household heads may also be earning higher incomes, or could be receiving more in the way of remittances from their children.

Results from all five study cities showed households headed by persons employed in the formal sector to be better off economically than those in which the head had an informal sector job. Three of these relationships were found to be statistically significant. Finally, the sex of the household head appeared to make relatively little difference as far as the ownership of consumer goods is concerned. Households headed by males tended to

Table 3.9

STANDARDIZED MULTIPLE REGRESSION COEFFICIENTS FOR A MODEL
OF CONSUMER GOODS OWNERSHIP, BY STUDY CITY

Independent Variable[a]	Medan	Pematang Siantar	Tebing Tinggi	Cebu	Cagayan de Oro
MIGSTAT	.08*	.04	.06	-.05	.02
SEX	.01	.02	.01	-.01	.02
AGE	.19**	.13*	.24*	.24**	.27**
EDUC	.43**	.32**	.40**	.54**	.53**
SECTOR	.14**	.17*	.11	.09*	.04
R^2	.27	.17	.22	.35	.35

[a]Dummy variables were use to represent the three nominal-type
predictors. In these cases, it was migrants (for MIGSTAT), males
(for SEX), and formal sector employees (for SECTOR) who were
coded positively.

**$p<.001$; *$p<.05$.

Source: Sample Survey Data.

fare better than those with female heads, but these relationships were weak
and in no case statistically significant.

A final way in which migrants and nonmigrants may be compared relates
to their housing conditions. As exemplified by La Greca's (1979) comments
about migrants living in "some of the worse slums imaginable" there exists
a very strong tendency in the literature to assert that migrants gravitate
disproportionately to slum and squatter communities once they arrive in
the city. An earlier paper (Costello and Palabrica-Costello, 1981) has shown
that this is actually not true as far as the great majority of migrants who
arrive in the city as *non heads of households* are concerned, since these
persons will most typically live with their employer or with a better-off
relative. The question remains, however, as to the housing conditions of
migrant heads, as compared to those experienced by urban natives.

Data on this question are presented in Table 3.10. The variable being
examined in this case is the tenancy status of the household head, with

Table 3.10

DISTRIBUTION OF HOUSING TENURE STATUS BY CITY OF RESIDENCE,
MIGRANT VS. NONMIGRANT (PERCENT)

Housing Tenure	Medan		Pematang Siantar		Tebing Tinggi		Cebu[a]		Cagayan de Oro[a]	
	M	N	M	N	M	N	M	N	M	N
Owns lot	65	60	60	66	72	75	14	29	11	20
Rents	16	16	28	22	17	15	40	27	54	30
Squatter	13	18	4	8	3	8	43	42	28	41
Other	6	6	8	5	8	2	3	3	8	9

[a]The differences between migrants (M) and nonmigrants (N) were statistically significant for the two Philippine cities (p<.001).

Source: Sample Survey Data.

comparisons being made between owners, renters, squatters and those holding other types of tenancy arrangements (chiefly persons who are staying for free with their relatives).

The results show a highly significant differential between migrants and nonmigrants on this variable within the two Philippine cities. In contrast, no significant relationship was found in the three Indonesian study sites. Inter-country comparisons also indicate that ownership of one's house and lot is much more common among the Indonesian respondents than among those from the Philippines. The reason for this differential is not immediately apparent to the authors, and would seem to be worthy of further investigation.

Of particular interest is the comparison between migrants and nonmigrants with regard to the proportion of each group who are squatters. The definition of "squatter" which has been used in this case consists of persons who are staying in rent-free dwellings on either private (the more typical case) or public land.[4] In general, squatters may be assumed to have little or no legal rights over the land on which they are living. This group, however, does possess the unique advantage of having to pay virtually nothing in the way of rental or amortization costs. For this reason, it is quite possible that squatting may in some cases be a valued type of tenancy arrangement, and one which can be regarded as being in some demand among members of the urban lower classes. Thus, in cases where a dispute has arisen over the legality of a title for some urban landholding, the area is likely to be invaded very soon thereafter by a number of squatter households (e.g., Cometa, *et al,* 1983). Most of these households, one would suspect, must have already been established in the city, since it is unlikely that information about the court proceedings would diffuse rapidly to other communities, or that, even if it did, many persons from such places would immediately move from their current residence in response to such a rumor.

These points are raised in an effort to explain the somewhat unexpected finding observed in Table 3.10; namely, that native urban household heads are equally or even more likely than citybound migrants to become squatters. In fact, nonmigrants were found to have a larger proportion of squatters in their midst in four of the five study cities, while the differential between these two groups for the remaining case of metropolitan Cebu is virtually negligible. Due to their longer term of residence in the city, urban natives may thus be in a better position to take advantage of the option to squat. Members of this group will have probably established more social contacts in the city and, as such, would be more likely to hear about coming "invasions" of public lands, or to establish a strong enough relationship with a higher status urbanite so as to be allowed to reside temporarily on some portion of his urban landholdings.

A second reason for the excess of nonmigrants falling into the squatting category could lie in the economic factors discussed earlier. The fact that nonmigrants appear to be faring somewhat more poorly on this dimension could thus be resulting in an increasing need, among members of this group, to squat. Whatever the explanation, though, it is again clear that the stereotyped identification of squatters with rural-urban migrants does not hold true for this particular sample of secondary urban centers.

As for the other types of housing tenure arrangements, it would generally appear to be the case that migrants are more likely to be renting their current dwelling. This is no doubt linked to the fact that members of this group have lived, on the average, for fewer years in the city and have thus had fewer opportunities to purchase or to inherit a residential lot therein. Indeed, further analysis of the tenancy status variable for the case of Cagayan de Oro (Costello and Palabrica-Costello, 1985) has shown that renting is most heavily concentrated among recent migrants to that city, while those who came ten or more years ago are about equally as likely as native-born urbanites to possess their own house and lot.

Summary

The purpose of this chapter has been to compare the characteristics of migrants coming to the five study cities with those of urban nonmigrants. Overall, our results provide little support for the stereotyped view of rural-urban migrants as consisting primarily of illiterate and unemployed slum dwellers. Most migrant household heads moved to the city while they were still young and unmarried. On the average, they had attained an equal, or even slightly superior, level of educational attainment as compared to nonmigrants in their city of destination. They also were found to be holding somewhat higher status occupations, and were more likely to be employed in the formal sector, than were urban natives. As a result, members of this group tended to be better off in terms of their ownership of consumer goods, with this relationship persisting (albeit somewhat weakly) even when such associated factors as age, sex, and educational status of the household head were controlled statistically. Migrants were also somewhat less likely than nonmigrants to become squatters. Finally, no significant differences were found between migrants and nonmigrants with regard to either the spouse's employment status or the probability that someone in the household had set up a family business.

These conclusions are not entirely novel. As we have seen, most empirically-minded researchers have obtained similar results to those presented in this chapter. Where our findings do go beyond previous studies, however, is with regard to our emphasis upon secondary urban centers. Data presented in this chapter may thus be interpreted as showing that the positive picture of the migration process which has been built up by studies conducted in the national primate cities of the region may well be extended to the smaller urban centers as well.

Notes

1. In the few cases where the migrant moved to the present city more than once, age and marital status at the date of the *first* move (after age fifteen) was used.

2. That is, there is no significant difference at the .05 level of probability. However, it is significant at the .10 level ($X^2 = 3.51$ with one degree of freedom).

3. For a discussion of the means by which formal and informal sector activities have been operationally defined in this study, see the more complete discussion of this topic in Chapter 5.

4. Persons who were staying rent-free on privately-owned land were defined as squatters whether or not they had permission from the owner to do so. Discussions of the squatting phenomenon are often based upon an implicit assumption that squatters do not have permission to reside in their current place. However, this is not always the case, since economically well-off urbanites may occasionally let a poor family stay on currently unused land, either because they pay some very minimal "rent" (e.g., one to two dollars per month) or because they can render some other service to the owner, such as to guard the property in question. In our opinion, such cases may still be characterized as squatting, since these persons do not have any tenure rights over the land on which they are residing. In any event,

it is virtually impossible to obtain valid information on "permission" from a survey-type study. This is especially true in the Southeast Asian context, where those staying without permission would be either afraid or ashamed to admit this. In the present case, an attempt was made to obtain information on this but the vast majority of households heads staying as squatters on private lands claimed that they were doing so with the permission of the owner.

4

Reasons for Coming to the City
and Subsequent Outcomes

What are the factors that cause people to move? In particular, what has brought about the heavy exodus of Third World inhabitants from their traditional rural homeplaces? One simple and effective way of answering these questions is to pose them directly to the migrants themselves. Migration, like any other social act, is a function not only of objective social conditions but also of the individual's subjective interpretations of these conditions, along with his or her perceived options for dealing with them. As Berger and Kellner (1981, 40) have observed, careful attention should be paid to these subjective factors, insofar as social science concepts must always "retain an intelligible connection with the meaningful intentions of the actors in the situation."

Our first concern in the present chapter will thus be to focus on the "meaningful intentions" held by migrants to the various study cities. What are these, and how do they vary among different groups of movers? A second issue stems naturally from the first, and is concerned with the extent to which the expectations held by migrants upon their arrival in the city have actually been met. For example, what are the patterns and correlates of economic and social mobility which have been manifested among this group? How has the migration process been affected by the presence of friends and relatives in the community of destination? Have such persons facilitated his adjustment to city life? Simultaneously, has the migrant managed to keep intact his social ties with those significant others who were left behind in the area of origin? These are the major questions to be posed in this chapter.

Among the many possible reasons for changing one's residence, economic motives appear to take precedence, especially in the less developed world. Such reasons can include the desire for economic mobility, either for one's self or for the household of origin; the drive to escape local economic problems, such as high unemployment or low wage levels; job transfers;

and the desire to utilize job-linked skills which are not in demand in the community of origin. Studies conducted in the Southeast Asian region have generally found a little over half of all migrants to be moving for motives of this type (e.g., Speare, 1976; Pryor, 1977; Ulack, 1977). Factors associated with family or kin ties also play a key role in this respect, usually accounting for about a third of all moves. This is perhaps to be expected, given the importance of the family in Southeast Asian social life. Persons who migrate to a particular city because they have kinsmen living there who can be called upon for assistance represent an important subtype of this general category, as do migrants who move at the time of major changes in the family life cycle, such as marriage, widowhood, or birth of the first child.

To date, only a few studies have sought to determine the major correlates of reasons for moving. One plausible hypothesis is that lower status (poorly educated, rural born) migrants would be disproportionately motivated by economic factors, due to their presumably greater financial need. Conversely, though, the precarious quality of lower class life might also have the effect of leading these respondents to stress family alliances and obligations as a form of risk minimization. This counterbalancing pattern may help to explain why it is that most previous Indonesian and Philippine studies have found only a modest tendency for lower status migrants to explain their move in terms of economic factors (Zosa, 1974; Speare, 1976; Palabrica-Costello, 1980).

To this point in the discussion we have been tacitly assuming that the locus of decision-making lies within the individual migrant himself. This, however, may not always be the case, especially in the less-developed world. An emerging perspective within the discipline, termed the household decision-making model, holds that the decision to migrate will most typically be made in conjunction with other members of the household, even in cases when only a single individual is moving (Simmons, 1981). In some cases, a young person's parents may encourage him to leave; in others he may be asked to postpone to a later date the move which he would like to now make. In either event, the major goal will be that of maximizing returns to the household as a whole, and not just to the individual migrant. Those who leave will be expected to remit much of their earnings for the upkeep of family members left behind. It will also be assumed that they will return home for occasional visits, or perhaps even permanently, should their presence be needed.

A contrasting picture is presented by the individual decision-making model. According to this view, migrants will tend to make the decision to migrate on their own, while the purpose for such a move will be to maximize returns for themselves, rather than for those left behind. This model would appear to approximate the Western pattern of geographic mobility, or, more generally, to apply in cases where the major units of economic production are business firms or the state, rather than the household; where individualism is emphasized; and where "wealth flows" (Caldwell, 1976) are directed more from parents to children than in the opposite direction.

Certain features of the mobility systems of Third World societies—such as the reportedly high rates of return migration and of cash remittances— would appear to indicate that it is the household model which is most appropriate for these settings. This, however, remains an empirical question, at least as far as Southeast Asia is concerned. Individualizing influences are by no means absent from the region and have, indeed, probably become more pronounced due to the growth of capitalism and of increasing exposure to the Western media. In addition, the stark poverty experienced by many of the families in the region may result in considerable departures from the household model as an ideal type. Thus, poor or landless household heads may lack the economic resources needed to legitimize their parental authority, while poorer in-migrants to the city may be too hard-pressed economically to remit much of their earnings to their family of origin.

In support of the household model, we may point to evidence from a number of less developed countries where it has been found that migrants prefer to move towards places and persons with whom they have already established some sort of contact. Thus, a major review article on the topic has concluded that "the great majority of migrants to large cities make the journey to, and the accommodation within, the large city as part of a kinship group" (Browning, 1971, 297). Relatives are an especially important source of information about job opportunities and local living conditions in countries where the mass media are poorly developed and employment agencies unlikely to be utilized. Kinfolk may also provide a place to stay or some sort of financial assistance to the newcomer upon his arrival in the city. Empirical studies from the region have shown that migrants— especially those in the lower status categories—do take advantage of such services upon their arrival in the city (Palabrica-Costello, 1980). Evidence also exists to the effect that the presence of relatives outside the source region tends to stimulate mobility from rural areas insofar as this variable is linked strongly to the intention to out-migrate (Lee, et al, 1985).

Having managed to establish himself in the city, the migrant is now faced with the difficult tasks of finding some form of permanent employment and of bettering himself economically. Most studies which have been conducted to date on these issues have concluded that the prospects for such mobility are by no means unlikely. Thus, Indonesian survey data have shown that rural- born migrants to Jakarta were earning higher wages than were non- farm workers in their areas of origin, even though most had only been able to find jobs in the "unproductive" service sector. As a result, over half of all such migrants claimed that their economic circumstances had improved since coming to the city, while only eight percent felt that their move had hurt them economically (Speare, 1976). Similar results have been reported for Brazil (Yap, 1976), Thailand (Fuller, 1981), and the Philippines (Ulack, 1976).

The prospects for such mobility, however, may often be contingent upon a number of background factors. Thus, the economic "payoff" accruing to migrants appears to be greatest among the better educated (Pernia, 1978; Connell *et al*, 1976), males (Pernia, 1978), and those coming from other urban areas (Speare, 1976).

Even though the migrant may be expected to eventually adjust himself to life in his chosen destination, it is unlikely that his ties to the area of origin will be completely broken. Bonds of sentiment and filial obligation will continue to unite him with members of his family of origin. In addition, it will often be to the migrant's economic advantage to maintain such ties. The risk of failure in the city is ever present, thus making it best to leave open the option of return migration. Temporary visits to the village of origin (e.g. during harvest time) may offer a source of additional income. In addition, migrants who have done well in the city may subsequently use their network of relatives and friends in the home community to recruit persons who could serve them as househelpers, or as low-skilled laborers in a family business (e.g., Adem, 1985).

Two means for maintaining social ties with those still residing in the community of origin are through periodic visits home and via the remittance of goods or cash. A lively debate exists in the literature as to the comparative magnitude of such remittances, with some authors viewing economic exchanges between rural-urban migrants and relatives in their home community as comprising a key source of rural welfare, while others have argued that these have an essentially minor, and possibly negative, impact upon the countryside (for a useful literature review see Hugo, 1983). Again, these contrasting conclusions appear to reflect the broader theoretical debate between household and individual models of migrant decision-making.

The Migration Process

Overall, about 70 percent of the migrating household heads in the five study locales claimed that they had been the one to make the final decision to move to their present community of residence. This finding fails to give clear support to either the household or individual migration model. On the one hand, the proportion of all migrants who moved in response to a request from some other family member is almost certainly higher than would be expected in the West. At the same time, it appears that well over half of all moves were brought about in response to the personal motives and aspirations of the migrant himself. Furthermore, more detailed data from Cagayan de Oro indicate that migrants who move in response to

Table 4.1

REASONS FOR MIGRATING TO PRESENT CITY OF RESIDENCE,
MIGRANT HOUSEHOLD HEADS (PERCENT)[a]

Reason	Medan	Pematang Siantar	Tebing Tinggi	Cebu	Cagayan de Oro
Economic	42.5	44.0	35.3	49.9	71.7
Family-related	37.6	28.0	29.4	24.4	11.1
Schooling	5.8	4.0	5.9	12.3	7.6
Other	14.2	24.0	29.4	13.4	9.6

[a]Sample sizes for all information presented in Chapter 4 are, with minor fluctuations, as follows: 205 cases (Medan), 32 (Pematang Siantar), 17 (Tebing Tinggi), 406 (Cebu), and 552 (Cagayan de Oro).

Source: Sample Survey Data.

requests from other family members are much more likely to do so in response to a discussion with their *spouse* than with their parents (Costello and Palabrica-Costello, 1985). This finding does not support the picture, provided by the household model, of young adults being sent out by their parents to find a job in the city so that they may remit some portion of their earnings homeward.

Given the greater impact which Westernizing forces have had in the Philippines and in the larger urban areas of the region, one might have expected that migrants in these settings would be more likely to move on their own initiative. This, however, is not the case. The percentage of respondents who said that someone other than themselves made the final decision to move was 36 percent in Medan and 31 percent in Cebu, as compared to 13 percent in Pematang Siantar, 24 percent in Tebing Tinggi, and 30 percent in Cagayan de Oro.

Some of the major reasons given by the migrants for moving to their present locale are given in Table 4.1. As expected, the economic motive predominates in this tabulation, with this category being found most frequently in each of the five study cities. Clearly, though, the commonly-expressed view that "virtually all" (Hardjono, 1980, 26) migrants in the region are motivated by such factors appears incorrect. About one in every four migrants cited family reasons as constituting their most important motive, while all other reasons combined, including the desire for additional schooling, comprise a roughly similar proportion.

Overall, there appear to be few consistent differences on this variable between the two larger cities (Cebu and Medan) and those in the smaller size categories. Some evidence does exist, though, that family reasons play a more salient role for the Indonesian respondents, while economic and educational motives are more frequently cited by Philippine migrants. This could be due to cultural differences between these two settings, although the fact that the Filipino family system has frequently been seen by social demographers as facilitating the migration process argues against this perspective. A more likely factor, perhaps, is the significantly younger age at arrival of the Indonesian migrants. The influence of family and kin ties might be expected to be especially strong at these ages.

Table 4.2 presents bivariate statistics depicting the relationship between the reason for migration and a number of associated variables. The measure of association in this case is Yule's Q, while the reason for coming to the city has been dichotomized into economic and noneconomic factors. The five associated variables have also been dichotomized; these include the migrant's year of arrival in his or her present community (YRARVL), the urban/rural character of the community of origin (URBORG), age and marital status at the time of migration, and the migrant's level of educational attainment. Positive coefficients in this table may be interpreted as showing that recent arrivals and those from other urban areas, along with older, married, and better educated migrants, were most likely to have been motivated by economic reasons.

Results from the four major study settings are approximately uniform. The primary exception is found for the case of URBORG, where the Q coefficients are neither large nor consistently patterned. This could be due in part to difficulties in obtaining a uniform definition of "urban" areas between Indonesia and the Philippines.

In general, recent arrivals tend to be more motivated by economic factors than were those who came ten or more years ago. Similar results are in evidence for older, married, and (in the two Philippine study cities, at least) less well-educated migrants.

That older and married migrants would place greater emphasis on economic factors is perhaps to be expected. The demands of providing for their own wife and children are likely to reduce their feeling of responsibility for their extended kin in their community of origin. Most such migrants will be too old to move for educational purposes and may also be less likely to be invited to stay with some other relative in the city. Indeed, the option of staying for an extended period with an urban kinsman appears to be most frequently extended to unmarried adolescents, insofar as such persons can be expected to lack dependents and therefore to make fewer demands upon

Table 4.2

MEASURES OF ASSOCIATION (YULE'S Q) BETWEEN HOLDING AN
ECONOMIC REASON FOR MIGRATING AND SELECTED INDEPENDENT VARIABLES,
MIGRANT HOUSEHOLD HEADS

Independent Variable[a]	Cebu	Cagayan de Oro	Medan	Pematang Siantar/ Tebing Tinggi[b]
YRARVL	.18	.15	.30	.35
URBORG	-.06	.19	.07	-.17
AGEMOVE	.06	.47***	.31*	.06
MARMOVE	.19	.27**	.40*	c
EDUC	-.28**	-.19**	-.06	.08

[a]All variables were dichotomized as follows: YRARVL (1970 or earlier vs. 1971-1983), URBORG (rural vs. urban origins), AGEMOVE (15-20 years of age vs. 21 years and over), MARMOVE (ever married vs. never married), and EDUC (less than secondary graduate vs. secondary graduate or above). Migrants who came more recently and who had moved from an urban community were scored positively, along with those who were older, married, and better-educated.

[b]Due to the small number of migrant household heads in Tebing Tinggi, respondents from this study city have been combined with those from Pematang Siantar in this and in several subsequent tables.

[c]Dropped from the analysis due to an insufficient number of migrants who had been married at the time of their move.

***$p < .001$; **$p < .01$; *$p < .05$.

Source: Sample Survey Data.

their urban kin. Young and unmarried relatives will also be more willing to take on some sort of quasi-servant role for the household in which they are staying.

Data from the two Philippine cities show poorly educated migrants to be significantly more likely to cite economic motives for their action than those who have attained a high school level of education or higher. No comparable pattern, however, is in evidence for the Indonesian data.

The explanation for the predominance of economic motives among recent migrants is not immediately clear. Indeed, one might well have hypothesized that the opposite pattern would prevail, since the earlier migration cohorts would have fewer relatives living in urban areas, thus decreasing their propensity to move for family-related reasons. Two possible explanations may be suggested for this finding, the first of which is that life in the Philippine and Indonesian countryside has become increasingly difficult over the past decade, thus forcing additional numbers of displaced peasants to seek their livelihood in an urban setting. Trends toward increasing rural population densities, the adoption of new forms of mechanized agriculture, displacement of small farmers by large-scale plantations, and the breakdown of traditional landlord-tenant relationships all represent examples of processes which might have brought about such a situation (cf. White, 1979; Costello, 1984). Another possibility is that those household heads who migrated a decade or so ago and who have by now gained a fairly secure foothold in the city have simply forgotten about their early hardships, such as are still being experienced by those who arrived more recently.

Initial adjustment to city life represents another important dimension of the migration process. Given the sharp cultural and economic discontinuities which may exist between urban and rural areas, this transition may at times be fraught with difficulties. These, however, can be ameliorated in cases where the migrant is incorporated into a network of friends and relatives already living in the city. Such persons can help in many ways: by providing a place to stay, as sources of information about employment opportunities, or by helping the migrant financially during the period before he finds his first job. Anthropologists have commented upon such patterns with some frequency but relatively little information has as yet been available from large-scale surveys on this topic, especially for those which have been conducted upon randomly chosen samples of all types of urban residents, and not just those from slum areas. Our statistics on this question, as shown in Table 4.3, are thus of particular interest.

The general picture provided by these data is one which shows pre-existing networks of relatives and friends to play an important, though scarcely universal, role in the migration process. A relatively large proportion of migrants asserted that they had made their initial move to the city without much help from friends or relatives already living there. About 60 to 70 percent of the migrating heads in the five study cities said that they did not stay with a friend or relative upon arrival, while even larger proportions claimed that they did not receive any financial help from acquaintances in the destination community. In addition, more than one-half of the migrants had never even visited their destination city before moving there.

The main exception to this overall pattern lies in the results from an item which inquired as to whether or not the migrant had known someone

Table 4.3

MIGRATION-FACILITATING CONTACTS WITH CITY OF DESTINATION,
MIGRANT HOUSEHOLD HEADS (PERCENT ESTABLISHING SUCH A CONTACT)

Type of Contact	Medan	Pematang Siantar	Tebing Tinggi	Cebu	Cagayan de Oro
Knew someone	59.8	73.9	57.1	53.6	61.9
Had visited previously	38.1	47.2	32.0	46.7	39.6
Stayed with someone on arrival	40.4	39.0	44.0	31.9	41.9
Obtained financial aid	20.3	31.0	16.7	20.1	31.3

Source: Sample Survey Data.

in the destination community before moving there. A majority of the migrants in all of the five study cities asserted that this had been true in their case. Noteworthy, though, are the rather substantial minorities in each setting who did not have the advantage of even this minimal level of pre-migration contact. As an overall conclusion, then, these data would appear to emphasize the individualizing nature of the migration process, with most migrants claiming to have moved of their own volition and with relatively little assistance from relatives or friends in the destination community.

Further insight into this question may be obtained by examining Table 4.4, which presents information on some correlates of the decision to stay with someone upon arrival in the city. As discussed earlier, there is some reason to suspect that older and married migrants would be less likely to take advantage of this option. This expectation is borne out reasonably well in the present case, particularly for the two Philippine cities. Results for the rural-urban origins of the (URBORG), however, are less conclusive. Weak inverse relationships are in evidence for the two Philippine study cities, indicating a pattern whereby urban-urban migrants are less likely than those coming from rural areas to seek out such help. This would appear to be the expected pattern. Confirming results, however, are not found for the Indonesian study settings.

That migrants of lower socioeconomic status are most likely to stay with a friend or relative upon their arrival in the city would appear to be a

Table 4.4

MEASURES OF ASSOCIATION (YULE'S Q) BETWEEN HAVING STAYED WITH
SOMEONE UPON ARRIVAL IN THE CITY AND SELECTED INDEPENDENT
VARIABLES, MIGRANT HOUSEHOLD HEADS

Independent Variable[a]	Cebu	Cagayan de Oro	Medan	Pematang Siantar/ Tebing Tinggi
URBORG	-.16	-.22*	-.01	.22
AGEMOVE	-.12	-.26**	-.04	b
MARMOVE	-.39**	-.38***	b	b
EDUC	.10	-.14	-.01	.67**

[a]All variables dichotomized as in Table 4.2.

[b]Less than five expected cases in one or more cells.

***p<.001; **p<.01; *p<.05.

Source: Sample Survey Data.

plausible hypothesis. Such migrants will be in greater need of such help
and may hold a more familistic perspective. As shown in Table 4.4, though,
no clear evidence could be found to this effect. Statistically insignificant
relationships were found for this variable, as proxied by the head's level of
educational attainment, in Cebu, Cagayan de Oro, and Medan, while a
significant *positive* correlation was found in the combined sample of respondents from Pematang Siantar and Tebing Tinggi. This latter finding,
however, must be interpreted with caution, since it is based upon a sample
of only 64 respondents. Two factors which might counterbalance the presumed
greater need for assistance of lower status migrants may be listed: first,
better-educated migrants have a wider circle of social contacts outside their
community of origin and, secondly, such persons may be more likely to
receive an offer of assistance from a city-based friend or relative, insofar
as they are perceived as constituting a more useful social ally than someone
with fewer skills and lower social status (for a discussion of social alliance
patterns in the Philippines, cf. Lynch, 1979).

Migrant Adjustment:
Changes in Occupational Status and Income

The changes which are brought on by migration continue to occur long after residence has been formally taken up in the city. In some cases, these will be for the worse, as the newcomer falls victim to the problems of poverty and social disorganization found in urban squatter areas; in others, a more fortuitous outcome may result, as the migrant begins to advance himself economically. One way of assessing the extent to which these contrasting alternatives may be occurring is to see how the occupational standing of migrants at the time of the survey compares to that which was held at the time of their initial arrival in the city. This has been done in Tables 4.5 (for Cebu and Cagayan de Oro) and 4.6 (for the Indonesian study cities).

The overall picture which emerges from these data is one of moderate upward mobility. In both Cebu and Cagayan de Oro there is a net out-movement over time from manufacturing, construction, and service occupations, all of which are associated with lower levels of socioeconomic status. At the same time, a larger proportion of Philippine migrants were found by the time of the survey to be in either a white collar (professional, administrative, clerical) or a sales position, as compared to the corresponding occupational distribution of this group at the time of their arrival. These data may be interpreted as showing evidence of upward mobility insofar as it is generally acknowledged that white collar work is more prestigious and better paying than that requiring manual labor, while sales workers in Southeast Asian cities have been shown to be earning reasonably high incomes, even when such economically marginal occupations as peddlers and sidewalk vendors are included in this category (Cabigon, 1980; Costello and Palabrica-Costello, 1985).

While the major occupational groupings employed for the Indonesian data set differ from those used in the Philippines, a generally similar pattern emerges in this case (see Table 4.6). By the time of the survey, a larger proportion of Indonesian household heads were working for either the government or the private sector than had been the case at the time of their arrival, with this differential being especially large for the city of Medan. Employment in these types of jobs is highly valued within Indonesian society. In contrast, declining proportions were in evidence, again for all study cities, for "daily" and temporary workers, both of which are characterized by low earnings and insecure job tenure.

A general tendency for migrants to initially find work in the informal employment sector, as followed by a subsequent net movement into formal sector jobs may also be noted in the data. This is most readily apparent

Table 4.5

OCCUPATION AT TIME OF ARRIVAL IN THE CITY AND AT TIME OF SURVEY,
EMPLOYED MIGRANT HOUSEHOLD HEADS IN PHILIPPINE CITIES (PERCENT)

Major Occupational Category	Cebu		Cagayan de Oro	
	Time of Arrival (N=281)	Time of Survey (N=332)	Time of Arrival (N=486)	Time of Survey (N=514)
Professional	3.2	8.4	3.3	3.9
Administrative	3.2	4.5	2.5	5.1
Clerical	3.9	6.6	6.8	6.6
Sales	13.5	14.8	19.5	22.0
Farming	3.9	4.2	4.3	6.0
Transportation and communications	19.2	17.2	17.1	17.7
Manufacturing and construction	34.5	30.7	33.7	28.1
Services	18.5	13.6	12.8	10.5
Total	99.9	100.0	100.0	99.9

Source: **Sample Survey Data.**

for the case of Cebu, where 51 percent of the migrant heads were working in the informal sector upon their arrival in this city, as contrasted to only 34 percent by the time of the study. Similar, though somewhat weaker, patterns were observed in Medan and Cagayan de Oro, while no substantial change was in evidence for the combined samples of employed household heads in Pematang Siantar and Tebing Tinggi. In Medan, 68 percent of the migrant heads had been employed in the informal sector at the time of their arrival, as compared to only 60 percent by the time of the survey; corresponding figures for Cagayan de Oro were 49 and 46 percent. Combined results for Pematang Siantar and Tebing Tinggi showed 66 percent of the migrant heads to be informal sector workers at both of these two points in time.

Table 4.6

OCCUPATION AT TIME OF ARRIVAL IN CITY AND TIME OF SURVEY,
EMPLOYED MIGRANT HOUSEHOLD HEADS IN INDONESIAN CITIES (PERCENT)

Major Occupational Category	Medan		Pematang Siantar/ Tebing Tinggi	
	Time of Arrival (N=192)	Time of Survey (N=298)	Time of Arrival (N=54)	Time of Survey (N=77)
Government service	12.5	18.2	11.1	20.8
Private sector	9.4	17.9	11.1	7.8
Retail trade	17.7	16.7	9.3	13.0
Farming	5.7	2.0	7.4	3.9
Manufacturing and construction	16.7	9.5	11.1	11.7
Transportation, services, and self-employed	12.5	16.2	5.6	13.0
Daily workers	7.8	3.1	9.3	3.9
Temporary workers	17.7	16.4	35.2	26.0
Total	100.0	100.0	100.1	100.1

Source: Sample Survey Data.

These findings stand in contrast to those obtained by Koo and Smith (1983) in their analysis, as based upon 1968 data, of secondary urban centers in the Philippines. Data from this early study showed larger proportions of recent male migrants (the most comparable group to our sample of household heads) to be employed in the formal sector than was the case either for long-term migrants or urban natives. Further analysis of these divergent findings seems called for; one possible hypothesis is that there has been a decline over time in the "quality" of migrants to secondary cities.

A second perspective on this issue may be obtained by comparing the socioeconomic status experienced by migrants when they were living in their community of origin, as compared to that for their present place of residence. Comparisons between occupational statuses held in these two locales will be of less utility for this question, given the substantial differences in occupational composition between urban and rural areas. Data are available, however, from an item on the survey which read as follows: "Do you think that by moving to this city your situation is better, the same, or worse with regard to the income you receive?" Overall, more than 60 percent of the migrants household heads responded to this item positively, while fewer than one in ten in each setting felt that they had experienced a decline in their economic standing (the balance felt that there had been no change in their income). More specifically, 67 percent of the Cebu migrants and 66 percent of those coming to Cagayan de Oro asserted that they had gained financially from their move. Comparative figures from the three Indonesian cities were 61 percent, 73 percent, and 48 percent in Medan, Pematang Siantar, and Tebing Tinggi, respectively. Thus, these figures, too, would appear to show migration as being correlated with the process of upward social mobility.

As an objection to the above findings it might be pointed out that our sample is limited to permanent migrants who were able to succeed in their efforts to establish themselves in the city. At least some migrants who failed economically in the city will not be "caught" by our sample, insofar as they would have decided to return to their home community. While this is perhaps true, several counterbalancing factors may be mentioned. In the first place, we may assume that return migrants, by re-establishing themselves in their former social position, have at least managed to attain socioeconomic stability. As such, the net balance between upward and downward social movements will still be in favor of the former category. Secondly, some persons who come to the city, only to subsequently move away, will not be return migrants at all, but will rather be moving to an even larger city, i.e., to Manila or Jakarta. Since such persons tend to be highly educated (Palabrica-Costello, 1980), it is therefore likely that they, too, will continue to show evidence of upward economic mobility. Finally, the rather impressive differential between those asserting that they had experienced an income gain, as compared to those whose income had declined, may also be noted. Overall, the former response was given more than six times as frequently as the latter, a differential which seems too large to be due solely to methodological factors.

We have hypothesized that the income gains accruing to migrants should be especially large among better-educated migrants. Data pertaining to this question may be found in Table 4.7. These figures show weak, but fairly consistent, support for the expected pattern. In all study locales the percentage of migrant heads who reported an increase in their income after coming to the city was larger among secondary school graduates than for those

Table 4.7

MIGRANT HOUSEHOLD HEADS WHO EXPERIENCED A POST-MIGRATION
INCREASE IN INCOME BY EDUCATIONAL LEVEL (PERCENT)

Educational Attainment	Medan	Pematang Siantar/ Tebing Tinggi	Cebu	Cagayan de Oro
Less than secondary graduate	59.8	61.4	65.6	61.5
Secondary graduate or higher	62.6	71.4	71.5	71.0
Yule's Q	.06	.22	.14	.21*

*p<.05.

Source: Sample Survey Data.

who were less well educated. In no case, however, did this difference exceed ten percentage points, and in only one city (Cagayan de Oro) was statistical significance attained.

One factor which may have attenuated the expected relationship concerns the relative nature of this comparison. Poorly skilled migrants will almost surely be earning less in the city than their more highly educated counterparts, but their comparative gain *vis-à-vis* their former residence might yet be greater. A majority of such lower status migrants will have come from rural areas, where cash incomes are low or even non-existent, as in the case of unpaid family workers in agriculture. Further study of this problem, in which controls have been instituted for the rural/urban origins of the migrant appear called for. Controls might also be made for the migrant's year of arrival, on the supposition that recent migrants tend to be somewhat better educated, but less successful economically, than those who have been in the city for a longer period.[1]

Post-Move Contacts with the Home Community

According to the household decision-making model, movement to the city does not usually bring about a sharp break with the community of origin. Rather, a majority of migrants will continue to regard themselves as

Table 4.8

POST-MOVE CONTACTS WITH PLACE OF ORIGIN,
MIGRANT HOUSEHOLD HEADS (PERCENT)

Type of Contact	Medan	Pematang Siantar	Tebing Tinggi	Cebu	Cagayan de Oro
Visited home-place in last three years	62.2	61.4	64.5	75.1	73.9
Sent remitt-ances in last three years	37.7	25.5	20.6	28.4	37.0
Received remitt-ances in last three years	21.7	13.3	14.3	24.4	20.4

Source: Sample Survey Data.

members in spirit, if not always in fact, of their original household. As such, they will want to make frequent visits to their homeplace and will also feel some obligation to extend financial help to those who have been left behind; for example, by sending money or goods to their parents, or perhaps by paying the tuition fees of one of their younger siblings. In contrast, the individual migration model predicts that visits home will be infrequent and that financial remittances will be small.

Unfortunately, data collected by the present study on this issue may not be of the sort which will allow us to make definitive conclusions about the comparative superiority of the household and individual decision-making models. Respondents interviewed in the present instance differ on several counts from those which have been analyzed in most previous studies of rural-urban remittances. These differences, it should be noted, are such as to make it likely that the level of reported remittances will not be particularly high.

One important characteristic of the migrants interviewed in this study is that they have all settled in the city on a more or less permanent basis. This contrasts with previous analyses of the remittances issue, which have tended to focus more upon temporary migrants, or circulators. Since the proportion of earnings remitted home tends to be much larger for persons falling within this latter category (Hugo, 1978; Fan and Stretton, 1985), this means that the household decision-making model will tend to be supported more when temporary moves are being analyzed. Research has also shown that remittances are lower among household heads and spouses than among more peripheral household members. This is also true for long-term migrants, as compared to those who have only recently arrived (cf. Hugo, 1983). Since the present migrant study population is composed largely of those who came five or more years ago, and exclusively of household heads, these factors, too, will tend to result in lowered levels of cash remittances.

Does this mean that our data are unsuitable for the analysis of this important topic? We believe not. Patterns of economic exchange between sending and receiving communities are relevant not only for circulators but also for migrants. Indeed, the very fact that permanent migration removes the person involved from his area of origin with such finality makes it of even greater importance to assess the extent to which this act has been compensated by return flows of cash or goods. If the predictions of household decision-making theory cannot be met in this regard, then this may be taken as evidence that this perspective is more applicable to circular movements in the region than to more permanent forms of population mobility. As Simmons (1981, 25) has observed:

We have insufficient information to indicate whether the household model is most appropriate in all cases. The household as a decision-making unit may be breaking down, and young migrants who leave home never to return may send few if any remittances. These are questions which only empirical information can answer.

With these considerations in mind, we may now turn our attention to Table 4.8, which presents findings on three major types of post-move contact with the migrant's place of origin: visits home, the sending of remittances (in cash or kind) to family members at the place of origin, and the reception of such remittances by the migrants themselves. This latter category has been included for analysis insofar as some observers (e.g., Lipton, 1980) have noted that rural-urban migrants are about as likely to receive financial help from their kin as they are to render such assistance.

In general, these data do not show migrants to be maintaining especially strong contacts with their homeplace after coming to the city. Visits home are fairly frequent, with about 70 percent of the migrants having done this at least once during the past three years. This figure, though, is scarcely remarkable, given the length of this time period and the relatively short distances involved for many of the migrants. Statistics on remittances are even less indicative of a continued affiliation with the home community. Overall, only about 30 percent of these respondents answered affirmatively when asked if they had sent any remittances during the past three years,

Table 4.9

AVERAGE AMOUNT OF CASH REMITTANCES SENT AND RECEIVED IN
PAST THREE YEARS (DOLLARS), MIGRANT HOUSEHOLD HEADS WHO
HAD SENT OR RECEIVED REMITTANCES[a]

	Medan	Pematang Siantar/ Tebing Tinggi	Cebu	Cagayan de Oro
Amount sent	26.54	29.63	86.67	56.35
Amount received	36.04	34.90	286.93	155.08

[a]Exchange rates at the time of the survey were approximately 10
Philippine pesos and 675 Indonesian rupiahs to the dollar.
Sample sizes were as follows: for Medan, 77 migrants who sent
remittances and 45 who received; for Pematang Siantar and Tebing
Tinggi, 15 and 9; for Cebu, 115 and 99; and for Cagayan de Oro,
204 and 113.

Source: Sample Survey Data.

while even fewer—about 20 percent—said that they had received some sort
of financial contribution.

In general, the migrant respondents in Cebu and Cagayan de Oro are
somewhat more likely to be maintaining contact with their homeplace
through visits or remittances than are those from the three Indonesian
study sites. This could be attributable to the somewhat shorter distances
found, on the average, between the Philippine communities of origin and
destination, or perhaps to the higher living standards found in the Philippines.
In either event, however, our Indonesian remittances data certainly do not
conform closely to the picture presented by other observers, such as Hugo
(1983), who have viewed this phenomenon as involving major flows of cash
and goods.[2]

Table 4.9 provides further information on this question. Shown in this
table are the mean values, in U.S. dollars, of the cash remittances sent to
and received by migrants during the three-year period preceding the survey.
Again, these figures do not provide much support for the argument that
remittances from migrants to their home community serve the function of
promoting rural economic welfare. The average amounts sent home over
the three-year period preceding the survey are not large. This is especially
true among the Indonesian respondents, where the average amount remitted
home comes to less than ten dollars per year. Furthermore, these figures

would be considerably reduced if the total population of migrants (i.e. including those who failed to send any money at all) had been included in the base population, rather than by limiting the analysis—as has been done in Table 4.9—solely to migrants who had actually remitted some amount.[3]

Also of interest is the fact that the average amounts *received* by the migrants are in every case larger than the corresponding figure remitted home, with the net inflow of funds to the migrant household heads being quite large in the two Philippine study cities. These results may be taken to indicate that in many cases migrants are actually receiving more financial help from their home community than they are sending back on their own accord.[4]

When one also takes into account the income invested in the migrant during his formative years, perhaps even computing the interest which could have accrued on these funds if they had instead been invested, there can be no doubt but that the process of permanent migration serves as a mechanism to drain fairly large amounts of capital from the countryside to the city.

Summary

This chapter has been concerned with what might be called the natural history of the migration act, starting with the original decision to move, then proceeding to the circumstances surrounding the move and ultimately focusing upon the migrant's situation as of the survey date. Patterns and correlates of the adjustment process undergone by all long-term migrants have also been investigated, with a view towards comparing the household and individual models of migration.

In general, findings presented in this chapter lend more support to the latter perspective. A clear majority of respondents in all study locales asserted that it was they, and not some other member of their family, who had decided on their first move to the city. As a correlate of this, the reasons for moving which were most commonly mentioned by the migrant household heads were economic in nature rather than being family-oriented. Economic reasons were cited more frequently by respondents in the two Philippine cities as well as by older and married migrants, upon whom the responsibility of providing for the members of their own household, rather than for those left behind, must clearly take precedence.

Other results from the study also support the individual, rather than the household, decision-making model. Thus, a majority of all migrants to the five study cities had not visited these locales earlier, had not stayed with a friend or kinsman upon their arrival, and had not obtained financial help from someone in the city. Again, such patterns were least commonly found among the older and married migrants as well as among (in the Philippines, at least) those coming from another urban setting.

A powerful factor supporting the individualization process is the functional connection between geographic and social mobility. Comparisons of occupational status between the time of arrival and that of the survey showed, for all study sites, a net movement towards the more prestigious and securely tenured occupational categories. A corresponding shift from informal to formal sector employment activities was also noted, while clear majorities of migrants reported that their income had risen in comparison to that experienced in their place of origin.

Finally, post-move contacts with the place of origin were not strongly in evidence. A majority of all migrants had not sent anything in the way of remittances to their homeplace during the past few years, while the average amount sent among those who had done so was not large.

These observations show the need for specifying more precisely the conditions under which the household decision-making model would appear to apply. It seems likely that this perspective serves best for the case of circulatory movements, rather than for permanent migratory acts; for young and unmarried movers instead of those in the older age groups; and for persons who have only recently left their community of origin rather than for those who have been away for half a decade or longer. It is among these latter types of migrants—who predominate among the geographically mobile respondents falling within our sample—that a more individualistic model is needed.

Indeed, permanent cityward migration would seem to be a pre-eminently individualizing experience, both by virtue of the enforced separation it brings between the migrant and his family of origin, as well as because of the life-cycle changes (e.g. marriage) and socioeconomic advances which will so often occur in the period following the move to a new community. In this sense the mobility process may be viewed as frequently functioning to promote the development of the individual migrant, as well as that of the larger society to which he belongs.

Notes

1. Evidence which supports both of these suppositions is available for the case of Cagayan de Oro (Costello and Palabrica-Costello, 1985).

2. Hugo (1978), for example, reports that 95 percent of the migrants in his West Java study had remitted some money to their parents, with the overall value of these remittances coming to fully 10 percent of the income earned by the migrants. In a subsequent publication, Hugo, (1983) argues that these findings may be attributed to the additional probes he used to elicit data on remittances. While this may be true to some extent we would suggest that the type and composition of the sample

being analyzed is of equal or even greater importance. Samples composed largely of temporary migrants, of those who have only recently arrived in the destination community, and of non-household heads may be expected to remit large amounts of money and goods. Those who do not typically hold these characteristics (as is the case with the present study) will not. That Hugo's sample is composed largely of younger and more recently arrived migrants is indicated by the fact that his remittances data refer specifically to the sending of money to the migrant's parents. In contrast, it is to be doubted if 95 percent of the respondents from the present study even have living parents to whom money may be sent. Among the Indonesian migrants, for example, fully one out of every three is aged fifty or over (Leinbach, 1984).

Philippine studies have generally not found high levels of economic exchange between migrants and their family of origin. Thus, Abad's (1981a, 134) review article on Philippine internal migration patterns concluded that "other forms of assistance to stayers—remittances in cash or kind . . . or periodic visits . . . —are not substantial enough to alter levels of living in the place of origin." Further details on ties to origin and remittances in the case of Cebu Province are provided by Ulack (1986).

3. If the total number of migrants are used as the base population for computing these figures, the mean amounts sent come to $17.69 in Cebu, $16.03 in Cagayan de Oro, $7.70 in Medan, and $5.15 in Pematang Siantar and Tebing Tinggi. The mean amounts received within these same settings are, respectively, $56.49, $19.73, $3.94, and $2.66.

4. It should be noted that not all remittances to the migrant household heads come from their source community. Some of the largest amounts have been sent by relatives working as contract laborers in the Middle East oil fields and elsewhere overseas, thus raising substantially the mean amount of remittances received by the migrants. This factor is also an important explanation for the very high level of remittances received by the Philippine respondents, since members of this group were more likely to have relatives working temporarily abroad (cf. Ulack, 1986 for a more complete discussion of this matter).

5

Employment Patterns of Migrants

We have seen in Chapter 3 the contrasts between the migrant and non-migrant groups within our sampled populations. Distinctions were drawn on a variety of characteristics including employment, occupations, and business operations. In Chapter 4 we began to focus on the migrant population as a means of coming to understand this important factor in the growth of intermediate-sized cities. In the current chapter we again focus on the migrant households in our samples and deal specifically with the topic of employment. Aside from a description of the occupational patterns among the cities, we seek to learn about pre-move employment information and the sources of the information as well as other details surrounding the search process. A major objective is to analyze the occupational data through a simple dual sector model in order to draw generalizations and compare these results with other research. Finally we seek to provide answers to the nature of occupational mobility within the city and the nature and extent of secondary employment.

Occupational Characteristics

The initial concern of this chapter is to examine briefly the major occupational categories at the time of the survey among the five cities in the study. The data have been generalized somewhat to achieve comparability. Despite this attempt it is obvious that some major distinctions in categorical definition remain. It must also be stated that in the Philippines, the labor force is defined as gainful workers 15 years old and over whereas in Indonesia the labor force includes all of the population over 10 years of age after deducting students, mothers, those retired, and other unemployable persons. At the national level, Indonesia now has a labor force of approximately 60 million which is increasing by over 1.4 million persons per year. Job opportunities in Repelita IV (1984–1989) are expected to increase by 2.7 percent per year while the numbers of those seeking employment is expected to increase by 3.1 percent per year. The labor force is expected to reach over 72 million by 1990 ("Manpower Crisis Centre," 1983, 2). In the Philippines, the labor force was 20.1 million in 1983. The annual employment level is projected to increase by about 2.9 to 3.3 percent for the period 1984–1987 (NEDA, 1984).

The Medan labor force in 1978 was estimated at 31 percent of the total population. The labor force, it is estimated, has grown by an annual growth rate of 2.8 percent between 1974 and 1979. The figures for Pematang Siantar and Tebing Tinggi are believed to be quite comparable. In Metro Cebu the total gainful work force in 1980 was 33 percent of total population and 54 percent of the population age 15 and over. The same figures from Cagayan de Oro in 1980 are 30 and 52 percent, respectively.

The data on occupational categories in the Philippine cities from Chapter 3 (Table 3.4) has been adjusted somewhat to provide greater comparability with the Indonesian cities. The various occupational categories held by the sampled migrant heads of household are shown in Table 5.1. In the Philippine cities the occupational categories are dominated by manufacturing, trading and retail activities, transport associated jobs and personal services. The transport category contains a significant number of drivers or vehicle operators which is a common employment source in many Southeast Asian, and indeed, Third World cities. The manufacturing group includes employment in a variety of formal industries ranging from food, textiles and footwear to handicrafts and shellcrafts as well as basic metal and chemical production. The trade category includes wholesale traders, *sari-sari* store (sundry goods) owners, vendors working out of stalls in the public market, and hawkers and peddlers. The personal services component also exhibits a variety of rather typical occupations extending from shoe and watch repair to welders and plumbers. In contrast to the Indonesian cities, there were in Cebu and Cagayan additional migrant heads who were enumerated as professionals and military personnel. Examples of the former are teachers, engineers, physicians, judges, and lawyers. The differences recorded among respondents in the professional category in the two countries may result from sampling design differences but more probably it is due to a stronger emphasis on professional development, training, and education in Philippine society.

For the Indonesian cities the most common occupational types are traders, temporary workers, trades/personal service, and private sector employment. Temporary workers (*mocok-mocok*) are those individuals who offer a specific skill or service but where the work is highly irregular and uncertain. Examples may include a broker in real estate or other commodities but more often simple labor skills such as operating a pedicab designed to haul goods (*becak barang*), not people. Private sector employees refer mainly to the wide variety of factory, commercial, and other non-government jobs where employment is permanent and usually long term. Daily workers, especially visible in Tebing Tinggi's sample, are individuals employed by

Table 5.1

DISTRIBUTION OF OCCUPATION CATEGORY,
MIGRANT HEADS OF HOUSEHOLD (PERCENT)

Occupational Category	Medan (N=325)	Pematang Siantar (N=48)	Tebing Tinggi (N=36)	Cebu (N=387)	Cagayan de Oro (N=561)
Government	16	27	8	1	9
Military	-	-	-	4	2
Professionals	-	-	-	4	2
Primary	2	2	8	4	5
Trader	18	12	19	18	25
Reg Daily Worker	4	-	11	-	-
Self Employed	9	2	3	-	-
Transport	5	8	6	12	17
Trades/Personal Services	10	11	9	17	9
Temporary Worker	15	21	33	-	-
Private Sector/ Manufacturing	19	13	-	23	22
Semi-Government	2	2	3	-	-
Unclassified	-	2	-	17	9
Total	100	100	100	100	100

Source: Sample Survey Data.

either government or the private sector on a daily basis. The job status in this category is less secure than the private sector category but more secure than that of the temporary worker. Those individuals who were enumerated in the self employed category are defined by the fact that they own their own equipment (for example they do not rent equipment such as a *becak* from an owner) and work independently (Scott, 1979). Retail traders include both mobile sellers (*pedagang kaki lima*) and those with a larger inventory who have a fixed or semi-fixed base of operation. The nature and locations of these operations may range from a spot on a sidewalk or roadside to a stall rented in a public market place or a full sized store (*toko*). Merchants working out of a smaller place (*warung*) in a main or peripheral shopping district are also included in this group. A final category, semi-governmental workers, is applicable only to the Indonesian data. Individuals who are employed, for example, by the electric utility, the housing authority, or non-private banks fall into this category.

There appear to be two obvious differences in the employment categories of the migrant househeads between the Indonesian and Philippine cities. First, manufacturing clearly provides a larger share of the jobs in Cebu and Cagayan de Oro. The figures of 23 and 22 percent respectively in the Philippine cities take on more importance because the private sector data in Medan and Siantar while including many manufacturing jobs are not exclusively so. Basic differences in the economic base of Cagayan and Siantar, two towns with roughly similar population sizes, are suggested in light of their respective job proportions in manufacturing. This interpretation however must be tentative in light of the quite different sampling proportions associated with the two towns. The difference between Cebu and Medan was expected given estimates of total employment by sector: the manufacturing sector in Cebu is considerably larger proportionately than that in Medan.

The second difference is associated with the employment in the government services category. Medan and Siantar, especially in the Indonesian city group, exhibit very high employment proportions in this category when compared to the Philippine cities. There appears to be a clear policy of job creation in Indonesia through the civil service. As a consequence the pay scale in government service, even for an upper level senior official, is very poor, often forcing individuals to seek out additional employment (Sethuraman, 1976, 118). This is most common at the lower ranks of government service (clerks, etc.) where individuals may supplement their basic income with a trading or personal services job on the side. Moreover it is suspected that multiple job holding is still very common among schoolteachers and lecturers in universities and IKIPs (teacher training institutions) (Jones, 1981, 261).

Aside from these two groups it is difficult to establish a concrete statement on the extent of multiple job holding. While it is believed to be very widespread, data from urban surveys in the early 1970s do not bear out the expectation. For example in Jakarta only 3.5 percent of workers were found to hold more than one job. Equal or even lower proportions were found in Surabaya, Bandung, Palembang, and Ujung Pandang. It may be, however, that occupational multiplicity may be much more pronounced in rural areas. Government surveys from the mid-1960s indicated that the rate of multiple job holding was twice as high in rural areas as in cities and also higher in the Outer Islands than in Java (Jones, 1981, 253–255). Given the significant economic progress which has taken place since that time, it is not at all certain that the rate of occupational multiplicity is as high today as the 8 and 14 percent respectively for urban and rural areas (both sexes, all Indonesia) in the mid-1960s. Further comment on this point with regard to the current study is reserved until a later stage in this chapter.

Recognizing these aspects of the employment pattern in Indonesia, it is clear that the general service sector in this setting is much larger than the figures indicated in the trades/personal services category in Table 5.1. The services category might quite legitimately be enlarged by including individuals from the trader, transport, daily worker, temporary worker, and self-employed categories. In addition we must recognize that some service employment has not been recorded where individuals count their main employment in the government sector. With respect to the Philippine data certainly the services component of employment may also be enlarged by adding the trader group and a portion of the transport category to the trades/personal services category. The obvious point is simply that the services and retail trade sectors are the dominant employment sources in all the urban economies. In order to give additional meaning to these common employment groups it may be useful to provide simple profiles of typical workers.

As evidenced from Table 5.1, traders or vendors in a variety of forms are quite common in the Indonesian and Philippine cities. In Cebu and Cagayan these individuals tend to be dominantly male (over 75 percent). It should be noted, however, that the limitation of the sample to *household heads* has inflated the proportion of males in this occupational group. The modal age groups are 40–49 and 30–39 years, respectively. They have high school educations, come from rural areas and most typically moved to the city in the period between 1976 and 1983. However, in Cebu a large number of traders moved before 1954. The modal income category for the Cebu traders is $87–$145, while in Cagayan the modal income category is somewhat less, $57–$87. In Medan traders also tend to be dominantly male but somewhat older and less educated than in the Philippine cities. The median age is 50 years with only 6 years of schooling. The income level for Medan traders is similar to Cebu. Individuals in this occupational category moved to Medan in the late 1950s from both urban and rural origins. Most were married when they came to the city. In Siantar and Tebing the traders are of roughly the same age as in Medan, but are less educated and earn slightly less. In the Indonesian cities traders tend to be associated with the Minangkabau, Batak, and Javanese ethnic groups.

Another important category is manufacturing and private sector employment. In Cebu and Cagayan individuals employed in manufacturing are slightly younger than in the trading group in both cities. In addition, manufacturing employees in both cities have less education and migrated at an earlier age than did those in the trading group. Perhaps of most significance is the fact that the average monthly income in both cities is lower among manufacturing employees ($90) as opposed to traders ($109). Also of interest is the fact that average manufacturing incomes are lower in Cebu ($88) than in Cagayan ($104). Private sector workers (not all are in manufacturing) in Medan and Siantar (no private sector workers were sampled in Tebing) tend to be slightly older than in the Philippine cities and have similar educational backgrounds. These individuals migrated to their destination in the late 1950s and early 1960s. Most significant is the fact that private sector workers in the two Indonesian cities earn, on average, somewhat more income than their counterparts in the Philippines. The average manufacturing wage in Medan is about $115 and in Siantar about $100. In Medan, private sector incomes tend to be higher than those for trade while in Siantar the incomes of the two groups are about equal. While there is the tendency for higher incomes to be associated with the larger cities in regards to trading activities, this generalization does not hold for manufacturing employment in the Philippine cities. It appears that, in general, one cannot expect to find higher incomes to be associated with manufacturing employment as opposed to other forms, specifically trading activities. Further evidence for this point is available from a more detailed analysis of occupation placement and levels of living in Cagayan de Oro (Costello and Palabrica-Costello, 1985), which showed that ownership of consumer durables tended to be well above average for household heads engaged in commerce, and very low for those in manufacturing and construction activities, even when such associated variables as age, sex, and level of educational attainment were statistically controlled.

Structural Differences in the Labor Market

The above discussion has compared migrant household heads with respect to rather specific job types within the five cities. As we suggested earlier, however, the urban labor markets in Third World cities are not homogeneous. Specifically, the notion of segmentation of the labor markets in terms of a conceptual distinction between 'formal' and 'informal' sectors has been shown to be quite useful as an analytic device in examining the character and composition of the labor force in urban areas. Initial definitions simply emphasized informal income opportunities as all those outside the formal wage market where the distinction was based upon wage earning versus self employment (Hart, 1973). The critical aspect here is whether labor was recruited on a permanent and regular basis for fixed rewards. Subsequently, various organizations (e.g., ILO) have suggested other definitions where variables such as low productivity, labor absorbing capacity, ease of entry, small scale, irregular hours of work, negotiable prices, labor intensity, and adapted technology are useful characteristic descriptions. Despite the common acceptance of the term it is possible to view the concept in two distinct ways. The first focuses upon the non-Western characteristics of essential enterprises within the urban economy while the second emphasizes the characteristics of a class of workers who do not form part of the formal or Westernized sector of the urban economy (Hackenberg, 1980, 412–415).

The idea of the informal sector has grown out of the tradition of dualistic models of the structure of Third World economies (Boeke, 1953). The popularity of the notion grew essentially in response to the growing need for employment opportunities in the Third World. Coupled with this were the observations of the widespread importance of small scale activities. Traditional attitudes, while recognizing the existence of such activities, have been unfavorable. The argument was simply that low incomes and productivity were not conducive to overall economic growth. This pejorative view was then countered by various authors who felt that informal activities may indeed play an important role in employment creation, income redistribution, and the satisfaction of basic needs (ILO, 1972; McGee, 1979).

The concept of the informal sector and its role in development has been the topic of considerable recent debate (e.g., Bromley and Gerry, 1979). The thrust of the debate is that essentially the simple definition outlined above does not elucidate the diversity and the complex web of interrelationships which exist in the urban setting. Hence, it is argued that the concept is inadequate as a tool in allowing the further development of theory. Other critics have suggested that the concept of the informal sector is ambiguous in its treatment and definition of organizational units and employment forms (Breman, 1976).

As a result of the perceived inadequacies in the concept, alternative treatments have emerged. One common alternative is the so called petty commodity production approach (Moser, 1978). This approach recognizes that considerable internal differentiation exists in the various sectors of the urban economy. Here the two sector dualist division is replaced by the recognition of multiple worker categories and a continuum of economic activities. The concept is essentially based on Marx's theory of different modes of production and utilizes his ideas on the interaction between two structures: the forces of production (technology, resources, labor) and the social relations of production (ownership and control of the means of production). The dynamics (a deficiency of alternative formulations) are derived from the accumulation of capital. Thus such analysis utilizes the articulation of a variety of modes of production and the way in which these modes adapt to and become dependent on one another. A useful application of this approach has been carried out using the example of peddlers and trishaw riders in Ujung Pandang, Indonesia (Forbes, 1981a & 1981b).

In addition to the above, other modifications have been suggested. One approach characterizes the dichotomy (corporate and noncorporate) as binary distinctions in management, ownership and power but continual in scale and level of technology (Dick and Rimmer, 1980). Still another is a fourfold classification of the labor force derived from one developed by

Gerry (1977) (McGee, 1982, 8–10). The classification scheme relates sectors of the labor force to the mode of labor-power reproduction, the function that the laborer performs for the capitalist mode of production, and the main type of labor mobility that occurs as a result of these relationships.

Perhaps even more useful in both a theoretical and practical sense is the notion of a *tri-sector* model of the urban economy (Friedmann and Sullivan, 1974). This modification of the conventional dual sector approach allows for some diversity by proposing two parts to the informal sector: a small-scale family enterprise sector and an irregular or 'street' economy. In the former incomes show great variability and some capital accumulation may take place as a result of competitive advantage and/or superior commercial skills. The 'street' economy is characterized by low-status, low-skilled trading and service activities where existence is essentially subsistence.

Empirical evidence for this diversity within the informal sector has been found in a recent study of Nairobi (House, 1984). In a detailed analysis of individual enterprises in that city significant differences appear between the 'intermediate' sector and the 'community of the poor' in terms of aspects of capital and its utilization. Enterprises in the former group are larger in terms of capital invested, the capital-to-labor ratio, and sales per week. These firms are also significantly more productive. In addition attitudinal and motivational differences also separate the two groups.[1]

In order to further compare the labor and employment characteristics in our set of cities it is necessary to simplify the occupational structures discussed above. The primary tool deemed most useful for this purpose is the informal-formal sector dichotomy. This choice seems to ignore the large body of critical research just discussed. We are fully aware of the limitations of this conceptualization yet it appears, for several valid reasons, to be the most reasonable approach. First, an abundance of both private and government research studies have used the informal-formal sector typology and thus provide a means of comparing our own results with other studies, especially in Southeast Asia (e.g., Koo and Smith, 1983; Aklilu and Harris, 1980). Second, there is not yet a clear consensus on a single, superior alternative method of characterizing employment relations. Finally, alternative typologies do not appear to be as useful and indeed are more difficult to generalize in cross cultural comparisons such as ours.

Essentially for the purposes of this study we subscribe to Hart's (1973) definition of informal sector employment. Where cash or other payment is not received on a set, regular basis the employment form is classified as *informal*. Coupled with this we have also frequently used employment type and job characteristics to provide a meaningful allocation. For example, domestic help and self-employed professionals clearly belong in the informal and formal categories respectively, despite the fact that the former group receives regular wages while the latter does not. According to this definition,

Table 5.2

MIGRANT HOUSEHOLDS: FORMAL-INFORMAL
EMPLOYMENT BY CITY (PERCENT)

	Medan (N=339)	Pematang Siantar (N=47)	Tebing Tinggi (N=36)	Cebu (N=316)	Cagayan de Oro (N=479)
Formal	40	42	22	66	54
Informal	60	58	78	34	46

Source: Sample Survey Data.

then, of the job types enumerated in the Philippine cities only manufacturing in larger private firms, government services, and professional occupations were included in the formal sector. In Indonesia only the categories of government service, daily work (regular wage), private sector, and semi-government workers (e.g., most state affiliated bank employees and utility company employees) are classified as formal employment.

Given the basis for distinction Table 5.2 provides the percentage values associated with each of the sectors in the five cities. The data show clearly that, among migrants, the informal sector is more dominant in the Indonesian than the Philippine cities. Allowing for some deviation as a result of the small sample size in Tebing Tinggi, it would appear that the informal sector accounts for at least 60 percent of the employment in urban areas of North Sumatra and it is likely that this generalization could be extended to the whole of Indonesia. Obvious exceptions might occur in cities where formal industry (private manufacturing firms) has concentrated either historically, naturally, or under specific government intervention strategies. The former case might be illustrated by the *kretek* (cigarette) industry in Kudus or Kediri (Java) and the latter by specially designed industrial estates that fall within an urban boundary such as the large scale industry complex at Lhokseumawe in Sumatra's Aceh Province. Cebu and, to a lesser extent Cagayan de Oro, are characterized by a stronger component of formal employment. This result is not unexpected and is consistent with our interpretation of estimated employment data by sector. The reader will recall that the manufacturing sectors in Cebu and Cagayan are considerably larger than in the Indonesian cities. Conversely the services component in each of the Sumatran cities accounts for more employment than in the two Philippine cities.

For a comparison of our results with other similar studies some evidence is available. In a recent study of migration to and employment within 24 Javanese cities it was found that 80 percent of the male and 81 percent of the female migrants were in the informal sector (Aklilu and Harris, 1980, 131). In another study, Koo and Smith (1983) found a higher proportion of formal employment in Manila (roughly 72 percent) but a somewhat lower proportion of formal sector workers (60 percent) in secondary cities of the Philippines. These results are consistent with our own findings. In addition, this study found significant employment sector differences by sex. Females were found in higher proportions in the informal sector, especially in secondary cities of the country (Koo and Smith, 1983, 225; Engracia and Herrin, 1984).

Findings from the present study on the sex composition of informal sector workers are not dissimilar. As mentioned previously, fewer female heads of household were enumerated in the Indonesian city samples, thus implying that the proportion of migrant female heads enumerated in the employment dichotomy will be lower. In Medan and Siantar, 5 and 8 percent, respectively, of all heads were female. Of these respondents, fully 75 percent of the females in both cities were enumerated in the informal sector. No female migrant heads were recorded in Tebing Tinggi. In Cebu the migrant female heads were double the proportion (10 percent) recorded in Medan and again were dominantly (73 percent) employed in the informal sector. The proportion of migrant female heads in the employment pattern of Cagayan was equivalent to that in Siantar but the proportion of females employed in the informal sector was considerably smaller, although still a majority (58 percent). The reason for this lower proportion in Cagayan is perhaps due to the tendency for female workers to dominate in clerical-type job activities (which are, of course, in the formal sector) in the Philippines.

In order to further establish distinctions with respect to migrant employment in the two sectors several additional criteria were assessed. The initial criterion, age, is depicted across the five cities in Table 5.3. The data show generally that migrants in the informal sector are somewhat older. Tebing Tinggi represents the only exception to this statement. In fact the age differences in the Indonesian cities under an ANOVA analysis are found to be insignificant. The age difference in the two Philippine cities are significant. This is so despite the relatively small gap in ages between the two sectors in Cagayan. The pattern found in the two largest Indonesian cities is reinforced even more dramatically with the very large age difference in Cebu. The most plausible explanation for this is that the formal sector age is lowered somewhat by the factory employment of younger adults. Older persons may also have an easier time entering some forms of informal work activities (e.g., market vendors) since they are likely to have greater access to the capital needed to get started in such jobs.

Table 5.3

MEAN AGE OF MIGRANTS IN YEARS:
FORMAL-INFORMAL EMPLOYMENT BY CITY

	Medan	Pematang Siantar	Tebing Tinggi	Cebu	Cagayan de Oro
Formal	43	42	44	40	38
Informal	45	44	42	47	36

Source: Sample Survey Data.

Table 5.4

MEAN SCHOOL YEARS:
FORMAL-INFORMAL EMPLOYMENT BY CITY

	Medan	Pematang Siantar	Tebing Tinggi	Cebu	Cagayan de Oro
Formal	10.1	11.2	9.3	10.2	10.4
Informal	6.6	6.9	5.9	6.6	8.1

Source: Sample Survey Data.

Another important characteristic by which the employment differences between the two sectors may be judged is education (Table 5.4). The data show a consistent relationship across all five cities: those employed in the formal sector are better educated. The education differences in each city are statistically significant. Comparative findings from the previously mentioned Javanese study show that the percentage of migrants in the formal sector increases with educational level (Aklilu and Harris, 1980, 134; cf. also, Engracia and Herrin, 1984, for compatible results for the Philippines). It was noted, however, that the formal sector was a relatively minor source of employment for Javanese migrants.

Three additional characteristics were utilized to evaluate sectoral distinctions. These were the rural or urban origins of the migrants, the age (over or under 25 years) at which they migrated to the city in question, and whether the migrants were recent movers (after 1970) or older migrants (before 1970). The chi-square analyses on each of these variables proved to be insignificant. Thus the origin, age, and timing of the migration appear not to be related to the nature of employment as categorized in a simple formal-informal employment dichotomy. Results from Koo and Smith's study of sectoral differences between older and recent migrants provide some comparable data on this question. These authors found that, within Manila, there was little difference between older versus recent male migrants and their participation in the formal-informal sector. Recent female migrants, however, did show a greater tendency to be found in the informal sector than did older female migrants (Koo and Smith, 1983, 225). In secondary cities within the Philippines nearly all recent female migrants were enumerated in the informal sector while a smaller yet heavy proportion (72 percent) of older females were found in the informal sector. Among male migrants to the secondary cities, as in Manila, high proportions of older and recent migrants are associated with the formal sector. These findings suggest that any relationship between migration and the urban labor market must be specific to male or female migrants. As the authors note, "the hypothesis that migrants are most likely to enter the urban occupational structure through the informal sector is not confirmed with regard to male migrants but is strongly confirmed with regard to female migrants" (Koo and Smith, 1983, 224). Furthermore, the authors suggest that if migrant status is associated with disadvantages or discrimination in the urban labor market, the evidence suggests that this applies largely to female migrants.

Income by Sector

A further useful contrast is provided by the examination of average income levels in the cities between the two sectors. Income, of course, is very difficult to estimate. This is especially so in Indonesia where government employees are given remuneration in kind (usually rice, but occasionally other items as well). In addition, individuals may have multiple occupations and this information is not always shared willingly. Thus, the usual caveats on reliability of income data certainly apply here. However, our feeling is that the figures reported were reasonable and accurate. In addition the data were screened for obvious false reportings which were subsequently discarded. The likelihood of obtaining accurate data was enhanced by instructing interviewers to use appropriate means in extracting information on this sensitive issue. Since the sample size for Tebing Tinggi was quite small, it was felt that these data should be omitted entirely. Comparative figures on employment earnings with respect to the timing of the move to Pematang Siantar are also omitted for the same reason.

It is not surprising to find that the average income is higher in the formal sector of all cities and that higher incomes are associated with the larger cities of Medan and Cebu (Table 5.5). This also supports our earlier, and similar, results for the analysis of the ownership of consumer durables (Table 3.8). The fact that higher earnings are associated with the Philippines overall is supported by basic data provided by the World Bank (World Bank, 1983, 200). It should be noted, however, that the formal sector earnings for Siantar and Cagayan are basically identical. Somewhat unexpected are the sharper gaps between sectoral incomes in the two Philippine cities in contrast to those in Indonesia. In Cebu, for example, informal sector workers earn just over one-third that of the formal sector employees while in Medan the same group earns 75 percent as much as the formal sector employees in the same city. The higher wage patterns in the formal sectors of Cebu and Cagayan are perhaps due in part to the fact that numerous professionals were interviewed in the sampling process. In Medan and Siantar many fewer professionals were enumerated.

The relatively high wages reported among heads in Medan and Siantar's informal sector was not anticipated. It is possible that, although few heads reported second jobs (only 8 percent in Medan and 7 percent in Siantar) this is indeed a possible explanation of the higher earnings relative to those in the formal sector. In Cebu, the rate of secondary occupation is identical to that in Medan while in Cagayan the figure is substantially higher (14 percent). It is likely that the higher wages in the informal sector relative to the formal sector in Medan and Siantar might be explained by the multiple jobs factor. However, given the same or higher rates of secondary occupation in the two Philippine cities and the sharp income gap between the two sectors there this argument does not appear to be valid. A more solid explanation is that there are distinct and in some cases dramatic differences among returns for various jobs performed in the informal sector (Leinbach, 1986a; House, 1984). A retail shop owner, for example, generally would earn considerably more than the operator of a pedicab. The latter might earn less than $1.50 daily after food and equipment rental have been removed from the gross earnings. It is likely therefore that the exact nature and composition of informal sector jobs and of their corresponding remuneration levels provide the explanation for the differences in income between the sectors in the two groups of cities.

Income by Sex of Head

Relatively few female migrant house heads were enumerated in the survey yet the question of income differences by sex is important. In Medan, Cebu, and Cagayan the percentages of female migrant heads were 5, 10, and 8, respectively. As the data reveal, there are differences in income by sex but

Table 5.5

MEAN MONTHLY INCOME (DOLLARS) OF MIGRANT HEADS OF HOUSEHOLD,
OCCUPATIONAL SECTOR BY SEX; BY RECENCY OF MIGRATION;
BY URBAN-RURAL ORIGIN

	Medan	Pematang Siantar	Cebu	Cagayan de Oro
SECTOR				
Formal	139	129	157	130
Informal	104	106	57	75
FORMAL				
Male	141	*	158	129
Female	87	*	138	132
INFORMAL				
Male	117	*	61	82
Female	71	*	46	59
FORMAL				
Recent Migrant	101	*	122	117
Older Migrant	137	*	182	149
INFORMAL				
Recent Migrant	104	*	49	70
Older Migrant	106	*	62	96
FORMAL				
Urban Origin	145	205	173	123
Rural Origin	132	110	153	132
INFORMAL				
Urban Origin	100	110	85	88
Rural Origin	109	102	50	77

*Insufficient Sample

Source: Sample Survey Data.

these are uneven (Table 5.5). For example in Medan, the only Indonesian city for which there is adequate data, the gap between male and female earnings in both the formal and informal sectors is quite large. In Cebu the male earnings remain greater but the gap between the sexes is not as large as in Medan. Finally, in Cagayan in the formal sector, female incomes on the average are actually greater than the male wages. A possible explanation is that this difference is due to spurious correlation with the age variable. That is, in general, older household heads have higher incomes, while female household heads (many of whom are widows) tend to be relatively old. In the informal sector of Cagayan, as in the other cities, female incomes are considerably lower than that of the males.

One possible explanation for the lower incomes among females in contrast to males in both sectors is the lower educational attainment levels. Education was found to be a very significant predictor of income in the Koo and Smith study (1983, 228). While lower educational levels among females in the informal sector of Cebu and Cagayan are consistent with income differences, they are not in the formal sector. For example, females are better educated in Cagayan's formal sector (consistent with the income difference) but this is not the case in Cebu where females earn less than do males, even though they are better educated. Still another factor which might explain differences in income are the hours worked in the job. It is not unreasonable to suggest that some females may only work part-time while devoting most of their time to the upkeep of a household.

By comparison with the Medan findings, differences in income arising from segmentation of the labor market in Javanese cities are small for males and non-existent for females. The conclusion is that the formal sector does not provide better opportunities than the informal sector and that there is little economic distinction between the two sectors (Aklilu and Harris, 1980, 151).

Recent Migrants: Income and Employment

A further consideration concerns differences in income and formal-informal employment among recent (since 1971) and older migrants (before 1971). The data show that, in all cities in both sectors, older migrants earn more than do more recent migrants. The gap between the two groups of migrants however, varies considerably from a very small difference in Medan's informal sector to a quite sizable difference in Cebu's formal sector. These results are quite consistent with our expectations, as well as with previous studies (e.g., Fuller, 1981; Yap, 1976). That is, a learning and advancement process occurs over time among migrants as they gradually adjust to city life. This advancement process occurs over time in the informal sector as well as the formal sector.

Origins of Migrants and Income

One final idea to be tested is that of the effect of urban versus rural origin of the migrant upon income levels in the two sectors. Our hypothesis is that urban origin migrants should have more experience and perhaps greater skills and thus would adapt more easily to life in their new surroundings. As seen in Table 5.5, the data results provide reasonably good support for this notion, with some exceptions. In the *formal* sector of Medan, Siantar, and Cebu urban origin migrants do indeed earn higher incomes. But this is not the case in Cagayan. In the *informal* sector of the Indonesian and Philippine cities urban origin migrants also earn more. An exception is the case of Medan. The explanation accounting for the exceptions is found no doubt again in the specific types of employment of the individuals in question. Basically the idea tested is valid; that is, generally migrants from urban areas will be more likely to 'succeed' in the city if we measure success in terms of earned income.

In order to further explore the variation in income among migrant households, an experiment using the Medan data was carried out. An OLS regression analysis was performed where income, the response term, was modeled as a function of predictor variables detailing rural-urban origins, informal-formal occupations, presence of family business, age of household head, and education of household head. While the level of explanation achieved was quite disappointing, significant regression coefficients were obtained for the family business and education variables. These results, especially with respect to the importance of education upon income variation, are quite consistent with nearly all analyses of this type (e.g., Aklilu and Harris, 1980, 138–145).

Search for Employment

Perhaps more important than the specific job characteristics and income of the migrants is the *process* by which the individual came to be employed in the city. If indeed the intermediate city has potential for enlarging its employment share we need to know more about the job search at this level of the urban hierarchy.

The knowledge of information about employment sources and how this is acquired remains as a critical gap in our understanding of the migration process. Respondents in the survey were asked whether they had information about a job before moving to each of the cities. In Cebu nearly 48 percent of the migrant heads responded positively while in Cagayan the positive response rate was nearly as high, 42 percent. In contrast only 17 percent of the migrant heads in Medan responded in the same way. An important qualification here is that a high percentage of the respondents in Medan could provide no information on this survey item. It is unlikely, however, that many of these respondents would have answered positively. Data and results from Pematang Siantar and Tebing Tinggi are excluded from this analysis because of the smaller samples and the few number of valid responses.

In Cebu, as in Medan, over 50 percent of the respondents could not identify a specific information source. Of those who did respond, friends were the most important sources of job information with relatives ranking second in this regard. In Cebu 78 percent of the valid respondents noted the importance of these two sources while in Cagayan and Medan the figures were 63 percent and 77 percent. The data show that the employer and employment agencies are somewhat important but these more formal channels are clearly less important than the friends-relatives category. The returns suggest also that employment offices may be more important in Medan and Cagayan, while the employer may be a more common source of information about employment in Cebu. The mass media (radio, television, and the newspapers), play a relatively minor role in the job search in all three cities. These findings do not differ greatly from findings gained from other researchers (Connell, *et al,* 1976; Pryor, 1979).

In terms of the accuracy of the information acquired on the potential employment a considerable difference was recorded between the two cultural settings. In Cagayan and Cebu over 90 percent of those responding felt the information was very accurate or mostly accurate while in Medan only 67 percent rated the information obtained in this way. In Medan a larger percentage of the migrants felt that the information was only somewhat accurate. This difference may be related to the fact, noted in the previous chapter, that migration for job-related reasons was more common in the Philippines than in Indonesia, where family-related reasons played a greater role. Further research on these patterns would certainly help to clarify the distinction. In addition, and perhaps most important, the lower information accuracy in Medan may relate to the generally greater distances of migration for the Medan migrants. In Cebu and Cagayan de Oro migrants often came from nearby and had better information about jobs as a result.

Of considerable interest too is whether the migrant was employed before moving to his or her destination. In Cebu and Cagayan, 13 and 8 percent of the migrant heads responded that they were working in the city before they moved on a permanent basis. The figure for Medan was 15 percent although in Medan a higher percentage of 'no information' responses was recorded. Clearly, most individuals find employment after they move to a destination on a permanent basis. Yet the opposite situation is of sufficient importance to warrant further research. Basically this category of responses reveals the possibility that people may be gainfully employed to some extent through a non-permanent movement scheme. That is, individuals will either

commute or circulate from their permanent residence to the employment
source before moving permanently. These individuals represent a special
category of employed migrants and a further analysis of their decision to
move permanently rather than continue commuting or circulating may be
warranted. We discuss non-permanent movement characteristics in Chapter
7. In addition, the policy importance of both permanent and non-permanent
movement in the employment situation of intermediate-sized cities is discussed in the final chapter.

All the migrant heads were asked whether they were ever unemployed
at some period since their arrival in the city and whether that period of
unemployment necessitated a search for work. In part this question is
directed to the matter of employment stability and occupational satisfaction.
Within our sampled cities remarkably similar responses were obtained in
answer to the question of unemployment and the ensuing search for work.
In Medan, 15 percent of the heads responded positively. In Cebu the identical
positive response rate was recorded while in Cagayan a slightly higher
positive figure was enumerated (21 percent). Obviously those individuals
who were searching for employment may come from a variety of employment
backgrounds. Individuals may find that while a particular employment type
is stable, that is there is little chance of losing a job, the income remuneration
may be insufficient which in turn will produce dissatisfaction.

Some occupational categories, on the other hand, are quite unstable.
The casual, temporary labor in Indonesia known as *mocok-mocok* is an
example. Another class of work exhibiting highly unstable employment is
construction work. Construction activities in many Third World countries
allow large numbers of workers, both migrant and native born, to gain a
foothold in the urban economy. But their work pattern is characterized by
uncertainty, both in duration of each job and the number of jobs they will
obtain each year. Most construction workers experience periods of unemployment between jobs but a surprisingly large portion of these workers
remain committed to this form of employment despite the uncertainty
involved. The committed laborers basically adjust to this employment
instability by adopting an employment-migration scheme based upon relationships which evolve between the foreman and his laborers. As a result
laborers are utilized more efficiently. One strategy for coping with this
problem is to utilize a circular migration pattern where workers will leave
their families in their hometown, returning for weekend visits once or twice
a month. This choice maximizes income and also offers a means of modifying
the effects of fluctuations in employment. When work is not available a
worker returns home to his village (Stretton, 1979, 267–281). One implication
of the above discussion is that unemployment rates should be higher among
informal sector workers, such as temporary workers and employees in the

construction industry. A separate analysis of the Cagayan de Oro data has confirmed this expected pattern (Costello and Palabrica-Costello, 1985).

All migrant respondents in the cities were asked several questions which would reveal their feelings about changes which they experienced since coming to the city. Two critical topics were changes in satisfaction regarding work status and income. Respondents in all three cities felt overwhelmingly that both their job status and conditions had improved after the move to the city. In Medan, 65 percent of the respondents replied that the work situation was better, while in Cebu and Cagayan approximately 69 and 65 percent of the respondents indicated the same. The responses on income status were basically the same. Over two-thirds of the individuals in each city felt that their income situation had improved. The obvious conclusion to be drawn is that a large percentage of migrants over time feel that their situation has improved by movement to the city. In addition these attitudes should result in a positive return flow of information regarding movement from the origin areas.

Occupational Mobility Within the City

Do migrants remain in the same occupation? The question of occupational mobility is an important one and one for which relatively little evidence is available, especially on a comparative basis. A related question which we seek to answer here is the nature of occupations after job changes. For example, do individuals gradually move toward occupations that provide higher income and/or more security?

Our occupational change data does not utilize job changes associated with previous moves to other cities. Thus if a migrant changed jobs in moving from Binjai to Medan this information while of considerable interest is not the subject of the current analysis. Rather, we are interested here in the migrant's occupational changes once he or she was resident in Medan, Cebu, and Cagayan. In addition, we focus in this section only upon the three year period prior to the date of the interview. This focus on a recent time period was done for several reasons. First, many migrants, especially those who have been in the city for well over a decade, would have considerable difficulty recalling the various employment changes. In addition, we are primarily concerned with recent occupational changes because these are more relevant to current policy decisions and options on the employment issue.

Within each city the specific job changes were enumerated. Thus, if an individual held a job in 1980 that was different from his or her current job this information was recorded. Of course, several jobs may have been held in the intervening period by an individual but it is the jobs at 1980 and

Table 5.6

OCCUPATIONAL CHANGES: 1980 TO 1982-83
(PERCENT)

	Medan	Cebu	Cagayan de Oro
Informal to Informal	50	49	43
Formal to Informal	25	21	16
Informal to Formal	21	7	9
Formal to Formal	4	23	32
Total	100	100	100

Source: Sample Survey Data.

the time of the interview which are being used to assess occupational mobility.

The three sample cities, in fact, reveal very different results. For example in Medan, only 9 percent of the migrant heads indicated that they had changed jobs in the previous three years. In contrast the proportions were 19 and 27 percent in Cebu and Cagayan, respectively. Responses reveal further that in Cebu 45 individuals changed their main job one time in the past three years and 12 more changed jobs at least twice. Data from Cagayan reveal an even more dramatic pattern where 94 individuals changed jobs once and 38 persons at least twice from a sample of 561 migrant heads.

Only 30 individuals from Medan's 325 migrants indicated different jobs at the two temporal points. What generalizations can be made with regard to these changes? First, one-half of the total changes involve occupational movement *within* the informal sector (Table 5.6). Examples are changes from self employment to temporary work, driver to retail trader, carpenter to driver, and so forth. Nearly 25 percent of the changes concern formal to informal sector movements. Typical of these are former private sector workers now employed as drivers, retail traders, or in other trades. A slightly smaller percentage, 21, is categorized by informal to formal sector changes. Nearly all of these movements are individuals traders or tradesmen now occupied in the private sector. Less than 5 percent of the changes are *within* the formal sector, for example, private sector worker to a government or semi-government position (Leinbach, 1986a).

For Cebu, 57 of the 387 migrant heads reported occupational changes over the period. As in Medan approximately one-half of the job movements are within the informal sector. In addition, another similarity shows that just over one-fifth of the changes occur from the formal to the informal sector. A typical example is a former manufacturing worker now employed in the personal services category or as a trader. A distinction between Cebu and Medan is revealed in the last two categories. For the former setting there is considerable occupational mobility within the formal sector. Virtually all of these movements consist of workers moving from one manufacturing job to another. There is, however, considerably less movement in Cebu from the informal to the formal sector. Rather than starting in the informal sector and eventually moving to a formal sector job, a migrant would perhaps more commonly move directly into the formal sector.

In Cagayan de Oro 140 of the 561 migrant heads reported occupational changes. This data pattern is not unlike that of Cebu insofar as a high level of formal to informal sector movement is in evidence. Once again the movements enumerated are largely within the manufacturing sector although numerous other intra-sectoral changes were found. For example, government service to the military or manufacturing or vice versa. As was the case for the other two cities, intersectoral movements by migrants in Cagayan are more likely to occur from the formal to the informal sector than vice versa.

What do these movements tell us? First, these data reinforce insights gleaned from the literature with respect to the informal sector. That is, these jobs, whether traders, personal services, or the like, are very diverse and fluid. Given the simple requirements of some jobs in terms of capital, equipment, and even skills, individuals can move in and out of occupations very swiftly. Second, considerable movement does occur from the formal to the informal sector. For example, a young adult may take a low paying formal sector job (e.g., a government clerk) and will eventually build up contacts and capital to launch into business on a part-time basis for himself or herself while still maintaining the clerical position. It is important to note here that these movements should not be viewed necessarily as 'downward' shifts but rather as part of a diversification and risk-spreading phenomenon. Individuals do not always acquire less secure and lower paying jobs in the movement to the informal sector. Indeed, certain manufacturing jobs can be very unstable while also providing relatively little in the way of remuneration. On the other hand, some traders have very stable demand for their goods and in fact may be earning high incomes (Hackenberg, 1980, 413). In contrast, the movement from the informal sector to the formal sector is of relatively minor importance, except in Medan (Leinbach, 1986a).

Formal industry, particularly consumer goods and wood products, has expanded over the past five years and so these occupational changes are not unexpected (Ginting and Daroesman, 1982, 67–68).[2]

Some related information on this topic may be extracted from the two studies we have cited frequently in this chapter. The study of migration to 24 Javanese cities found that the majority of the male migrants remained in the occupation they were in prior to migrating; the major exceptions were male domestic servants, daily workers and production workers. The majority of female migrants, other than those engaged in prostitution and scavenging, changed their occupation after migration. This was attributed to the fact that women often have to give up their previous occupation when they migrate with a spouse or family. In addition however, and directly related to our analysis here, was the proportion of migrants whose current job was the same as the first job they obtained after migration. In contrast to our findings, for both males and females there was very little occupational mobility subsequent to migration (Aklilu and Harris, 1980, 129, 138).

In addition to the Javanese study, Koo and Smith (1983) have examined the question of occupational mobility within Metro Manila. They found that roughly 10 percent of the individuals interviewed had changed occupations between 1960 and 1968. Among these occupationally mobile persons 22 percent moved from the informal to the formal sector and 10 percent moved from the formal to the informal sector. They conclude that movement from the informal to the formal sector is more likely than movement in the opposite direction. The opposite is true from our findings in Cebu and Cagayan. In Medan there is a slightly higher chance of moving from the formal to the informal sector than the reverse. Their conclusion is that it is very unlikely that migrants (with respect to Manila) will move out of the informal sector and the same is true with respect to the formal sector. While the intersectoral movement patterns fail to conform to our findings, the conclusion of the dominance of intrasectoral stability, that is that it is very unlikely that migrants will move out of either the informal or formal sector, does fit well with our observations. Occupational mobility in the three present study sites is more likely to occur within the sectors than between them. In addition they note, "that Philippine cities offer very limited opportunities for occupational mobility, and the main cause of this may not be in the duality of the urban economic structure itself but in other characteristics of the Philippine economy" (Koo and Smith, 1983, 229). We cannot completely agree with the restriction of opportunities conclusion based upon our findings. We would maintain that occupational mobility is first obviously a function of an individual's attributes. Aside from this, locational and structural advantages may accrue to cities which are further down on the urban hierarchy and these influences in fact may foster and encourage occupational mobility. It is very clear that economic structure, both in a static and dynamic sense, does play a major role in occupational mobility. An example of this in North Sumatra would be towns within or adjacent to major agricultural districts. Here the growth of agricultural processing industries will allow considerable mobility.

Secondary Employment

As was suggested earlier the SUSENAS survey of the mid-1960s notes that occupational multiplicity in a cross section of large urban areas in Indonesia was not significant. We would expect that this rate is unlikely to have risen considerably, given overall improvements in living conditions since then. Our survey directed questions to the existence and nature of secondary occupations. Among the Medan migrant heads, approximately 8 percent indicated that they had some form of secondary employment. The most common job enumerated was irregular work. In addition individuals who held second jobs identified trading (*pedagang*), farming, daily wage labor, self employment, and even private sector work as the supplementary form of employment. Again the small samples from Pematang Siantar and Tebing Tinggi prohibit us from generalizing with a high degree of certainty. But in these two cities the proportions of positive responses were 5 and 9 percent, respectively. Farming and irregular work were the most common forms of work mentioned in the lower order Sumatran towns. In the Philippine cities secondary occupations were also recorded. For Cebu approximately 7 percent of the migrant heads responded positively to this question. While the jobs were scattered over a wide variety of categories, farming, personal and other services, and general commerce were the most commonly cited. Cagayan de Oro produced the strongest positive responses to the secondary employment questions. Fourteen percent of the heads acknowledged employment in addition to the primary job. As in Cebu, personal services, trading, agriculture, and manufacturing were the most important types.

Our expectation was that lower rates of occupational multiplicity would exist in the Philippines as opposed to Indonesia. In fact it would appear that quite similar rates of secondary employment exist among *migrant* households. Given the dated information available for Indonesia and the specific migrant population we have used it would be difficult to compare our results for Java or Indonesia as a whole. A recent study in the Philippines has found that in one rural area high levels of secondary job holding are quite common (Kerkvliet, 1980). Similar conclusions have been drawn elsewhere regarding the increasing level of occupational multiplicity in rural areas throughout Southeast Asia (White, 1979).

Summary

The topic of employment and employment creation obviously has a very central role in all development efforts. This concern becomes even urgent when we consider how employment and incomes will be affected by a rapidly expanding supply of labor combined with a slower growth in output— a situation which confronts both Indonesia and the Philippines today. The focus of this chapter has been the employment patterns of the migrants in our study cities. Our objective has been to learn more of the occupational characteristics and the search for and changes in employment.

Two major differences occur in the employment categories of the migrant household heads between the Indonesian and Philippine cities. Government service provides a much larger share of employment in the former while manufacturing accounts for more jobs in the latter. In all cities the broad services sector is clearly dominant.

If employment is allocated to formal-informal shares, our data reveal that the informal sector is more dominant in the Indonesian cities. Across all cities informal sector job holders tend to be older than those in the formal sector but formal sector workers are considerably better educated. Rural or urban origins of the migrants, age at, and the time of migration appear not to be related to the nature of employment as depicted in the dual sector model. Formal sector workers clearly earn higher incomes. In general, in both sectors male earnings exceed those of females. Again, with only a few exceptions in all cities, regardless of sector, older and urban origin migrants earn higher incomes, than do recent and rural origin migrants.

Some differences do exist between the Philippine and Indonesian cities with respect to prior knowledge about potential employment. There is a higher incidence of such knowledge in Cebu and Cagayan de Oro than in Medan. Differences in the perceived reliability of information may be related to the distance travelled and the fact that migration for job-related reasons is more common in the Philippines than in Indonesia. Most individuals in both regions find employment after they move to a destination on a permanent basis. A large percentage of migrants in both areas felt that their situation had improved by movement to the city.

Recent occupational mobility within all of the cities is dominated by intra-informal sector movements. Formal to informal sector movements appear to be more common than the reverse. The results reinforce the growing body of literature which details the complex and varied opportunities available within the informal sector. There is little evidence in our findings to contradict the conclusion that segments of the informal sector allow for the expansion and accumulation of capital and that there is considerable potential in this sector for increased incomes and employment opportunities. The importance of this is amplified when evidence suggests that linkages to the formal sector in general appear to be benign rather than exploitative (House, 1984, 298). The critical question, especially for policy, is how to best encourage these positive qualities of the informal sector in intermediate cities and how also to spread the benefits among a larger share of individuals.

Notes

1. The intent here has been to present several of the most important research themes related to the informal sector. For more detailed and exhaustive reviews the reader is encouraged to peruse other materials. Especially important and recent essays which provide generalizations and suggestions for new research are those by Richardson (1984) and Moser (1984).

2. Versions of the Todaro model, e.g., the Harris-Todaro model, attempt to explain rural-to-urban migration between an urban manufacturing sector and a rural agricultural sector. It is maintained that rural outmigration will continue as long as expected urban real income exceeds real agricultural product at the margin. This model, which fails to explain ASEAN rural-to-urban migration, assumes that rural-to-urban migrants are unemployed until they find jobs in the modern urban sector (Ogawa and Suits, 1985). The failure of the model in the ASEAN region is in part accounted for "because of low educational requirements and easy access which allows most migrants to enter the informal sector immediately after they move to urban areas" (Ogawa and Suits, 1985, 142). Even here there is stated the view that entry level jobs are largely in the informal rather than the formal sector. Clearly, initial employment may be found in the formal *or* the informal sector. The importance of one or the other in a certain spatial setting is dependent upon the structure of the urban economic base, personal contacts, access to capital, and a host of other factors.

6

Migrant and Nonmigrant Perceptions

In this chapter our focus shifts from the migration and employment characteristics of the sampled population to perceptions about the decision to migrate. We are particularly interested in determining how respondents view differently sized places, from rural hamlets to the very largest metropolitan centers. This topic is of special importance since government agencies may find it useful to know the perceptions and attitudes that potential migrants hold if policies designed to encourage movement toward middle-sized and smaller places are to be successful. As we have noted in Chapter 1, such decentralized urbanization is favored both by many Third World policy-makers, as well as by various social scientists who have conducted studies on this topic (Simmons, 1979; Hackenberg, 1980; Rondinelli, 1983).

As has been clearly pointed out in the literature, examination of the differences between perceptions and "reality" is important in gaining an understanding of migration decision-making and, furthermore, the migration literature is lacking in this regard (Gardner, 1981, 76–77). A large number of researchers have emphasized the importance of individual perceptions; in sociology Everett Lee (1966) was among the first and in geography the early work of Julian Wolpert (1965) on place utility and behavioral aspects of migration decision-making was of singular importance. Consideration of individual perceptions is also crucial for policy makers as Ricardo Abad (1981b, 301) tells us:

. . . it is evident that microlevel approaches to migration posit a complex series of causal linkages among the factors involved in the decision to move or stay. In this series of linkages, the migrants' perceptions of the macro world are critical variables, which serve as entry points for understanding policy interventions.

Only limited evidence is now available on the question of how individuals in Third World nations view the option of residing in different-sized places. One study completed in Southeast Asia demonstrated that migrants who moved from rural areas to small urban places in Thailand were satisfied with life in such places (Fuller, 1980). The conclusion was that secondary centers can retain such cityward migrants.

It is our purpose here to examine how both migrants and nonmigrants in our five study cities view different-sized places. Beginning with an examination of the levels of satisfaction of respondents regarding their present community and their hypothetical residential preferences, we next turn our attention to questions about migration expectations, potential destinations, views about achieving various goals in different-sized places, and value-expectancy scores. It is our hope that the information presented here will aid in understanding and planning for migration to secondary urban centers.

Level of Satisfaction with Current Residence

One of the first questions asked on the perception section of the questionnaire related to perceptions about the current place of residence. As has been found elsewhere (Fuller, 1980), we expected that respondents would relate positively to their present residence situations. As shown in Table 6.1, this is indeed the case. In all study cities and for all subgroups (except migrants in Tebing Tinggi) more than one-half of all respondents stated they were satisfied or very satisfied with the place in which they currently resided. Those in Cagayan de Oro were the most satisfied with their city and those who resided in the two smaller Indonesian cities were the least satisfied. Relatively few stated they were not satisfied; again, the two smaller cities in Sumatra had the greatest share of respondents in this category but in no case did more than 15 percent of the respondents state they were dissatisfied. In general, figures for migrants and nonmigrants were quite similar and only in Tebing Tinggi were intracity differences statistically significant. Furthermore, levels of satisfaction were remarkably similar across the five study cities suggesting that Filipinos and Indonesians have similar perceptions, at least with regards to satisfaction levels. These satisfaction findings reinforce our general or intuitive impression that cities hold strong attraction for potential migrants and that such attraction includes intermediate cities as well as the largest city in various nations. We explore this notion further in the next section.

Residential Preferences

A question of particular interest for the present study relates to preferences towards places of varying size. The rapid growth in Third World primate

Table 6.1

PERCEPTIONS ABOUT PRESENT PLACE OF RESIDENCE
BY CITY OF RESIDENCE, MIGRANT VS. NONMIGRANT (PERCENT)

	Medan (N=1050)		Pematang Siantar (N=231)		Tebing Tinggi (N=135)		Cebu (N=485)		Cagayan de Oro (N=335)	
	M (318)	N (732)	M (47)	N (84)	M (36)	N (99)	M (200)	N (285)	M (238)	N (97)
Very Satisfied	10	9	9	7	3	3	17	15	19	34
Satisfied	55	57	45	54	36	57	51	55	46	40
Somewhat Satisfied	24	24	32	28	50	27	23	19	27	22
Unsatisfied	12	10	15	11	11	13	10	11	8	4

Note: The differences between migrants (M) and nonmigrants (N) were not statistically significant for any city.

Source: Sample Survey Data.

cities would seem to indicate that perceptions about such locales should be basically positive, whereas loss of migrants from rural areas and towns, and slow growth in many smaller cities, suggests more negative views about these places. Given the evidence presented above, however, one would also expect that respondents would prefer to live in places similar to their current residences; that is, in small and medium-sized cities.

We obtained information on the question of residential preferences by asking respondents about the type of community in which they would most like to live (Table 6.2).[1] In general, the data show the not unexpected tendency for respondents to be satisfied with the type of place in which they are currently residing. Thus, nearly two-thirds of the respondents in Medan said they preferred to live in a city the size of Medan, while one-third and two-fifths of the respondents in Cebu and Cagayan de Oro, respectively, answered likewise. In Pematang Siantar and Tebing Tinggi, the most often cited city type was that which is nearest to the size class of these two, that is, smaller cities. As was the case for satisfaction levels, it is again clear from the data that, except for Tebing Tinggi, differences between migrants and nonmigrants are not significant. That is, both groups exhibit similar residential preferences. This is somewhat unexpected as it

Table 6.2

PREFERRED TYPE OF COMMUNITY BY
CITY OF RESIDENCE, MIGRANT VS. NONMIGRANT (PERCENT)

	Medan (N=1046)		Pematang Siantar (N=234)		Tebing Tinggi[a] (N=140)		Cebu (N=477)		Cagayan de Oro (N=336)	
	M (313)	N (733)	M (48)	N (186)	M (36)	N (104)	M (195)	N (282)	M (239)	N (97)
Rural	21	23	19	12	14	35	23	17	20	21
Town	5	3	4	4	8	12	13	12	7	4
Small City	6	9	65	72	61	46	22	25	23	30
Medium City	64	64	10	10	14	4	35	33	42	41
Large City	4	2	2	2	3	4	7	13	8	4

[a]The differences between migrants (M) and nonmigrants (N) were statistically significant for this study city (p<.05).

Source: Sample Survey Data.

would seem, for example, that the large number of migrants in Cebu from rural areas might mean that a greater share of migrants would cite a preference for rural areas. It is also evident from these findings that the bulk of migrants to the small- and medium-sized cities in our study feel psychologically committed to the city size grouping which their new residence lies within.

Another finding of interest is the fact that a fairly large proportion, around 20 percent on the average for all groups, stated that they would prefer to live in a rural community. One might expect this from those migrants who came to the cities from rural origins but the data in Table 6.2 show that approximately the same proportion of nonmigrants hold this viewpoint. Such findings confirm those made in Chapter 4; that is, return migration to a rural community of origin remains an important option among migrants in the cities. Reverse-stream migration could also be a potential option for urban nonmigrants as well, especially if greater economic opportunities existed in rural communities.

Table 6.3

EVER VISITED PRIMATE CITY BY
CITY OF RESIDENCE, MIGRANT VS. NONMIGRANT (PERCENT)

Ever Visited?	Medan[a] (N=990) M (299)	N (691)	Pematang Siantar (N=216) M (45)	N (171)	Tebing Tinggi (N=130) M (35)	N (95)	Cebu[a] (N=481) M (198)	N (283)	Cagayan de Oro (N=336) M (239)	N (97)
Yes	34	18	22	16	14	12	41	32	39	31
No	66	82	78	84	86	88	59	68	61	69

[a]The differences between migrants (M) and nonmigrants (N) were statistically significant for Medan ($p<.01$) and Cebu ($p<.05$).

Source: Sample Survey Data.

Also readily apparent in Table 6.2 is the distaste that respondents in all cities have for the very largest cities in the two nations, Jakarta and Manila. Apparently this perception is based on some knowledge of these largest cities since a considerable number of respondents from our study cities had visited either Jakarta or Manila (Table 6.3). Migrants had more often visited the primate city in all locales, but differences between migrants and nonmigrants were generally quite small on this variable and thus apparently perception and preference is not strongly influenced by actual behavior or direct visits. With regard to differences between countries, respondents in the Philippine cities were more likely to have visited Manila than were persons from the northern Sumatran cities to have visited Jakarta. Finally, relatively fewer respondents from the two smaller Indonesian cities had visited their nation's primate city.

Intuitively speaking, this finding of low preference level for the largest city may not be unexpected. Nevertheless, this observation must be considered as surprising, given the thousands of migrants who move every year to the largest city, as coupled with the fact that value-expectancy scores for the largest cities were highest from all study cities (see below). This latter finding of course implies that our respondents are more likely to move to the largest cities should they move, at least based on their values and goals.

In summary, it is clear that those who live in medium-sized cities of varying size in northern Sumatra and the southern and central Philippines

Table 6.4

MIGRATION EXPECTATION BY CITY OF RESIDENCE,
MIGRANT VS. NONMIGRANT (PERCENT)

Expect to Move?	Medan[a] (N=1042)		Pematang Siantar (N=229)		Tebing Tinggi (N=137)		Cebu[a] (N=475)		Cagayan de Oro[a] (N=332)	
	M (309)	N (733)	M (48)	N (179)	M (33)	N (104)	M (196)	N (279)	M (235)	N (97)
Yes	16	12	17	9	6	4	22	14	15	5
No	84	89	83	91	94	96	78	86	85	95

[a]The differences between migrants (M) and nonmigrants (N) were statistically significant (p<.05).

Source: Sample Survey Data.

are satisfied with their own cities, have a higher preference for living in rural areas than expected, and do not wish to live in the very largest metropolitan areas in the country.

Migration Expectations

Given that respondents were generally satisfied with their current places of residence we expected that few would be anticipating migration. Our data clearly support this expectation in the sense that the great majority, when asked whether or not they planned to move, responded that they did not plan to leave their current place of residence (Table 6.4). The fact that our sample includes only household heads and spouses must be kept in mind, however, since no doubt the proportion intending to migrate would be greater if, for example, respondents had been young and unmarried. It is also worth pointing out that these data do not necessarily indicate a high level of satisfaction with the community of residence. In many cases, perhaps especially among nonmigrants, the respondent may simply feel that he has nowhere else to go, or that a move could involve too many risks (Goodman, 1981, 140–141; Haberkorn, 1981, 254–258). In the three largest cities, a significantly greater share of migrants stated they expected to move. This is not surprising given that migrants have already had the experience of moving and do not have the long-term attachment to their current place of residence that nonmigrants have.

Table 6.5

PREFERRED DESTINATION OF THOSE WHO STATED THEY EXPECT
TO MOVE, BY CITY OF RESIDENCE (PERCENT)

Preferred Destination	Medan (N=105)	Pematang Siantar and Tebing Tinggi (N=25)	Cebu (N=86)	Cagayan de Oro (N=41)
Urban	61	76	33	32
Rural	24	20	34	54
Foreign	-	-	2	10
Uncertain	15	4	31	4
Same Region[a]	50	90	40	22
Jakarta/Manila	15	10	7	2

[a]North Sumatra Province, central Visayas region, or northern
Mindanao region.

Source: Sample Survey Data.

The preferred destinations of those who stated that they expected to
move from their present community are presented in Table 6.5. While the
sample sizes are quite small (because relatively few stated they expected
to move) and it is therefore difficult to make broad generalizations, some
of the perceptions already discussed are confirmed by these data (Table
6.5). For example, the importance of rural destinations is clearly evident.
In each of the three largest cities at least one-quarter of those who said
they expected to move said they would move to a rural destination. In
Cagayan de Oro, over one-half of this group stated they would move to
such a destination. As already mentioned, a number of such persons would
be return migrants illustrating both the importance of this type of movement
and circular mobility.

Another finding of importance is that whereas a large portion of those
who stated they expected to move were intending to go to an urban area,
few expressed a desire to move to the very largest city of the nation. The
largest share was the 15 percent from Medan. Among the total 257
respondents from all five study cities who said they expected to migrate,
less than 10 percent (25), said they wanted to move to Jakarta or Manila.
Thus again, our data support the notion of the more or less negative
perception of the largest cities of each nation. Another finding is the greater

tendency for potential migrants from Medan and Cebu to move to Jakarta or Manila. This, together with the fact that potential cityward migrants from Cagayan de Oro responded they would most likely go to larger cities like Davao or Cebu (and those from Pematang Siantar and Tebing Tinggi would travel to Medan), would seem to indicate some conformity to a step-like pattern of movement to larger urban places.

We also asked respondents about whether or not there were good effects or bad effects in moving to cities. The majority of those who responded that there were good effects, which included anywhere from almost three-quarters of the respondents in Cebu to only one-third in the two smaller Indonesian cities, gave economic or social mobility as the predominant good effect. Worth noting, however, is the fact that in the Philippine case and to some extent in Indonesia many responses had an associated qualifying phrase which indicated an awareness that not all migrants would be able to achieve economic advances. The most typical response along these lines was the notion that an urbanward migrant can improve his or her economic position, but only "if he can find a job," "if business is good," or "if he has an education." The essentially contingent nature of the results of moving to the city is, it would seem, well understood by the respondents. The second most important good effect of city life was that life there would be more "interesting" or more "stimulating;" educational factors ranked third.

The economic dimension was also cited frequently in answers to the question about the bad effects of moving from the countryside to the city. In Cagayan de Oro, for example, of the 62 percent who said there were bad effects of such a move, nearly two-thirds expressed concern about finding employment in the urban destination, or about the "hard life" in the city. A further one-quarter cited the deviant life styles found in the city (crime, prostitution, etc.) as the principle bad effect. Ecological factors, such as noise and air pollution were also cited as bad effects, but only a few respondents seemed to be concerned about such conditions. In Indonesia the results were somewhat similar except that the crowded nature of the large city was seen as the principle bad effect of such a move. In Medan, for example, of the 40 percent who stated there were bad effects, some 40 percent cited crowded conditions (which presumably related to poverty) as the principle bad effect. This factor may emerge or be pronounced because of the relatively low population densities throughout North Sumatra. As was true in the Philippine cities, few noted pollution or environmental deterioration or other ecological factors as bad effects.

It is perhaps surprising that not more of the respondents stated they expected to move since a greater share of respondents in most of the study cities felt that migrants were better off than were nonmigrants (Table 6.6). This was especially so in the case of the Indonesian cities; in Cebu the perception was that migrants were somewhat better off but in Cagayan de Oro the view was that there was little difference between movers and stayers.

Table 6.6

OPINIONS AS TO WHO IS BETTER OFF--MOVERS OR STAYERS,
BY CITY OF RESIDENCE, MIGRANT VS. NONMIGRANT (PERCENT)

Opinion	Medan (N=626)		Pematang Siantar (N=112)		Tebing Tinggi (N=67)		Cebu (N=469)		Cagayan de Oro (N=336)	
	M	N	M	N	M	N	M	N	M	N
	(299)	(327)	(45)	(67)	(35)	(32)	(193)	(276)	(237)	(97)
Migrants Better Off	36	33	20	28	51	44	35	29	27	26
Same	35	37	56	37	34	22	31	28	35	38
Stayers Better Off	18	15	16	22	-	3	20	29	28	27
Uncertain	11	16	9	12	14	31	14	14	9	9

Note: Differences were not statistically significant in any of
the five study cities.

Source: Sample Survey Data.

In nearly all cases the modal response was that the two groups could be
rated about the same economically and in no case were migrant-nonmigrant
intracity differences statistically significant. The conclusion, and this is
reinforced by our findings regarding reasons for migration as discussed in
Chapter 4 (see Table 4.1), must be that economic factors and perceptions
about poverty are predominant in one's assessment of migration to cities.

Thus far, our conclusions have been based upon answers to questions
that directly ask the respondent about how they perceive their level of
satisfaction, whether or not they expect to migrate from their present place,
and their residential preferences. A more indirect, and perhaps more objective,
method by which to determine how individuals view different-sized places
and the possibility of moving to such places, is through the value-expectancy
model of migration.

Value-Expectancies

In this application the value-expectancy model, developed in psychology,
has been shown to have considerable utility in analyzing migration behavior
(Chemers, *et al*, 1978; De Jong, *et al*, 1983). With respect to migration,

"the model calls for a specification of the personally valued goals that might be met by moving (or staying) and an assessment of the perceived linkage, in terms of expectancy, between migration behavior and the attainment of goals in alternative locations" (De Jong and Fawcett, 1981, 47). It is, in short, a cognitive model that is cast in a cost-benefit framework.

The basic components of the model are thus goals (values or objectives) and expectancies (subjective probabilities). In order to determine the intention to migrate, the value of each goal is multiplied by the expectancy of achieving that goal in each alternative location and the goals are then summed for each location:

> The multiplicative assumption means that if either the importance of a particular value is low or the expectancy concerning it is weak, that component will contribute little to total intentions. . . . (and) multiple values or goals may be involved in the migration decision-making process. The value-expectancy model includes this possibility by summing the product of individual values and expectancies in developing a final measure of the strength of the intention to move. (De Jong and Fawcett, 1981, 47–48)

An important consideration in the application of this model, of course, is the decision as to the relevant values or goals. This is even more critical in a cross-cultural study since some values which are given great emphasis in certain cultural contexts may be held to be less important in another. The problem in the present study is not insurmountable but differences in culture (e.g., religion) and current events (e.g., the insurgency in the Philippines, periodic droughts), for example, will tend to put a greater emphasis on certain values. In short, our comparisons, where they are possible, must be viewed in the context of such differences.

It was possible to agree on eleven, more or less mutually exclusive, values which seemed to be psychologically meaningful to respondents in both nations (Table 6.7).[2] Respondents were asked the importance of each of these values and responded with one of four possible answers from "very important" to "not at all important."

With one exception (entertainment in Cagayan de Oro), the majority of respondents stated that each of the eleven values was at least "a little important" to him or her (Table 6.7).[3] Furthermore, differences among the five cities were not great. The values held most important by the respondents in all cities were income, availability of jobs, education, housing, access to health care, their security, and access to transportation. Entertainment, "adventure," independence (from living with or near family), and living among people of similar ethnic stock, while of some importance, were significantly less important than the seven previously-cited values. One difference between the two nations is that respondents in the two Philippine

Table 6.7

THE RELATIVE IMPORTANCE OF VALUES,[a]
BY CITY OF RESIDENCE (PERCENT)

Value	Medan	Pematang Siantar	Tebing Tinggi	Cebu	Cagayan de Oro
Income/High Wages	91	92	91	96	98
Job Availability	91	94	97	94	97
Education	88	92	89	94	99
Housing	83	86	91	96	95
Health Facilities	90	94	94	94	99
Entertainment	58	52	81	51	39
New Experience/ Adventure	76	81	87	76	86
Independence	64	60	64	72	81
Live Near Same Kind (Ethnic Group)	57	52	62	77	82
Safety/Security/ Peace and Order	94	97	97	96	99
Transportation	88	91	96	94	94

[a]Figures include all respondents who stated the value was at least a little, or somewhat, important. Figures do not include those who claimed the value was not important. The number of respondents in each city varied slightly for each value since some did not respond for all values. See Table 6.1 for the approximate number (N) of respondents for each city.

Source: Sample Survey Data.

cities view independence and living near the "same kind" as more important than did the Indonesian groups. The former pattern appears to support our earlier finding, as noted in Chapter 4, that the Indonesian respondents were more likely to have moved for family-related reasons than were those from the Philippines.

After the importance attached to each value was determined, respondents were asked to rate the perceived possibility of achieving each of the eleven values in three hypothetical settings: a rural area, a small city, and a large city. These data provide a profile of the perceptions about life in three different-sized communities held by the respondents (Table 6.8).

The findings are not unexpected in that the respondents perceived that the largest cities were the places wherein the possibility for high incomes, attaining jobs, high educational levels, health care, entertainment, adventure, and access to transportation were the greatest. On the other hand, and also not surprisingly, the largest cities were perceived as places wherein one was least likely to find persons of the same ethnic group and where one's safety was at greatest risk. It is not possible to make generalizations about housing since the percentage of respondents who perceive the attainability of comfortable housing was similar for the three different-sized places in at least two of the five study cities (Pematang Siantar and Cebu). In only one city, Tebing Tinggi, was there a clear distinction among the three hypothetical locations for the housing value. Respondents in this city perceived good housing to be most attainable in the largest city, and least attainable in rural areas. Another value wherein there was no clear difference in the percentage of respondents who perceived the value important among the three hypothetical places was independence. Generally, the perception is the larger the place, the more attainable is comfortable housing and independence, but differences by size of place are not as great as was expected. One reason for the former finding is no doubt the visible pattern of city slum and squatter areas, which may be perceived as offering few advantages or even some disadvantages in comparison to the type of housing available in the countryside.

One clear finding, at least in the case of the three Sumatran cities, is that respondents from the two smaller cities perceive that goals are more attainable in the largest places than do respondents who live in Medan, a large city. A greater share of those surveyed in Tebing Tinggi and Pematang Siantar viewed the largest cities as the place where higher incomes, improved educational levels, and better jobs could be had. On the other hand, those in the larger cities (both Medan and Cebu) apparently view values such as income and education as being at least slightly more attainable in rural areas than do those in the smaller cities. This is not surprising in that the residents of the smaller cities tend to have a more negative view of rural areas than do large city residents.[4]

Table 6.8

PERCEPTIONS ABOUT THE POSSIBILITY OF ACHIEVING GOALS[a]
IN RURAL AREAS, SMALL CITIES, AND LARGE CITIES,
BY CITY OF RESIDENCE (PERCENT)

| | Medan | | | Pematang Siantar | | | Tebing Tinggi | | |
Value	Rural	Small City	Large City	Rural	Small City	Large City	Rural	Small City	Large City
Income	20	33	72	18	34	75	10	24	87
Job	24	39	70	24	44	73	11	24	84
Education	27	44	84	15	37	82	10	28	88
Housing	33	45	58	36	51	51	21	41	76
Health	42	57	81	33	46	79	25	46	93
Entertainment	24	37	86	28	39	83	22	39	93
Adventure	28	41	81	27	32	85	16	31	93
Independence	45	42	51	46	52	68	46	46	47
Same Kind	76	57	32	75	64	29	81	68	33
Security	84	70	29	76	67	19	80	83	30
Transportation	37	45	67	32	43	56	44	56	64

| | Cebu | | | Cagayan de Oro | | |
Value	Rural	Small City	Large City	Rural	Small City	Large City
Income	13	44	90	13	45	91
Jobs	10	46	94	9	47	92
Education	16	57	94	11	53	94
Housing	65	60	64	42	56	68
Health	19	62	94	14	59	96
Entertainment	20	61	94	9	47	96
Adventure	37	62	87	22	53	93
Independence	43	54	79	45	47	69
Same Kind	81	46	37	74	29	25
Security	91	41	28	92	36	17
Transportation	26	63	90	17	50	91

[a]Figures include all respondents who stated the value was
"possible" to achieve; two other choices, "a little possible" and
"impossible," could be given. The number of respondents in each
city varied slightly since some did not respond. See Table 6.1
for the approximate number (N) of respondents in each city.

Source: Sample Survey Data.

In summary, respondents in all study areas were found to rate cities as superior to rural areas in terms of a widespread number of specialized institutional facilities, including those for education, health, entertainment, and transportation. Furthermore, large cities were uniformly rated superior in this regard to small cities. Cities, and large cities in particular, were also rated much higher in terms of high wages and availability of jobs, a pattern which fits well with our earlier discussion on urban-rural differences in incomes and living standards (Chapter 2). Perhaps as a consequence of this a positive relationship between city size and perceived housing quality may also be noted in the data, though the differences in this case are less clearly manifested. Interestingly, in the case of Cebu no such relationship existed between city size and housing.

One somewhat surprising result in the case of the Philippines, and especially Cagayan de Oro, regards the question about safety and security, or peace and order. We had anticipated a considerably more negative response toward the rural areas since at the time of the study numerous violent incidents were reported occurring in Mindanao's countryside, including military incursions against the Communist-led New People's Army, assassinations of government officials and military leaders, military abuses, and forced relocations of the rural population. However, instead of scoring rural areas low on this value, most respondents apparently chose to interpret this question in terms of such qualities as the peaceful, easy-going nature of life in the ideal rural community, as opposed to the hectic life styles associated with urban living.

For nearly all comparisons in all five study cities, the small city category took an intermediate position between the rural and large city responses. This would seem to indicate that our respondents perceive small cities as being unable to offer all of the advantages of life in the big city, but also that smaller cities have fewer of the large city disadvantages, like crime.

Overall, these data would appear to indicate that programs designed to improve the attractiveness of small cities should concentrate on helping such cities gain parity with the primate centers on a number of dimensions including income levels, jobs, educational and health facilities, and transportation. Conversely, educational campaigns designed to attract more migrants to small cities (or rural areas for that matter) could start by emphasizing those values where smaller cities are already perceived as holding an edge over the primate city, such as security and being with one's own ethnic group.

The overall value-expectancy scores are consistent with the previous results. Thus, the scores for rural areas are in each case the lowest, while those for the large city are uniformly the highest (Table 6.9). Scores for rural areas are remarkably similar among all cities, with the two smallest study cities, Pematang Siantar and Tebing Tinggi, recording the lowest mean

Table 6.9

VALUE-EXPECTANCY SCORES,[a]
BY CITY OF RESIDENCE, MIGRANT VS. NONMIGRANT (PERCENT)

	Medan		Pematang Siantar		Tebing Tinggi		Cebu		Cagayan de Oro	
	M	N	M	N	M	N	M	N	M	N
Rural Score	71.8	71.1	70.6	68.1	64.8	69.4	77.4	74.2	72.2	75.0
Small City Score	81.6	80.2	79.9	77.1	83.4	82.6	98.8	96.2	93.5	94.5
Big City Score	87.1	87.8	90.3	85.3	103.8	96.1	104.4	102.5	101.8	102.3

[a]The highest possible score is 132. The number of respondents in each city is smaller than the total possible because of missing values. The number may vary slightly for each score for the same city. The approximate total number of respondents is 880 (263 migrants, 617 nonmigrants); 200 (42 migrants, 158 nonmigrants); 120 (30 migrants, 90 nonmigrants); 460 (189 migrants, 271 nonmigrants); and 334 (237 migrants, 97 nonmigrants), respectively.

Note: Differences between migrants (M) and nonmigrants (N) were not statistically significant for any city.

Source: Sample Survey Data.

scores in this regard. This finding is consistent with our previous discussion of the more negative perception of rural areas from these smaller cities. The mean scores of respondents among the Indonesian cities were quite similar for the small city whereas small cities received a considerably higher score from respondents in Cebu and Cagayan de Oro. This, too, is not unexpected given the fact that respondents in these medium-sized cities were considerably more satisfied with their situations than those in the Sumatran cities (Table 6.1). Also worthy of note is the fact that the value-expectancy scores for migrants and nonmigrants were quite similar overall, with this comparison attaining statistical significance in only one of fifteen comparisons.

While it is somewhat difficult to make comparisons between the results from the Philippine and Indonesian study cities, the difference between the scores of the small cities and large cities is clearly greater for Medan, Pematang Siantar, and Tebing Tinggi than it is for either Cebu or Cagayan de Oro. This implies of course that value-expectancies for respondents in the two Philippine cities are quite similar for small and large cities. The implication of this finding is that small cities are viewed as being more attractive than they are in the Sumatran case. From the standpoint of policy, this may mean that migrants can more easily be directed toward smaller cities in this setting than is the case for Indonesia (see Hugo and Mantra, 1983). Such an implication of course must be corroborated against other research findings.

Summary

Our findings have shown that relatively few respondents are planning to leave their present communities, while most claim to be generally satisfied with their current places of residence. Those few who do plan to migrate tend to prefer another urban place but not the nation's primate center. In fact, a surprisingly large share of those who say they will move have decided to go to a rural area, with this destination being chosen much more frequently than the primate city. The apparent unpopularity of such locales is evident in our early discussion (e.g., see Table 6.2) even though respondents did seem to perceive their national capital regions as offering much in the way of economic opportunities and specialized institutional facilities (Tables 6.7–6.9). The unwillingness to move to the primate centers may thus be attributable to the fact that respondents, who are located some distance from Jakarta and Manila, are not well enough integrated with the socio-economic networks of these large cities so as to feel confident about moving there (although a fair share had visited, see Table 6.3). Another possibility is that they are already aware of the extreme urban diseconomies which are seen as present in the primate cities. In any event, a strong foundation, on the attitudinal level, appears to exist in this area for programs designed to deflect migration streams away from the national centers.

Thus, our sample generally appeared to dislike the largest urban center of each nation from the standpoint of living there. However, the data from the value-expectancy items suggest clearly that respondents perceive the very largest cities as the place wherein subjectively important goals may be most easily achieved. In turn, smaller cities, especially among the Indonesian respondents, fared less well, though better than rural areas, where the achievement of most goals was seen as being least likely. Thus, even though our early discussion showed respondents as viewing such areas at least somewhat favorably, it is unlikely that many of these would actually consider locating permanently in such areas.

It also appears from the relative importance given to the values (Table 6.7), that socioeconomic factors such as income, education, and the availability of jobs are the factors most important in decisions about migration. This is not surprising, given the predominance of economic motives for migration, as shown both in our earlier findings in this regard (Chapter 4) as well as from studies conducted in other Third World settings (e.g., Pryor, 1977). On the other hand, at least one study which specifically examined value-expectancies among a small sample of Iranian nonmigrants, migrants to Teheran, and return migrants, found the cultural values of religion and family to be more important than economic opportunities in location choice (Chemers, et al, 1978).

Another interesting finding is that perceptions with regards to satisfaction, residential preferences, goals, and so forth do not differ very significantly between migrant and nonmigrant groups in any of the study cities. This is interesting because it may imply that nonmigrants are no more or less resistant to moving than are migrants, at least based on their own statements and values. On the other hand, there is some limited evidence that migrants have a greater expectation of moving (Table 6.4).

One of the purposes of this study is to make cross-national comparisons. That is, do the sampled groups in the Philippines and Indonesia differ with regards to their migration, employment, and cognitive characteristics? In earlier chapters we have seen that our study populations are similar in many respects when comparisons are made by city size. Our findings in this chapter, too, clearly demonstrate that the Indonesian and Philippine populations are quite similar with regards to level of satisfaction with current residence, residential preferences, plans to migrate, and value-expectancies.

Notes

1. The question read as follows: "Other things being equal, where would you prefer to live?" Five precoded responses to this question were then read aloud to the respondent. These included "rural area or village" (translated as *barangay* in the Philippines), "town" (*poblacion* in the Philippines), "small city," "medium-sized city," and "large city" (like Jakarta or Manila). Examples of different-sized cities were given to the respondent in order to make this concept more concrete. However, the names of the study cities were consciously avoided as an example of the city-size concept in order to be sure that preferences for one's home community were not to be confused with ideas about life in the hypothetical category.

2. Based on an extensive review of the theoretical and empirical literature on the subject, De Jong and Fawcett (1981, 49–51) developed a list of seven conceptual categories of values or goals that they felt represented psychologically meaningful clusters. The seven categories are: wealth, status, comfort, stimulation, autonomy, affiliation, and morality. At least one indicator for each of these seven categories is to be found among our list of eleven values.

3. Migrant-nonmigrant differences are not reflected in Tables 6.7 or 6.8 since the differences between the two groups were not significant in any of the study cities. This is evident in Table 6.9, the value-expectancy scores, which is of course based upon the preceding two tables. Migrant-nonmigrant differences are given in this table to demonstrate that differences are very small.

4. An analagous finding was found in the Cagayan de Oro study area in that residents of this city tended to hold more favorable impressions of life in rural communities than did a sample of respondents actually living in three rural settings in the same province (Costello and Palabrica-Costello, 1985).

7

Characteristics of Circulation
and Circulators

Thus far our analysis has emphasized that aspect of human mobility known as migration, that is, permanent movement. It is becoming increasingly clear that much human mobility in Third World nations is of a more temporary nature: movement which is "usually short-term, repetitive or cyclical in nature, but all having in common the lack of any declared intention of permanent or long-lasting change of residence" (Zelinsky, 1971, 226; Standing, 1982). This form of mobility, known as circular migration or circulation, is not a new phenomenon in the Third World but its widespread significance is only now beginning to become well-documented (e.g., Prothero and Chapman, 1985; Standing, 1985). How long circulation will continue to be a significant form of mobility is questioned: some maintain it is but one stage in the mobility transition and others see it as a more long-lasting form of mobility. As is true for the other two types of mobility, commuting and migration, the temporal and spatial aspects of circulation vary greatly from one area to another. Operational definitions of circulation also vary and may include people temporarily absent from their permanent homeplaces from one day to several decades.

The earliest studies on circulation in the Third World were focused upon Black Africa due to the heavy male labor migration to cities and mines found in that region (Wilson, 1941–1942; Prothero, 1958; Elkan, 1967). Since then research has been conducted on the topic in many other Third World regions, most notably in Southeast Asia (Goldstein, 1978; Jones and Richter, 1981). Most studies on circulation conducted in this region have been carried out in Indonesia or Thailand and have focused either on rural communities or on particular groups within the very largest cities which are characterized by high rates of circulation, such as various informal sector jobs (Meinkoth, 1962; Forbes, 1978, 1981; Hugo, 1978, 1982; Mantra, 1981; and Lightfoot, Fuller, and Kamnuansilpa, 1983). Virtually all studies on the topic agree that circulation is now an important component of mobility in Southeast Asia.

Several researchers maintain that it is stimulated largely by economic motives (Standing, 1985) and that it will become more dominant as internal transport systems continue to improve (Hugo, 1985b).

It is our purpose in this chapter to examine the characteristics and implications of circulation in our three largest study cities: Medan, Cebu, and Cagayan de Oro.[1] More specifically, we will examine the characteristics of those identified as circulators, including their age, sex, income, occupation, homeplace, and educational level. Once the characteristics have been established, the implications of this movement for the study areas can then be examined. In terms of policy, a basic question is whether circulation should be facilitated or discouraged.

Because of differences in survey techniques and questions asked with regard to circulation, it is not possible to directly compare the Indonesian and Philippine results. In the two Philippine cities, the findings reported on here are based upon information from the major survey instrument. That is, household questionnaires were utilized to isolate individuals who were identified by the spouse as temporarily visiting from another municipality or city and who were staying at least overnight in the households we sampled. Separate interviews were then conducted with temporary visitors, in which it was established whether or not they did indeed intend to return to their home community; respondents who said that they did not intend to do so were eliminated. We also asked the head or spouse (almost always the latter) of these households whether any household members who permanently resided in the household were temporarily elsewhere. If there were such members, and if the head or spouse said they were certain that they would return to reside there, we then asked the spouse a number of questions about the persons temporarily absent. We eliminated from consideration all those visitors or persons temporarily absent who were under fifteen years of age.

Thus, for the Philippine cities our definition of circulation is based more upon the *intent* of the mover than on the length of time the circulator had been absent. In this manner, 100 individuals were found to be temporarily absent among the 1,000 households surveyed in metropolitan Cebu, while there were 122 absentees among the 800 households in Cagayan de Oro. On the other hand, there were 113 temporary visitors in the Cebu households and 154 such visitors in Cagayan de Oro.

In Medan a different approach was used to gather information about circulators and therefore our results are not entirely comparable with regard to circulation. In Medan, a select group of interviewers was instructed to randomly halt individuals at bus depots and minivan stops, work places, and other locations within the city where circulators were likely to be found. Individuals were asked simply whether they were permanently residing in the city. If they were not, a follow-up question inquired whether they were in the city for employment purposes. In this way it could be determined if the individual returned to his residence outside the city on a daily basis (commuted) or stayed there for a more extended period of time (circulated). A sample of 300 non-resident individuals was thus isolated from within five *kecamatan* of the city (Leinbach and Suwarno, 1985). Following the initial contact, arrangements were made for a more lengthy and detailed interview. Of the 300 individuals sampled, 233 (78 percent) were evaluated as commuters, and 67 (22 percent) were judged to be circulators. It is with this latter group that this chapter is largely concerned. Thus, it is important to bear in mind that in Medan only those who were temporarily visiting the city are included here. In the two Philippine cities, characteristics of both persons temporarily visiting ("in-circulators") and those temporarily absent ("out-circulators") are examined.

Circulation to Medan

Just as migrants to Medan tend to be young and male so, too, are circulators to the city. Nearly 45 percent were in the 20 to 30 year age category and a further 14 percent were under 20 years of age; only 3 percent were over 50. Nearly all (98 percent) of the 67 circulators were male, and 58 percent of these individuals were married. While about 14 percent of the commuters were under 20 years old, the median age in the two groups was identical, 28 years.

In terms of origin, the circulators came from a variety of locales. Approximately 40 percent came from North Sumatra province, with about one-third of these coming from Deli Serdang, the North Sumatran *kabupaten* which surrounds Medan. Nearly one-quarter came from West Sumatra province. A much smaller proportion, six percent, came from provinces on Java, while the remainder came from other provinces, mostly on Sumatra. Of interest is the fact that a lower percentage of circulators came from the nearest province (North Sumatra) than was found for the more permanent movers or migrants; in the case of migrants, more than one-half moved from North Sumatra (Table 2.8). Overall, about 35 percent of the circulators travelled over 85 kilometers, while the proportion travelling under 12 kilometers was 25 percent. Clearly, the commonly-held view that circulators travel only relatively short distances is not supported by our limited evidence. In contrast, nearly 30 percent of the commuters travelled distances under 11 kilometers whereas only 10 percent travelled a daily distance of over 24 kilometers.

Information gathered on ethnicity fits the expected pattern, i.e., that circulators would be dominantly Javanese and Minangkabau. Over one-third of the circulators were Javanese and 30 percent were Minangkabau. The circulation behavior of the latter group is well known through the tradition

Table 7.1

JOB TYPES OF CIRCULATORS TO MEDAN (PERCENT)

Job Type	Circulators (N=67)
Motor becak driver	9.0
Becak driver	10.5
Trader	44.8
Carpenter	9.0
Factory worker (temporary)	1.5
Factory worker (permanent)	4.5
Domestic help	1.5
Motor mechanic	3.0
Salesgirl	1.5
Restaurant worker	1.5
General laborer	4.5
Tinsmith	4.5
Tailor	4.5

Source: Sample Survey Data.

of *merantau* (temporary population movement). Among members of this group, economic goals among individuals are encouraged by *adat* (traditional law) and the desire for prosperity in the matrilineal extended family (Naim, 1973). This special form of movement is unusual in that individuals are supported while they are away from their home region. Young males are given a great deal of freedom to leave and can return to the household when they choose. The other significant ethnic groups represented among the circulators were the Toba Batak, Mandailing, Tapanuli Batak, and Melayu. Given the importance of the Batak community in the immediate hinterland of Medan, it was not unexpected that a significant proportion of circulators should have come from this ethnic association.

While a wide variety of job types were held by the circulators to Medan, those who were traders outnumbered all other groups (Table 7.1). The second most important source of employment for circulators was transportation services; many circulators were employed as drivers. A variety of personal and other service jobs were also held. Thus, among the circulators in our sample, nearly all (over 95 percent), worked in the informal sector. Findings in West Java have indicated that among temporary migrants there, about two-thirds were employed in the informal sector (Hugo, 1977, 65).

Classification differences between that study and our own could account for this difference but, in any event, it seems clear that most circulators are informal sector workers. In contrast, over 40 percent of the commuters in Medan, on the other hand, were employed in government service and factories (temporary and permanent jobs), while only about 15 percent of the commuters were employed as traders.

Given the importance of the employment motive in circulation behavior we also sought to learn about the job search process. Among the circulators to Medan, 45 percent learned about the employment opportunity in their village or origin area, whereas 36 percent learned about the job only after arriving in the city. Friends and relatives were clearly the most important source of information, with 73 percent of the circulators citing such reasons. Formal sources and official channels were of only minor importance.

A major question in our investigation concerns income. While the matter of remuneration is always a difficult question, especially in Indonesia where some payment is often given in kind and multiple job holding may occur, we believe our data to reflect actual earnings. The average monthly earnings of the circulators was nearly $100 (Rp 16,300, or $24.20 per week). This is slightly less than the monthly income of US$113 found for migrant heads of household in Medan (see Table 2.4) but more than the $78 monthly income of the commuting group. Given that commuters may hold their job for a longer period of time than the circulators (who will by definition be returning home eventually) this result is somewhat surprising. One might have expected that circulators would not normally have the opportunity to "mature" in their jobs and thus move up the wage scale in terms of experience, knowledge, and seniority. Conversely, such a result might occur in the case of commuters, although the nature of the job and of the employer-employee (patron-client) relationship is obviously critical for such an outcome. The large proportion of commuters found in Medan to be engaged in government service, as compared to the predominance of traders among the circulators, could account for this differential. As we have noted earlier, government service tends to be very low paying in Indonesia, whereas many traders (especially those who have managed to rise above the "street" economy) can be earning fairly high incomes. A further major question that has emerged in the literature concerns remittances (e.g., Hugo, 1983; Ulack, 1986). In West Java, it has been reported that all circular migrants remitted money and that 80 percent of them brought back goods to their families (Hugo, 1977, 65). Circular migrants in the West Java study remitted from 21 to 44 percent of the incomes they earned in the city. In South Sulawesi it was found that one-third of the *becak* drivers interviewed in Ujang Pandang sent money back to their home villages, usually to wives and parents on a monthly basis (Forbes, 1978, 229). In addition, Naim (1973) suggests that as part of the tradition of *merantau* by the Minangkabau, migrants leave with the idea of bringing home everything they earn. However, there appears to be a wide range in variation in this regard. Thus, one study of eleven West Sumatran villages (Maude, 1975) found that the proportion of households in those villages that relied on remittances for income ranged from 0 to 73 percent. Naim (1973) has also suggested that there may be ethnic differences in the propensity to remit.

Our respondents were asked whether they sent money to their normal place of residence and, if so, how frequently, to whom, and how much was sent. Of the 67 circulators, 48 percent reported that no money was sent home. This was not surprising since about 42 percent of the circulators were not married and therefore did not have an immediate family to support. Of the 52 percent who did remit, money was sent on average four times per year. The average annual amount sent was Rp 29,000 ($48), which is a relatively small share of total income earned. Perhaps one reason for this is due to the high expenses incurred by circulators while staying in the city. A typical individual reported weekly expenses of Rp 5,500 for food, Rp 1,500 for shelter, Rp 2,000 for transportation, and Rp 2,100 for miscellaneous expenses, for a total of Rp 11,100, or nearly 70 percent of earned income. In additon, some individuals have specific rental costs associated with their employment. For example, costs reported for equipment rental (motorized *becak, becak dayung*), a market stall, or pedicab for goods (*becak barang*) ranged from Rp 500 to Rp 5,000.

In summary, our findings show that the typical circulator to Medan tends to be young, male, and married, although over 40 percent were single. He is usually Javanese or Minangkabau in terms of ethnic background and most often resides permanently in the nearby *kabupaten* of North Sumatra, or in West Sumatra. He is typically employed in the informal sector, most often in trading or as a driver. His income is perhaps adequate, but not as high as that of the permanent migrant city resident. A large portion of his earned income is spent on basic living expenses during his temporary stay in the city, whereas only a relatively small proportion is sent home to his wife and family.

Circulation to and from
Cebu and Cagayan de Oro

In contrast to Medan, nearly 10 percent of all households surveyed in the two Philippine cities had one or more persons residing temporarily elsewhere, while a slightly larger percentage had at least one person temporarily visiting. More specifically, 100 persons in 82 households were temporarily absent from metropolitan Cebu whereas similar figures for Cagayan de Oro were 122 and 91, respectively. On the other hand, there were 113 temporary visitors in 77 Cebu households and 154 such visitors in 110 households in Cagayan de Oro. Cities like Cebu and Cagayan de Oro, as was the case in Medan, are "magnets" for circulators because of a relative lack of opportunities in nearby areas compared to those available in the city.

Our evidence suggests that the characteristics of Cebu and Cagayan de Oro's circulation fields conform closely to the characteristics of migration fields. That is, the frictional effect of distance is evident and circulation appears to occur in some rather well-defined streams, for both temporary visitors and those who are temporarily elsewhere. While the frictional effect of distance was also a factor for the circulators to Medan, it should be recalled that circulation fields in that case were also influenced by the cultural tradition of West Sumatrans. As was so in Medan, the largest number of temporary visitors to both metropolitan Cebu and Cagayan de Oro City came from municipalities in the same province, though not necessarily from those closest to the cities (since such individuals could commute). Just over one-half of the circulators to metropolitan Cebu came from other places in Cebu Province and 47 percent of those visiting Cagayan de Oro came from Misamis Oriental Province. The next largest group of circulators came from nearby provinces in the same region. For Cebu, this meant the nearby provinces of the Visayas (34.5 percent) and in Cagayan de Oro it meant other provinces in northern Mindanao (31.8 percent). Fewer than two percent of all circulators in either city came from the more distant Luzon region. A similar pattern was noted in Medan, where only six percent of the circulators came from Java.

Origins of temporary visitors were often quite specific; for example, nearly all of the circulators in Cagayan de Oro who were from the Visayas came from only one of the region's fourteen provinces: Bohol. This reflects long-term patterns of interaction between these two places as Cagayan de Oro has been a destination for Boholanos for some time (Palabrica-Costello, 1979). In terms of ethnicity, the great majority of those who live in Misamis Oriental and Cebu Provinces are of the Visayan ethnic group. As such, a heavy preponderance of circulators are ethnic Visayans.

Of those circulators who were absent from Cebu, nearly two-fifths were in Manila and over one-fifth were at foreign destinations. Similarly, over one-half of those temporarily absent from Cagayan de Oro were in large or middle-sized cities or at foreign destinations. In addition to Manila, though, another important urban destination for circulators from Cagayan de Oro was Cebu City, which is relatively close and thus an intervening opportunity between Cagayan de Oro and Manila. A further 30 percent of those temporarily away from Cagayan de Oro were at urban destinations elsewhere on Mindanao because of the new industrial job opportunities in several Mindanao cities including Davao, Iligan, and Butuan.

Table 7.2

DEMOGRAPHIC CHARACTERISTICS OF CIRCULATORS,
CEBU AND CAGAYAN DE ORO

Characteristic	Cebu	Cagayan de Oro
Those temporarily absent:		
Number	100	122
Sex ratio	222.6	130.2
Average age (years)	30.0	23.6
Married (percent)	51.0	22.1
Educational level (average school years completed)	10.4	10.2

Source: Sample Survey Data.

As was the case for migration, economic motives were by far the principle reasons for circulating. Evidence of this is held in the fact that nearly 58 percent of those circulators absent from Cebu and Cagayan de Oro were working at jobs in their place of destination. Furthermore, the greater the distance of circulation, the more likely it was that the reason for circulation was job-motivated; virtually all of those who were temporarily away in distant urban or foreign destinations were working. Education is an important reason for temporarily leaving one's home if the homeplace is a rural area, but smaller proportions leave cities for such reasons. Nevertheless, some 13 percent of those absent from Cebu had gone elsewhere for schooling. In Cagayan de Oro, a smaller city with fewer opportunities for education, the comparable figure was 21 percent. Visitation of relatives was the reason given by about 12 percent of all circulators and "other" reasons comprised a further 4 percent.

In terms of socioeconomic characteristics, we found that circulators, like migrants, tended to be young, male, single, and relatively well-educated (Table 7.2). There were more than three males for every two females among those temporarily absent; the sex ratio for the two cities together was 164.3.

As was so for Medan, circulators were young, with an average age of 26 years. Those circulators who were absent were predominantly single; only 29 percent of all those elsewhere were married. In addition, the majority (two-thirds) of those temporarily visiting in the two cities were also single. Finally, circulators who were temporarily elsewhere tended to be relatively well-educated. Those from the two Philippine cities had completed an average of more than ten years of school. The average years of schooling for those circulators who were visiting the two cities (mostly from rural areas nearby) was more than eight years, which is considerably higher than the average for the origin rural areas. These findings conform with conclusions from earlier migration studies which have shown that educational levels of migrants tend to be between those of the population at the origin and the destination (Lee, 1966). It should be noted that in the case of some of these characteristics there are important differences between the results from Cebu and Cagayan de Oro (Table 7.2). In particular, the Cebu circulators were somewhat older and more likely to be male.

As we have already noted, about 58 percent (123 of 222) of all temporarily absent household members in the two-city sample left because they had jobs elsewhere. In contrast, only about one-third (88 of 267) of the temporary visitors in the two cities were there because they had jobs. As is shown in Table 7.3, a wide variety of jobs were held among both groups. Among the more important job types were maids and other kinds of domestic help, various kinds of skilled workers, and unskilled laborers. In general, those circulators who were temporarily absent from the two study cities had jobs with higher salaries and skill levels. Such workers included some who worked in the Middle East oil fields or were skilled workers on ocean-going ships (included under "transport services"). Workers who were temporarily visiting included larger shares of unskilled laborers and domestic helpers, which reflects the rural origins of many circulators to the city.

Unlike the case of Medan, nearly all circulators knew of job opportunities at their temporary destinations before going there. For this reason few travelled to cities in search of work as is often the case for migrants. In most cases the source of such information was friends and relatives, with this finding paralleling the results for Medan.

Among those who were temporarily absent and working elsewhere, over 80 percent knew of a job before they left. For working visitors nearly two-thirds said they were assured of a job in the city when they arrived. Furthermore, those visitors were apparently satisfied with their jobs in the city, at least when compared to work opportunities at their place of origin. Over 44 percent said that they would not want to return to their homeplaces to work, even if jobs were available there, as compared to 32 percent who said they would and 24 percent who were unsure or who did not respond. This is not surprising given the significant differences in urban and rural incomes and employment opportunities discussed in Chapter 2. Most circulators could expect to earn less at a job, if one were available, at their rural origins.

In Medan we found that most employed circulators worked in the urban informal sector rather than the formal sector. Our findings for the two Philippine cities generally support this notion in the typical case when the

Table 7.3

JOB TYPES OF CIRCULATORS TO AND FROM THE TWO
PHILIPPINE CITIES (PERCENT)

Job Type	Temporary Visitor		Temporarily Absent	
	Cebu (N=37)	Cagayan (N=51)	Cebu (N=69)	Cagayan (N=54)
Professional	2.7	2.0	18.8	1.9
Transport services	8.1	2.0	20.3	7.4
Carpenter	0	3.9	7.2	5.6
Skilled worker	10.8	5.9	10.1	35.2
Unskilled worker	21.6	9.8	10.1	5.6
Domestic help/ personal services	48.6	45.1	20.3	18.5
Salesperson	2.7	11.8	7.2	9.3
Clerical	2.7	5.9	1.4	7.4
Waiter	0	5.9	0	0
Farming/fishing	0	0	1.4	5.6
Other	2.7	7.8	2.9	3.7

Source: Sample Survey Data.

circulator in the city is from a rural origin. Those temporary visitors who
were working in Cebu and Cagayan de Oro were employed predominantly
in jobs in the informal sector. Of the temporary visitors employed in
metropolitan Cebu, over three-quarters were employed in informal sector
jobs. These included sixteen maids and four unskilled laborers who worked
at various jobs (Table 7.3). Those who were formal sector workers worked
chiefly as sales personnel in department stores or as regular laborers in
the city's rattan factories. Similar patterns were found in Cagayan de Oro,
where about three-quarters of the visitors worked in informal sector jobs.

On the other hand, those circulators temporarily absent from the two
cities most often worked in formal sector jobs at other urban, or foreign,
destinations. This in part reflects their higher educational and skill levels.
The majority of those overseas, for example, worked in skilled or semi-
skilled positions in the oil fields of the Middle East. As for those persons
who were working elsewhere in the informal sector, these occupations
included a high proportion who were working as maids or in other domestic
and personal service jobs.

As Todaro has suggested with respect to the migration process in the Third World, people move in response to urban-rural differences in expected rather than actual earnings as well as with regard to the probability of getting an urban job (Todaro, 1981, 239). This model appears relevant to the circulation phenomenon in the Philippines and, to a lesser extent perhaps, in Medan. We have already seen that circulators seeking work had a high probability of gaining a job. It is also true that incomes in the mostly foreign and urban destinations justified their mobility as shown by comparative figures on the current earnings of circulators and nonmobile household heads in the source areas of the circulators. In Cebu, those who were absent earned an average of $200 monthly compared to $125 for all Cebu heads of household surveyed. Even if we exclude those working in higher-paying foreign jobs, persons temporarily away from Cebu still earned more, with an average of $133 per month. In Cagayan de Oro, the situation was somewhat different in that all persons temporarily absent earned only slightly more than one-half the amount earned by all household heads ($61 compared to $109 for all heads surveyed). On the other hand, if we included those absent in foreign lands, then the average income of the circulators increases to $125. In short, the urban circulators who were away were doing well at their destinations compared to what they would earn at their origins. Similarly, those circulators who were visiting the city were earning substantially more than they would at their mostly rural origins.

As we discussed in our analysis of the Indonesian data, substantial research has been completed on the subject of migrant remittances in the Third World, with much of the literature supporting the notion that migrants remit a significant portion of their earnings to their origins. One would expect that remittances by circulators would be more substantial than that of migrants since circulators are residing at their destinations only temporarily and are there presumably to supplement earnings of other household members at their permanent residences. Our findings in both Sumatra and the Philippines, however, provide only mixed support for this expectation.

In the case of temporary visitors to the two Philippine cities, only 38 percent of the working circulators in Cebu had remitted money to their homeplace at some time since their absence. On the average, the total amount sent, among those who had remitted, was only 368 pesos. However, it is true that the majority of these visitors had only been in the city for a short time (two-thirds had been there one year or less) and total remittances may be expected to increase the longer a circulator remains at his or her job in the city. On the other hand, a significant minority (19 percent) of the employed temporary visitors had received money from their origins. The average for visitors who received money was more than double (881 pesos) the amount sent to homeplaces. Thus, the amount sent home by our Cebu sample was more than cancelled out by that received. The results for the temporary visitors in Cagayan de Oro were similar.

Remittances home appear to be more substantial for temporarily absent circulators who were employed elsewhere, both for Cebu and Cagayan de Oro. Some 58 percent of all those falling into this category were reported to have sent an average of about $375 to their origins since they had been away. The percentage remitting and the amount remitted is of course less if those working at foreign destinations (mostly in the Middle East) are excluded. Just over one-half of those working elsewhere in the Philippines sent money remittances home for an average of $211. Remittances from Filipinos working abroad contributed a great deal to the national economy.[2] It is worth noting that circulators who were elsewhere did not usually receive cash remittances; in only a very few cases did respondents report that they had sent money to household members who were temporarily elsewhere.

Implications and Conclusions

There are several basic conclusions that can be derived from these results; some have theoretical importance and others are more applied in their implications. We should again caution the reader that comparisons suggested between the Philippine and Indonesian study cities are only tentative given the different populations and sampling procedures utilized. Nonetheless, it seems to us that many of our findings, especially when compared to those of other studies on circulation in Southeast Asia, warrant comparisons.

Broadly, we found that levels of circulation were high in all the places studied with this finding agreeing with most other microlevel studies carried out in Southeast Asia. This means that intermediate-sized cities often have higher populations than are reported by the national census because of the large number of persons *temporarily* residing in these cities who are not usually counted for census purposes. Such persons either reside with family or friends in the city (such as most of the temporary visitors reported on here) or live in such places as construction sites (Stretton, 1981) or in *pondoks* (dormitories), as reported by Jellinek (1978). While temporary visitors such as those surveyed in the Philippine cities only give a partial view of those residing temporarily in a place, it is instructive to consider their numbers and characteristics. As we have seen, in Cebu there was approximately one temporary visitor for every ten households and in Cagayan de Oro there was about one for every five households. That means that in Cebu just those circulators who are residing in private households add two percent to the city's population, since the average household size was 5.95 persons. Thus, a *de jure* enumeration would have counted over 13,000 persons in that city who were temporarily staying in private households.

Given that this figure does not include the even larger numbers staying in other types of living arrangements (e.g., at construction sites or in boarding houses), it is not unreasonable to assume that the population of circulators in cities like Cebu add at least five percent to the population estimates given by national censuses, like that of the Philippines, which follow the *de facto* principle of enumeration. The impact of the circulation process appears to be even greater in Cagayan de Oro, given the higher proportion of temporary visitors found therein. Of course, it should also be noted that there is a significant number of persons who were temporarily elsewhere from these two cities, as will tend to mitigate the impact of the numbers who are temporary visitors. Nonetheless, during average and, especially, poor economic times, such cities no doubt have a net positive balance of circulators since even fewer jobs are available in rural areas and small cities, or at international destinations, during such times. For example, recent declines in oil demand have brought about a decrease in the number of foreign workers in the Middle East.

It is also instructive to examine how circulation affects a rural area. During the field research period, separate surveys were completed in randomly-selected households in rural areas of Cebu Province. One such area was Alcoy Municipality, located about 100 kilometers south of Cebu City, where 100 households were surveyed utilizing the same questionnaire used in the city. We found, that because of the large number of persons residing temporarily elsewhere, such poor rural villages like Alcoy do in fact have much smaller resident populations than those officially reported. For example, in Alcoy the average household size was found to be 5.15 persons, yet an average of one person per household was temporarily absent. In short, about 18 percent of the permanent population was absent at the time of the survey.[3]

Since circulation is so significant, an important research question is whether or not this form of movement "represents a transition stage in some evolutionary sequence of mobility change . . . which will eventually lead to movers settling permanently in the city" (Hugo, 1985a, 97). While we cannot, of course, answer this question it does seem likely that this temporary form of mobility will continue for a considerable time, certainly for the forseeable future. One reason for this, and one of several explanations for such temporary mobility, is that it is a risk-minimizing strategy insofar as the actual costs of permanently settling a family in cities like Medan or Cebu are perceived as prohibitive. In contrast, expenses are relatively minimal for circulators, especially for those who stay with friends or relatives. In other cases circulators often stay at construction sites or in lodging provided by the employer; for example, maids living in homes where they work or foreign workers living in company-owned dormitories. As we saw in the case of Medan, circulators sometimes do have to pay for temporary lodging, with this being found more often in Indonesia. Overall, though, it seems that the high cost of living in cities, as coupled with the fact that the absorptive capacity of even the largest cities is limited, suggests that individuals or families may prefer some other alternative to migrating to the city. Circulation and commuting provide such alternatives.

Another explanation for high levels of circulation is the "intrusion of capitalism into subsistence-based economies" (Bedford, 1981, 39). The economic influences from the First World have exacerbated, it is argued, spatial inequalities, with the resulting pattern of uneven development bringing about huge movements of populations, including circulation to cities and to commercial agricultural opportunites. Among other things, this has facilitated the growth of the urban informal sector since the formal sector cannot absorb all those seeking work. Since such inequalities are very much a reality in the Philippines and Indonesia, this further supports the argument for the continuance of high levels of circulation. It is difficult to foresee a voluntary reduction in mobility levels in the near future, even with the major structural changes in the economy that are advocated by some researchers (Young, 1982, 4).

Given that circulation is likely to continue as a major form of mobility and that this process temporarily affects population size and composition, it is imperative that we consider its implications for both sending and receiving areas. From the standpoint of policy formulation the basic question is whether circulation and commuting should be facilitated. Those who favor such policies do so largely because of the high social, cultural, and economic costs of permanently relocating entire families; since movement to cities is inevitable, the demands of temporary workers are less expensive than those of permanent residents. Those who would discourage circulation do so because it is argued that by-and-large temporary migrants are not really improving their lot, but only moving from one kind of poverty to another. Our results do not support this latter contention. Rather, we have found circulators to (and from, in the case of the Philippine cities) the study cities to be generally productive and certainly better off than they would be in their origins.

If circulation is to be abated then policies need to be directed at improving economic opportunities in sending areas. Based on our findings, however, we suggest that the more appropriate strategy would be to facilitate circulation. We did not find that circulators were the poorest and most unskilled; indeed, circulators who worked at their destinations were typically better educated than those at the origin. Working circulators usually knew of jobs at their destinations before they went. In short, circulation is an important coping strategy for individuals and a significant alternative to migration. At the very least, planners and policy-makers should be aware of the characteristics, impact, and role of circulators, both upon receiving and sending areas. For this reason, more research is needed on these, and related, topics. In addition, it is important to keep in mind that, while circulators are similar to migrants in many of their characteristics, there remains one major difference: they are not permanent residents. Therefore, the needs of circulators, such as for housing and transportation, differ from those of migrants. Facilitating access to jobs through relatively inexpensive improvements in transportation, or in providing temporary shelter for workers, could significantly affect the growth of population both at origins and destinations.

Notes

1. As reported also in Leinbach and Suwarno (1985) and Ulack, Costello, and Palabrica-Costello (1985).

2. In 1982 there were reported to be over 300,000 Filipinos working overseas. Approximately 85 percent of the total were working in the Middle East. It has been reported that this group remitted 70 percent of their estimated $650 million annual earnings ("324,000 Filipinos Overseas," 1983, 3; Parazo, 1983, 1).

3. Data gathered in a technique similar to that used for our analysis of circulators in Cebu and Cagayan de Oro revealed that nearly 8 percent of the population of Mae Sa, a village in northern Thailand, was temporarily absent at the time of the survey (Singhanetra-Renard, 1981, 143).

8

Synthesis and Policy Implications

The ultimate rationale for the present study lies in the policy implications which it holds for migration and employment patterns in Indonesia and the Philippines. In order to draw these out, however, some recapitulation is needed. Our findings have been many and varied, so that it will be necessary to reduce them to a more general set of observations. Also needed is a brief review of Indonesian and Philippine government policies which affect mobility, employment, and intermediate-sized cities. This will provide an historical foundation for the chapter's concluding sections, which deal with suggested alterations in these policies and future research needs.

Major Findings

Given the scanty knowledge on interlinkages between migration and employment in intermediate-sized cities of Southeast Asia, we have attempted to answer some basic questions. The chief goals of the study have included first, a delineation of the characteristics of the five selected study sites. This included a description of their social and economic structures, as well as their patterns of inmigration and population growth. Also of central concern were the twin questions of migrant selectivity and adjustment, that is, who is coming to these cities and how well are they faring once they get there? In particular, how do migrants go about earning a living and what happens to those who end up in the informal sector, as opposed to formal sector employees? How do the residents of intermediate-sized cities perceive their present community, especially in comparison to rural areas and the national primate city? And finally, what is the nature and extent of non-permanent movement? These were the major questions posed at the onset of the study. What follows is a list of tentative generalizations on these issues, as based upon the study's empirical results.

1. *There are distinct, and important, differences in the social and economic structures of the various settings compared in this study.* This is true for comparisons between the two national settings, for different-sized urban

places within the general category of "intermediate-sized cities," and for the distinction between rural and urban settings.

Formal sector employment in general and the manufacturing sector in particular seem to play a more important role in the economic structure of the two Philippine study sites than was the case for the Indonesian cities. Simultaneously, though, agricultural densities in Cebu Province and northern Mindanao were markedly higher than in North Sumatra. Perhaps as a result of these factors, inmigration levels were somewhat higher to the cities of Cebu and Cagayan de Oro than was the case for Medan, Pematang Siantar, and Tebing Tinggi. The population composition of the two Philippine cities also differed in some ways from that obtained for the Indonesian locales, as shown in particular by a larger proportion of female heads of households and a higher average level of educational attainment.

Various indications were found to support the notion that a city's economic structure varies according to its position in the urban hierarchy. The more heavily populated cities (Medan and Cebu) were characterized by more developed urban infrastructure, more frequent employment in formal sector jobs (including work for private corporations and in the government, as well as employment in professional occupations and in manufacturing), and higher levels of living. As such, it is apparent that the conceptual distinction between "primate" and "intermediate" cities is not an entirely satisfactory one, since the range of variation within the latter category may in some cases be fairly wide.

Despite these important differences, it must also be stressed that the study has been able to identify a number of similarities in mobility and employment patterns in the five study cities, as brought out in the following generalizations.

2. *Migration patterns in the region are as much a function of certain key geographic factors as of the more commonly stressed economic and social forces.* As seen in Chapter 2, migrants to intermediate cities tend to travel within well-defined streams. The areas which serve as the major recruiting grounds for these migrants can to a large extent be described as being *nearby, ethnically compatible, and rural* in character. Migrants are more likely to come from a locale within the region itself (or from an adjacent and historically-linked region, as was the case in Cagayan de Oro) than from an extraregional source area. As expected, inmigrants come heavily from the countryside, rather than from other cities, most often from areas characterized by high agricultural densities and dwindling resource bases. However, considerable urban origin movement was noted in the case of Medan.

When urban outmigration occurs it most typically takes place within this same stream-based framework. Thus, persons who wanted to move from their present city of residence were generally more likely to plan on returning to a rural area (usually within their present geographic region) than to go to the national primate city.

3. *The individual-level effects of spatial mobility on the small- and medium-sized cities in our sample are almost uniformly positive, at least as far as the migrants themselves are concerned.* Migrants to these cities are positively selected in terms of such variables as educational and occupational attainment. When asked if their move to the city had resulted in a net financial gain or loss, a much larger proportion of migrants said that the former had been the case. Migrants were also found to be doing reasonably well on such indicators as housing status, ownership of consumer durables and operation of a family business, ranking in many instances ahead of urban natives on these variables.

The perception data, too, showed migrants to be every bit as satisfied with their present community of residence as were natives. Only a small minority said they planned to return home or to leave for yet another destination.

4. *The more or less permanent type of cityward migration analyzed in this study tends to have more of an individualizing influence, rather than to approximate a more conservative or familistic orientation.* While contacts between the migrant and his home community are perhaps more frequent than would be found in a Western setting, it is nevertheless apparent that feelings of obligation to kin and friends who have been left behind tend to become weakened over time. These changes result both from the migration-induced separation from the household of origin as well as from the processes of social and economic mobility which seem to so frequently accompany cityward movements. Life-cycle changes that occur during the migrant's absence from his home community—such as marriage and initiation of family building—also play a key role in this process.

Some indicators of this individualizing pattern include, in the first instance, the small number of respondents who are planning to return to their place of origin. When we keep in mind the low standard of living experienced by a majority of the study's respondents, this in itself is a noteworthy finding. Also tending to support this perspective are such findings as the large majority of migrants who claim to have made the move to the city on their own initiative (rather than under pressure from other family members), the relatively small proportion of migrants who are still sending regular economic remittances to their home community, and the somewhat infrequent nature of homeward visits, even though most migrants did not come to their present destination from a far distant locale (Ulack, 1986).

In all five study locations, the great majority of moves were for economic rather than familistic reasons, particularly for those who migrated at an older age or after they had already been married. Many migrants had already established some social contact (friend or relative) in the city before coming, but the majority did *not* stay with such or accept any economic assistance along these lines.

Indeed, as Thomas and Znaniecki (1927) observed in their landmark study of Polish immigration to the United States, geographic mobility often serves the function of isolating the individual physically and culturally from his primary village and family groupings, leaving him open to more innovative attitudes and behaviors, including an increasing emphasis upon egoistic rather than familistic influences. To the extent that cityward migrants in contemporary Third World settings are caught up in a similar process, we might well expect them to be more dynamic, open to change, and willing to take risks than those left behind (cf. Browning, 1971, for a similar argument).

Conversely, the overall impact of permanent migration upon the areas of out-migration is unlikely to be on balance positive. Such areas lose the most talented of their young adults, as well as the capital which has been invested in their care and education. In return, they are receiving relatively little in terms of economic remittances, a finding which supports Michael Lipton's (1980) argument in this regard. In this sense our data would appear to show that patterns of temporary migration can have a more beneficial impact upon rural areas than do more permanent moves.

5. *Findings with regard to informal sector employment are on balance positive, given the numerous functions performed by this occupational alternative.* In general, somewhat lower levels of living (income, consumer durables) were associated with the informal sector, as compared to formal sector jobs. This is only to be expected given the higher levels of capitalization and skill requirements associated with the formal sector.

On several associated dimensions, though, a more positive picture emerged. For example, our multiple regression analysis of household income levels in Medan found no significant difference on this variable by employment sector of the head, while a significant and positive coefficient was found for ownership of a family business. Most such enterprises, it should be recalled, are really informal sector establishments; they are typically small in scale, involve low capitalization and little formal training in business management practices. Not dissimilar results were also reported for a special analysis of the standard of living data for Cagayan de Oro. Respondents from this city who were employed in commercial-type jobs (including such informal sector roles as vendors and peddlers) were found to be better off economically than blue collar, clerical, and even professional workers in the same city. But this was not true of educational attainment.

One way in which these apparently conflicting findings might be reconciled lies in Friedmann and Sullivan's (1974) tri-sector model of the urban economy discussed in Chapter 5. Again this modification of the conventional dual sector approach allows for some diversity by proposing two parts to the informal sector: a small-scale family enterprise sector and an irregular or "street" economy. In the former, incomes show great variability, although some significant capital accumulation may take place as a result of competitive advantage or superior commercial skills. The "street" economy is characterized by low-status, low-skilled trading and services activities where existence is on a day-to-day subsistence level.

In the present study, just as in the study of employment patterns in Nairobi (House, 1984), the higher incomes earned by commercial workers in general, and family business owners in particular, would appear to reflect the superior standing of the intermediate, or family enterprise, portion of the informal sector. In contrast are low skilled and underemployed service workers (e.g., carpenters, repairmen, tricycle drivers) along with self-employed and poorly capitalized sales workers. These occupations make up the bottom level of the informal sector and appear to be unable to generate adequate income.[1] Since representatives of the irregular economy invariably outnumber those in the intermediate grouping, income levels associated with the general category of informal sector workers tend to be low.

The possibility of achieving upward mobility from the irregular economy to the intermediate level is one of the many functions of the informal sector. As we have seen in Chapter 5, occupational shifts in the five study cities tend to be from one informal sector job to another, though the fact that many respondents had moved from a formal sector position to an informal sector job is also worthy of note. In many cases these will have been low-paid formal sector workers (e.g., government clerks) who have finally acquired enough contacts and investment capital to set up their own small-scale business.

Another important function played by the informal sector lies in its labor absorptive character. One result of this is the surprisingly low level of unemployment (though not of *underemployment*) which has been noted in this study. Informal sector activities also tend to provide additional economic opportunities for women as shown by the disproportionate number of female household heads employed in this sector.

Contrary to our initial hypothesis, permanent migrants were not always found to be disproportionately represented in informal sector jobs. Indeed, in the case of Cebu and Cagayan de Oro significantly higher proportions of migrants were formal sector workers (see Table 5.2). Similar evidence with respect to recent migrants in Peninsular Malaysia has been reported (Blau, 1986). This would appear to indicate that in the Philippines at least the prospect of informal sector employment, *per se*, does not function strongly to induce cityward migration. As such, attempts to control or restrict employment opportunities in this sector are unlikely to dampen rural-to-urban flows.

6. *Education continues to play a key role in the processes of spatial and social mobility.* Migrants to the intermediate-sized cities included in our analysis are equally as well, if not better, educated than urban natives. As such, they hold considerably higher levels of educational attainment than rural stayers. Educational achievement was found to be very strongly related to consumer goods ownership in all five study cities, as well as to income levels in Medan (the only city in which this particular dependent variable was analyzed). Some evidence was also found, in Chapter 4, that the process of economic adjustment to city life was more successfully carried out by the well-schooled migrant respondents than by those who had only a low level of educational attainment. These findings point to the need for continued efforts to expand and upgrade educational services within the region, while also serving notice that such efforts are likely to accelerate the rural-urban drift.

7. *A fairly strong basis, at the attitudinal level at least, now exists in both countries for policies designed to deflect migration streams away from the primate city and towards intermediate-sized urban centers.* Respondents in all five cities reacted negatively to the thought of changing their residence to the national capital. Small- to medium-sized cities were much more frequently chosen as the desired type of community, with towns and villages (i.e., essentially rural areas) ranking a distant second. All other factors being equal—which in this case means equal employment opportunities and equal access to modern educational, health, and transport services—the respondents whom were interviewed would much rather stay in an intermediate-sized urban place than move to Manila or Jakarta. The one caveat here, of course, lies in the widely held perception that all other factors are not really so equal, after all.[2] The value-expectancy results showed very large cities as ranking consistently higher in terms of their perceived ability to offer a wide spectrum of services and employment opportunities to their inhabitants. Unless these perceptions are changed—whether through a propaganda campaign on the virtues of smaller urban places or through programs designed to actually upgrade government services and urban amenities in these locales—they may come to outweigh the more basic antipathy held by provincial respondents toward life in the primate city.

8. *Circulation is an important component of the total mobility pattern associated with intermediate-sized cities.* Evidence from Medan, Cebu, and Cagayan de Oro reveals that, in addition to permanent movement, temporary movements in the form of circulation and commuting are important. These movements are largely, although not entirely, motivated by economic factors. Overall, circulators in our Indonesian and Philippine study cities are productive and better off than they would be in their area of origin. In addition, cash remittances from temporarily absent household residents are fairly significant. For these reasons, and because circulators make fewer demands upon urban

services, it seems more appropriate to formulate policies which will facilitate, rather than discourage, circulation. In addition, more research appears needed to identify the possible transition to permanent residence versus the continued growth of circulation behavior in lieu of migration. An improved theory of mobility must also explain under a variety of settings the structural forces which stimulate temporary oscillations.

Indonesian and Philippine Urban Policies

In any discussion of migration and urbanization an important consideration must be the development of policy formulations. Policies and programs which have the objective of influencing population distributions have a long history in Indonesia. Given the size of her population as well as its growth and uneven distribution, numerous attempts have been made to influence migration patterns in order to seek a better match between the distributions of resources and people. The best known of these attempts is the trans-migration program. This was initiated by the Dutch in the early 1900s in order to resettle people from the densely populated islands of Java and Bali to the Outer Islands in a colonization effort. The successes, difficulties, and modifications undergone by this program have been treated in the literature (Hardjono, 1977; MacAndrews, 1978; Babcock, 1986) and will not be recapitulated here. There have also been several attempts in Indonesia to prevent migration to specific destinations. The policy which attracted the most attention in this regard was the "closed city" legislation which was enacted for Jakarta in 1970. The effectiveness of this policy in discouraging migration to the capital city is now recognized as quite limited (ESCAP, 1981, 149–150).

Of more direct concern to us are the policies with respect to urban development in our respective areas. Indonesian development policy, as enunciated through a series of five-year plans, has been dominated by the threefold goals of equity, growth, and stability. Since 1970 the country has also emphasized spatial development objectives, with particular emphasis being placed on the goals of achieving stronger social and economic integration and a greater development balance between regions. Urban areas play a key role in achieving these spatial objectives. In recognition of this, a national urban development strategy (NUDS) has been undertaken by the Government with assistance from the United Nations Development Program (UNDP) and the United Nations Centre for Human Settlements (UNCHS).

Essentially, this urban strategy is linked with a broader analysis of economic growth which was carried out in light of declining oil prices and a deep international recession. Forecasts suggest that cities will account for a much larger share of total population growth than the 35 percent which occurred between 1971 and 1980. In fact, the urban share of growth could be as high as 70 percent between 1980 and 2000, so that, by the beginning of the next century the urban population will have increased to about 76 million.

The NUDS recognizes no independent urban objectives but has rather been designed to use the development of cities to contribute to broader objectives. Over 500 cities throughout the nation are classified by policy/ action categories based upon their similarities in future development roles and potentials, as well as upon government program responses. These categories are: mature national development centers (the three major metropolitan areas of Java); emerging national development centers (nearly all other cities of over 200,000 population); interregional development centers; regional development centers; and local service centers. Associated with all of these groups are a series of policy instruments affecting infrastructure placement, spatial regulations and subsidies, industrial location, and guidelines for the internal development and management of urban areas. Implementation of the strategy calls for the strengthening of units for local urban development administration, as based upon the view that many cities do not now have appropriate administrative status. Coupled with this is a call for adjusting administrative boundaries to coincide with their entire functional urban areas.

Trends in urban growth have been, and continue to be, a major concern of policy-makers. In Indonesia, a review of *kotamadya* data alone suggest that during the 1970s large cities grew most rapidly while medium and small cities were losing their share of the total urban population (Hugo and Mantra, 1983). It is generally agreed that there is no "optimum city size" and that it is desirable for a nation to have a mixed hierarchy of urban centers. Thus there is a potential danger if the largest cities are increasing out of proportion to the other size classes. However, the old *kotamadya* urban definition is apparently misleading. When an improved urban definition is utilized, the largest cities grew at a rate of 4.2 percent annually between 1971 and 1980. The fastest growth rate of 4.4 percent is associated with cities in the 200,000 to 500,000 population range. Even small cities (20,000 to 100,000 population), however, grew at a rate above 4 percent (Government of Indonesia, 1985, 97). While Indonesia has a reasonably balanced distribution of cities, national policy must still, it is argued, aim at slowing the growth of the largest cities and stimulating smaller and intermediate cities (Douglass, 1985). It is recognized in the NUDS that policies and programs must be designed to respond to differing urban problems in differing regions. As a general policy, however, it would appear that some emphasis is being placed upon upgrading small or *kecamatan* towns throughout the archipelago (Hariri, 1984). In this way, it is hoped that various agro-processing industries will crop up in the small towns. Such industries may provide significant employment opportunities, especially insofar as they require little in capital outlay. It is reasoned that the *kecamatan* town is the appropriate point in the urban hierarchy at which to restrain the rural overflow of people. Clearly, though, considerable investment must be made before such places become attractive and capable of luring even modest industries.

Government policies toward migration and population distribution in the Philippines have long tended to be vague and poorly integrated. Writing during the 1970s, such observers as Laquian (1975, 235), Ocampo (1972), and Carino (1974, 4) criticized the national government's apparent lack of concern towards these issues. In line with this, the final report of a Special Committee to Review the Philippine Population Program noted that, as of 1978, the program "had remained essentially a family planning program," and recommended that efforts be made to achieve a closer integration between population and development planning in the country (Herrin, n.d.).

Early efforts to influence population distribution in the Philippines included: (1) Attempts to reduce inmigration to Manila or to send less affluent inmigrants back to rural areas (e.g., squatter removal, denial of city services to non-residents of the city); (2) rural colonization schemes (especially in Mindanao); (3) rural development policies (with a latent goal of slowing rural-urban migration); and (4) "growth pole" strategies (regional development strategies, industrial dispersal plans, e.g., through tax incentives). Such policies show a fairly consistent strategy of reducing movements toward the cities, especially towards Metro Manila. For the most part, however, these efforts were not very successful (Carino, 1974; Pernia and Paderanga, 1980). Questions have also been asked as to the validity of these goals. As Pernia (1976) has pointed out, the rate of urbanization in the country has not been unusually rapid, while the experience of other countries has tended to show a positive connection between urbanization and economic growth. From a micro perspective it has also been argued that urban squatters and slum dwellers in the Philippines tend to be hard-working, upwardly mobile, and committed to city life (e.g., Laquian, 1971; Ulack, 1978), thus raising the question as to why such strong efforts are being made to send them back to the countryside. However, most Philippine social scientists do feel that the very rapid growth of the Manila Metropolitan Area does pose a number of problems for the country, and have therefore recommended that migrants be redirected towards smaller urban centers (e.g., Pernia, 1976).

So far as the current situation is concerned the Population Program *per se* is still heavily oriented towards the twin goals of fertility reduction and increased adoption of family planning. Thus, a recent article entitled "The Philippine Population Program: An Overview" by the National Director of POPCOM under the Marcos administration (Jamias, 1985) failed to even mention such concepts as migration, urbanization, or population distribution.[3] Economic planners within the country, however, are now devoting increasing attention to these topics. The most recent economic plan for the country makes a brave attempt to take these variables into account, as well as to integrate them logically with one another and with the overall economic strategy of the country.

In general, the major goals of the Philippine government regarding population distribution have changed little in the past decade. In his 1981 Manila address to the members of the International Union for the Scientific Study of Population former President Marcos (1981) spoke of "headlong urbanization," the "loss of vitality in some of our rural areas" (due to out-migration), the country's growth pole policies, and of efforts to "encourage people to return to the countryside." At the same time, the official government position, as expressed in response to a number of United Nations surveys was that the spatial distribution of the country's population was "extremely unacceptable" and in need of "radical intervention" (Fuchs, 1983). Indeed, the Philippines was at this time one of only six Asian and Pacific governments (along with such Communist countries as Laos, Kampuchea, and China) calling not only for a deceleration but actually for a *reversal* of rural-to-urban migration trends. More recent pronouncements by the Aquino administration have not been dissimilar to the general perspective taken during the Marcos years, at least insofar as these have concentrated heavily upon the need for rural self-sufficiency and income generation.

At the same time, and as earlier critics have charged, government policies on the issues are not always well-integrated. A good example of this is provided by Laquian's (1979) analysis of "accommodationist" policies in the less developed nations. This paper reviews efforts to take a less punitive stance towards rural-urban migrants. Interestingly enough, many of his examples come from the Philippines in general and Manila in particular (e.g., migrant reception centers, sites and services schemes, and urban employment generation through labor-intensive development strategies). This seems in some ways to run counter to the above-noted anti-urban statements of the national government, but may well represent a more or less rational strategy from a political standpoint, since it can help to win the votes of urban squatters. (Indeed, *local* political officials may be quite willing to grant tenure rights to organized groups of urban squatters if it suits their political interests to do so, even when *national* plans seeks to discourage inmigration to the cities.)

This brings us to the most recent national development plan (NEDA, 1984). This is an "updated" development plan, for the period 1984–87, and one in which a fair amount of attention is given to the current economic crisis in the country. Briefly, the emphasis is upon "balanced" economic development, with a strong emphasis upon primary (agricultural, fishing, forest products) economic activities, along with regionally-based agro-processing industries. An obvious implication of this strategy, and one which is clearly noted in the development plan, is that it will tend to dampen rates of rural-urban migration. The plan also calls for the further development of small- and medium-sized cities and for decreasing "urban-rural welfare gaps."[4] Interestingly, some awareness is shown in the plan of the possible contradictions between the overall strategy of limited urban growth and the various *de facto* accomodationist policies. Thus, it notes that while the urban land reform program will continue, "care will be taken so as not to encourage further urban inmigration." Also of interest is the fact that the regional level plan for the National Capitol Region (i.e., Metro Manila) calls for reduced population growth through "vigorous information campaigns," the "monitoring of inmigrants," and the "strict enforcement" of "regulations governing squatting." It is stated as an explicit goal of the plan that population growth rates in Metro Manila will be reduced to a level of three percent per year by 1987.

In summary, it is important to emphasize the extreme difficulties faced by most Third World governments in their attempts to alter ongoing patterns of migration and population redistribution.[5] Migration policies typically represent but a small portion of the larger population program, which may in turn be the recipient of only a minuscule portion of the national budget. Generally speaking, resources are small, and expenses high. Many of the more direct efforts along these lines, such as "growth pole" policies and colonization schemes, have been characterized by high costs, especially in light of their limited results. Furthermore, programs designed to discourage or forbid migration to certain locations (e.g., the primate city) may be virtually unenforceable, given the ease with which inmigrants may escape detection or buy off those local officials who are responsible for apprehending them. Such, at least, has been the experience of both Indonesia and the Philippines when this approach has been attempted (Fuchs, 1983).

Viewed from a cross-cultural perspective, the difficulties involved in reducing in-movement to the country's largest city, or "core urban area," appear monumental, insofar as nearly all Third World nations are concerned. Indeed, the argument might be made that such movements have been so commonly found in these settings during the past few decades as to represent a virtual social science "law" (e.g., Vining, 1985), against which it would be futile for governments to resist. This is perhaps too strong a conclusion, since a few such efforts appear to have met with success, but these are the exception and not the rule.

Another stereotyped image which must be challenged is that of a central body of government planners, acting in unison and with the necessary authority so as to implement effectively the country's overall development plan. In actual fact, the picture is much more diverse and confusing than this. Marked disagreements with regard to urbanization policies may exist among the various sectors and levels of government, to say nothing of the plethora of powerful interest groups who may also be concerned with such issues. As a result, policies which pertain to migration and population distribution may appear to be uncoordinated and poorly integrated, as when two quite different policies or programs are found to be operating simultaneously (e.g., Carino, 1974).

Rather than viewing this situation as a result of unintended oversights or communication breakdowns between demographic and economic planners, such as could be overcome by a more vigorous effort to integrate population issues into the sectoral planning process, we would argue that such patterns are tied intimately to the complex balance of power which exists between various socially significant groupings, only one of which is the planners.

What is evident, though, is that concern with small and medium-sized urban centers as alternates to the primate city is becoming more firmly entrenched in the planning process, with economists and development specialists now showing as much sensitivity to this issue as demographers and geographers have previously. As such, results from the present study may be expected to contribute much to the widening discussion of ways in which intermediate-sized cities can contribute to national development and equity, as well as to point out implementing mechanisms by which these goals may be more readily met.

Policy Implications

A specific intention of this research was to relate our findings to policy formulation. Given the restatement of our findings and the discussion of current urban policies we turn now to this matter.

A first issue to be dealt with is the question of whether migrants should be directed to small and intermediate-sized cities through official government efforts. It should be noted that these are really two separate questions involving different circumstances. Population redistribution policies focused upon intermediate-sized cities are based upon the premise that such cities are large enough to generate significant positive attractive qualities or external economies of agglomeration but yet not so large that these positive attributes are outweighed by negative qualities or diseconomies. Encouragement of movement to smaller towns must first consider the opportunities for development found therein (Hansen, 1979, 114). Our findings indicate that a major impediment towards programs designed to deflect migration streams away from the primate city and towards intermediate-sized cities seems to lie in the dearth of employment opportunities and services obtainable therein, rather than in any innate desire on the part of small-city inhabitants to move to the national capital. This discussion is extended in reflections on the role of secondary centers which follows this current section on policy implications.

As stated above our research confirms that migration tends to take place within well-defined streams. Consequently, any formulated migration policies should reflect this reality. For example, if we wish to accelerate or impede migrant flows to Cebu or Medan or wish to alter the composition of migrants going to these locations, rural-based information or development programs must be directed towards the specific origin areas found to predominate in these cases. For example, an experimental information program in Thailand has shown that migration can be encouraged from rural to urban places in the same region (Fuller, Lightfoot, and Kamnuansilpa, 1985). The higher levels of inmigration to the larger cities (in Indonesia at least) also imply that growth pole policies can be implemented more successfully in big cities, as compared to smaller and more isolated urban centers. But, as is pointed out later, often such schemes have not been successful. It is clear that the development support must be carefully considered before migration is encouraged.

Another point concerns migrant selectivity and adjustment. The generally positive findings along these lines which have been obtained by the present study suggest that an accomodationist, rather than a punitive, stance should be taken towards rural-urban migrants. If migrants are 'voting with their feet' to live in one locale, rather than another, this must be for fairly rational reasons. As such it would seem to be impractical and inefficient to try to overcome this overall trend.

The functions of migration for maintaining rural living standards (the household decision-making model) have, we believe, been overstated, at least as far as permanent migration is concerned. Actually, such permanent movements drain much in the way of talent and capital from rural areas. Efforts, of whatever form, designed to expand the development potential of these rural areas must receive serious consideration as policies toward migration are formulated. At the same time, policies aimed at population redistribution must first consider the growing importance of temporary migration, both commuting and circulation forms. The encouragement of people to obtain employment in cities while maintaining their residence in rural areas is clearly an important policy alternative.

As indicated in Chapter 5, our findings point to the significance of the informal sector in generating employment and raising incomes. It is clear that this category of economic activity is not temporary and that it will continue to expand and become more firmly established. It is difficult to predict from our data whether the informal sector will or should provide a bridge from the traditional to the more formal modern sector. Our view is that the informal sector is flourishing because there exists a clear demand for it. Goods and services produced by the informal sector are required by those people with low incomes as well as those who work in the formal sector. From this point of view, punitive policies which severely restrict *becak* or jeepney drivers, vendors, scavengers, and other operations should not be pursued. This is not to say that efforts at control are not needed. Control can mean the abolition of illegal levies on enterprises in the informal sector, for example, the imposition of proper sanitation standards upon food vendors, or the removal of enterprises such as begging. Greater attention to the control of such enterprises must be shown by urban authorities. In this examination such factors as demand and social acceptability must be considered.

In addition, more constructive policies which serve to upgrade informal sector enterprises might also be considered. Government policy in the area of guidance of the informal sector must be based upon the premise that this sector is necessary and inevitable. Policies are needed which create a climate of encouragement and allow scope for them to be upgraded and become efficient. At present in both Indonesia and the Philippines, such policies are either absent altogether or contradictory in nature (Soetjipto, 1984, 83).

As research in other regions has indicated, the informal sector has an intermediate component which consists of dynamic entrepreneurs. Government policies should be directed toward assisting especially this segment by increasing educational opportunities and training programs. In addition, small scale credit and management improvement efforts should be evaluated for possible implementation. There is considerable potential for increased incomes and employment opportunities in this subsector. Investment induces significant increases in incomes and, because of the labor intensity employed, improved job opportunities. With these suggestions we turn back to the broader aspects of secondary centers in development and ways in which such cities might provide a stronger role in the development effort.

The Role of Secondary Centers in Development Planning

An initial premise in this study was that the role of intermediate cities in development has been neglected and that such cities can provide an important asset to progress in a variety of ways. Key functions may include the reinforcement of rural-urban linkages, stimulation of agricultural productivity, a more efficient provision of public services, and the improvement of incomes and welfare levels of the resident and hinterland populations through job creation. In addition, an important, and often overlooked, aspect of intermediate and smaller cities is their stimulative capacity. The historical record shows clearly that economic growth has not necessarily been initiated in the urban cores that have dominated world economies. In fact, innovations which took place in small and intermediate cities that were closely linked to rural areas formed the basis for Europe's sustained long term development (Hansen, 1982, 301).

Obviously, medium and small towns exist in virtually all developing countries yet their role in spurring development thus far has been quite limited. One important reason for this is that such towns rarely form a functional hierarchy and they therefore fail to provide an interlinked system of exchange that will facilitate the application of labor, capital, and skills (Johnson, 1970, 70–71).

Another view is that small centers may siphon off financial and human resources. They can drain taxes and human capital from rural areas and absorb most of the regions' educational resources. At the same time they act as impediments to the flow of resources from national governments. This often occurs through corruption and use of funds to promote private interests. It is also argued that many industrial and commercial firms in smaller cities have few downward linkages but many strong upward linkages (Schatzberg, 1979, 173).

Another problem is that growth center strategies, which have become equated with dependency models and multinationals, seem to have been generally unsuccessful in stimulating regional development. In part this has occurred because such strategies often have been inappropriately adapted to their institutional settings, have been badly designed and implemented, or have been promoted without sufficient recognition of a region's economic structure and interchange. Occasionally they have even been abandoned prematurely where they might have enjoyed considerable success. In other cases the overall goal of these policies has remained unclear. While these strategies have often been applied directly to higher order centers, the intent of trickle down impacts to lower order cities and towns has also been frequently present (Richardson, 1982, 333).

A current focus of the debate on the viability of intermediate places concerns the utility of 'top-down' versus 'bottom-up' planning (Hansen, 1982, 316–318; Richardson, 1982, 331–336). The former is often associated with highly centralized decision-making, large scale investments and an urban-industrial bias. It has been said to result in a strategy which aims at investment concentration in large cities with the anticipation that smaller urban places and rural areas would benefit as benefits diffuse downward. Most of the 'bottom-up' planning strategies, on the other hand, place emphasis on the need for local participation and self reliant development. Agropolitan development and selective spatial closure schemes are generally associated with this approach. The former idea aims at districts which have small centers of 10,000 to 25,000 inhabitants. It views agriculture as the propulsive sector, while also promoting small scale industry and giving priority to the informal sector. The concept of selective spatial closure also emphasizes small-scale industrial organization and nonmarket and informal sectors, in this case with the intent of minimizing negative linkages between underdeveloped regions and the core area. This notion rejects innovation diffusion down the urban hierarchy as the dominant mode of development. While both approaches can serve to stimulate smaller centers, they require strong intervention by the central government in order to be effective. In fact, an obvious reason for the lack of growth being transmitted through smaller centers is that these entities have all too frequently received inadequate resources and direction from the national government (Rondinelli, 1983, 178).

The essence of this discussion, then, is that agropolitan development, integrated spatial development, and especially growth center strategies may not be ideal vehicles for aiding the rural poor. One current alternative to these approaches is to encourage 'urbanization-from-below'. Such growth, however, does not occur naturally. As such, public investment policy has an important role to play in national development. These investments must be made selectively in areas where there exist natural advantages and strong chances for success. Simultaneously, it must be recognized that adjusting the settlement system is not a panacea. Also important are matters of taxation, land reform, and credit, as well as the distribution of political power (Hansen, 1982, 321).

Given these deficiencies, the question must therefore be asked as to the basis upon which intermediate cities and their surrounding hinterlands may be assisted. First, it would appear that such cities must be analyzed and understood in relationship to their hinterlands. Efforts to promote and strengthen small cities must recognize the importance of rural-urban linkages and the importance of a host of agriculturally-related developments including feeder roads, marketing, and agro-based industries. In addition, vast improvements must be made in water supply, sewerage, and electricity as well as in the basic social services of health and education.

Beyond these, economic development for small cities must begin with appreciation of their economic structure. Most cities with populations from 20,000 to 200,000 persons are regional service, financial, and administrative centers. As was noted in the case of our five study cities, the dominant economic sectors tend to be wholesale and retail trade, small businesses, and personal services. Where industry is present it is typically represented by small establishments which process local agricultural production or which produce consumer and intermediate goods for consumption within the town and the surrounding area. Even cities as large as Medan are dominated by small and medium size firms in the industrial sector. Assistance to such firms in order to stimulate growth and to insure viability can take on a variety of measures. Financial aid, management training, provision of skill training, and facilities, as well as marketing assistance are all important.

Given the rather limited economic base and range of capabilities, the potential to generate employment in small cities is not great. The emphasis must be upon stimulating the demand for informal sector goods and services. It has been noted that much of the informal sector is dependent upon the formal sector, either from the demand side (consumer goods and personal services for workers) or on the supply side (intermediate or simpler goods for higher order industry). Thus, stimulating the formal sector would expand demand for informal sector services. Unless a city has a natural advantage or a demanded resource, however, it may not be feasible or wise for a government to decentralize industries from larger cities (Richardson, 1982, 341–43). In the present case, this can be seen in terms of the larger profile taken on by the manufacturing sector in Medan and Cebu.

One other formal sector prospect is government. The important role of the central government as an employer in Indonesia has already been pointed out. Further administrative decentralization may be critical for choosing and implementing development projects and increasing local decision-making and self reliance. This process may strengthen the employment base of small cities while further increasing, through a multiplier effect, the demand for informal sector goods and services. At the same time, however, caution must be exercised in ensuring that additional employment opportunities created by the government sector in the smaller cities must be truly productive in character (e.g., through the use of appropriate and labor-intensive technology in infrastructure projects), rather than through the creation of additional and unnecessary white-collar positions in the already overstaffed government bureaus. Other possibilities in the informal sector include the development of domestic import substitution industries such as household utensils and other simple consumer goods. Here again success will be determined by sufficient demand and the ability to market and distribute the product not only at the source of production but also throughout a regional hinterland. Handicraft industries, such as shellcrafts in Cebu, may further develop and create employment. In this case, though, marketing for export for such a specialized product will be particularly crucial.

It goes without saying that the stability of these simple industries and the employment which they create will be dependent not only on credit, marketing, and management but also upon the adequacy of urban infrastructure and public services. In many small- and medium-sized cities infrastructure quality is very deficient. Nor will it be possible to decide simply to provide these cities with the resources they need, given the woefully inadequate supply of public funds. One suggestion for solving this dilemma which has been put forth is to reduce the public investment burden by introducing a degree of cost recovery so that both the rich and the poor would bear some of the burden of supporting lower cost public services (Richardson, 1982, 346).

Future Research Needs

As a final topic it may be useful to provide some reflective comments on issues not addressed in this monograph but which warrant future research attention. One of these topics is the role of the transport sector in population mobility, urbanization, and employment.

Too often the role of transport has been taken for granted. It is obvious that the type and degree of transport provision, as measured by network density and vehicle numbers, and the cost of these factors will exert a major impact on mobility (Cooley, 1894). Yet only recently has this relationship been examined to any degree (Hugo, 1981; Leinbach, 1983). An initial point to be made here is that, while travel costs and distances play a role in the decision to move permanently, these influences may not constitute a major factor. Especially with migration to the large and easily accessible primate city, distance and its cost may play only an insignificant role (Temple, 1975). On the other hand, with temporary forms of mobility, these variables become more critical as an element in the decision process. Transport costs, especially for commuters, constitute a significant and regular cost in the accounting matrix. In addition to cost, the simple availability and scheduling convenience of transport vehicles are important factors influencing movement patterns. Thus, the vast improvements in the availability of both private and public transport as well as in the road network in Indonesia over the past decade have been related to the growth of circular mobility (Naim, 1973; Hugo, 1981; Leinbach, 1986b). For example, it has been argued that major improvements in roads and road transport facilities in Yogyakarta have made it possible to commute relatively quickly to nearby centers of employment without having to spend the night there (Mantra, 1980). Of special significance is the claim that these transport changes have brought about strategy shifts from circulation to commuting and from migration to circulation. This same pattern is also existent in the Philippines where circular mobility appears also to have been facilitated by decreases in the friction of distance (Ulack, Costello, and Palabrica-Costello, 1985; Leinbach and Suwarno, 1985).

The upgrading of transport facilities has also had a role in increasing the amount and quality of information regarding employment opportunities at various destinations (Hugo, 1978; Leinbach, 1983). By widening commuting and circulation fields improved public transport has in effect also widened the feasible options which are available to underemployed individuals in rural villages. As such, it is clear that an important benefit of transport is to enhance the potential for employment. In focusing on smaller cities it must also be recognized that hinterland transport improvements can allow rural villagers access to services and employment within or adjacent to a city without further burdening its already poorly developed infrastructure and facilities. Thus, intraregional or secondary transport infrastructure investments may forge tighter urban linkages while facilitating more efficient marketing and increasing access to small town services (Richardson, 1982, 346).

Despite such preliminary evidence and findings much more research must be focused on the transport and mobility interrelationship. First, there now exists no real evidence for causal links between mobility levels and the quality of life. We must establish through carefully laid research designs how social and economic conditions change under mobility improvements. In addition we do not know who are the main beneficiaries of such improvements or the extent of the benefits derived from them. For example, will additional investments in public transport systems benefit small farmers by increasing their access to the urban-based market? Another important area for which we have little information is the transport industry and its impact. For example, how are profits from transport investments disbursed? To what extent are they reinvested in productive enterprises which create local employment? How much additional employment is being generated as vehicle numbers and roads grow? Spatial mobility clearly has grown over time in both Indonesia and the Philippines but we need to investigate the overall impact of this mobility much more than has been done to date.

In addition, the process of information acquisition in the migration process is only imperfectly understood. We have provided some broad data with regard to this topic for our study cities but further information is required which will provide insights into the decision making process. For example, is the accuracy of information received related to the strength and nature of the migration stimulus? In this respect exploration of village-community ties and social networks may indeed bear considerable fruit in our search for a more general understanding of all forms of movement (Hugo, 1981).

Two empirical findings from the present study appear to call for further, and more detailed, analysis. The first of these refers to the overrepresentation of nonmigrants among the squatter population. This finding suggests either that the urban-born are less well equipped to compete in the city's labor market than are migrants from the countryside or that the option to squat represents a scarce resource which is generally desired, but often available only to those with greater experience in city life. More research would be helpful in settling this question. Also needed is more information as to why it is that, in each of the five study cities, economic motives were found to predominate more strongly among recent arrivals than for those who came to city a decade or two ago. Does this represent a general shift towards greater valuation of the pecuniary factor by migrants, or is it better interpreted as a sign of increasing hardship and exploitation in the Indonesian and Philippine countrysides?

Lastly, the role of the informal sector in the encouragement of migration and migrant adjustment deserves further attention. This is particularly true for the case of female migrants. While the present study has been forced to pay relatively little attention to this numerically important group of migrants, clear evidence was found for the importance of the informal sector in generating employment opportunities for women. Such research must also probe further the nature of the apparent bifurcation of the informal sector into intermediate and irregular components. An analysis of successful enterprises in the intermediate sector and an assessment of their specific operational characteristics should be made. Especially important here is the role of management, capital sources, and connecting linkages within and outside the sector. Just as it may be useful to investigate possible improved linkages between the informal and formal sectors so also may it be worthwhile to explore ways of strengthening the ties of the poor or irregular segment of the informal sector with the intermediate sector (Weeks, 1975). In this instance, too, microlevel case studies would be valuable as an initial way to gain insight, with the hypotheses generated from such an approach being subsequently tested at a broader scale and with a larger sample of respondents.

Notes

1. The occupational groups scoring lowest in Cagayan de Oro in terms of their levels of living were workers employed in manufacturing, construction, transport, and services. After controlling for age and education, sales workers scored higher than any other group, including professionals, except for managers and administrators (Costello and Palabrica-Costello, 1985).

2. Recent research has shown that population movements to and from Indonesia's smaller cities and towns differ substantially from that of the largest cities: "Small cities and towns are not recording substantial gains of migrants. In addition the stepwise nature of the migration up the urban hierarchy has meant they are losing their most skilled and entrepreneurially oriented people to the largest cities" (see Hugo and Mantra, 1983, 30).

3. The Population Commission (POPCOM) has recently been placed under the Ministry of Social Services Delivery (MSSD) within the Philippine government. The traditional orientation of this bureau towards "social work" probably accounts for POPCOM's continued concentration on family planning advocacy.

4. The extent to which this proposed redirection of priorities towards rural areas and less developed regions will actually be put into practice is, of course, another question. The last yearly budget for the Government of the Philippines which was formulated under the Marcos regime was in fact criticized for the increased funds

which it directed towards the military, while the Ministry of Agriculture received no proportionate increase in its already small budget (Danao, 1985).

5. A recent work that includes sections on past, present, and future migration trends and policies in Indonesia and the Philippines, as well as the other ASEAN nations, is that edited by Hauser, Suits, and Ogawa (1985).

Bibliography

Abad, Ricardo G.

    1981a   "Internal Migration in the Philippines: A Review of Research Findings." *Philippine Studies,* vol. 29, pp. 129–143.

    ———— .

    1981b   "The Utility of Microlevel Approaches to Migration: A Philippine Perspective." Pp. 291–302 in Gordon F. DeJong and Robert W. Gardner (eds.), *Migration Decision Making.* New York: Pergamon Press.

Adem, Elisea S.

    1985   Reasons for Migration: A Case Study of Bohol Outmigrants. Unpublished Master's Thesis. Xavier University, Cagayan de Oro City.

Aklilu, B. and J. R. Harris.

    1980   "Migration, Employment, and Earnings." Pp. 121–154 in G. Papanek (ed.), *The Indonesian Economy.* New York: Praeger.

Babcock, T.

    1986   "Transmigration as a Regional Development Strategy." Pp. 157–189 in C. MacAndrews (ed.), *Central Government and Local Development in Indonesia.* Kuala Lumpur: Oxford University Press.

Banerjee, T. and S. Schenk.

    1984   "Lower Order Cities and National Urbanization Policies: China and India." *Environment and Planning A,* vol. 16, pp. 487–512.

Bedford, Richard D.

    1981   "The Variety and Forms of Population Mobility in Southeast Asia and Melanesia: The Case of Circulation." Pp. 28–29 in G. W. Jones and H. V. Richter (eds.), *Population Mobility and Development: Southeast Asia and the Pacific.* Canberra: Australian National University, Development Studies Centre Monograph No. 27.

Berger, Peter L. and Hansfried Kellner.

    1981   *Sociology Reinterpreted: An Essay on Method and Vocation.* Garden City, N.Y.: Anchor Books.

Birdsall, N. and W. P. McGreevey.

    1978   "The Second Sex in the Third World: Is Female Poverty a Development Issue?" Paper prepared for International Center for Research on Women Policy Roundtable, Washington, D.C., June 21.

Biro Pusat Statistik.

    1979   *Statistical Yearbook of Indonesia, 1977–1978.* Jakarta: Biro Pusat Statistik.

Blau, D. M.
1986   "Self Employment, Earnings, and Mobility in Peninsular Malaysia." *World Development,* vol. 14, pp. 839–852.

Boeke, J. H.
1953   *Economics and Economic Policy of Dual Societies as Exemplified by Indonesia.* New York: Institute of Pacific Relations.

Booth, Anne and Peter McCawley, eds.
1981   *The Indonesian Economy During the Soeharto Era.* Kuala Lumpur: Oxford University Press.

————— , and R. M. Sundrum.
1981   "Income Distribution." Pp. 202–205 in Anne Booth and Peter McCawley (eds.), *The Indonesian Economy During the Soeharto Era.* Kuala Lumpur: Oxford University Press.

Bose, Ashish.
1982   "The Role of Medium-Size Cities in the Urbanization Process." Paper prepared for the Third Asian and Pacific Population Conference, ESCAP, Colombo, Sri Lanka, September 20–29.

Breman, Jan.
1976   "A Dualistic Labor System." *Economic and Political Weekly,* vol. 11, pp. 1870–1876; 1905–1908; 1934–1944.

Bromley, Ray and Chris Gerry, eds.
1979   *Casual Work and Poverty in Third World Cities.* Chichester: John Wiley & Sons.

Browning, Harley L.
1971   "Migrant Selectivity and the Growth of Large Cities in Developing Societies." Pp. 273–314 in Roger Revelle (ed.), *Rapid Population Growth.* Baltimore: Johns Hopkins Press.

————— , and Waltraut Feindt.
1969   "Selectivity of Migrants to a Metropolis in a Developing Country: A Mexican Case Study." *Demography,* vol. 6, pp. 347–356.

Cabigon, Josefina V.
1980   "A Socioeconomic Index for all Occupations in the Philippines." Paper presented at the Second National Convention on Statistics, Manila, December 2–3.

Caldwell, John C.
1976   "Toward a Restatement of Demographic Transition Theory." *Population and Development Review,* vol. 2, pp. 321–366.

Carino, Benjamin V.
1974   "Managing Migration Streams and Population Redistribution: Alternate Strategies and Research Needs." Paper presented at the Experts Meeting on Philippine Population Research, Makati, October 10–12.

Castillo, Gelia T.
1979   *Beyond Manila: Philippine Rural Problems in Perspective.* Ottawa: International Development Research Centre.

Chapman, Murray.
1985 "Policy-Makers and Circulation at the Grass-Roots: South Pacific and Southeast Asian Examples." Pp. 382–407 in Guy Standing (ed.), *Labour Circulation and the Labour Process.* London: Croom Helm.
Chemers, Martin M., Roya Ayman, and Carol Werner.
1978 "Expectancy Theory Analysis of Migration." *Journal of Population,* vol. 1, pp. 42–56.
Cometa, Reynaldo, *et al.*
1983 "It Sprouted Overnight: A Study of the Bagting Squatter Area." Paper presented at the First Annual Student Research Symposium, Xavier University, Cagayan de Oro, December 10.
Connell, John B., Biplab Dasgupta, Roy Laishley, and M. Lipton.
1976 *Migration from Rural Areas: Evidence from Village Studies.* Delhi: Oxford University Press.
Cooley, Charles.
1894 "The Theory of Transportation." *American Economics Association Journal,* vol. 9, pp. 1–370.
Costello, Michael A.
1984 "Social Change in Mindanao: A Review of the Research of a Decade." *Kina-adman,* vol. 6, pp. 1–41.
————— , and Marilou Palabrica-Costello.
1981 "Slum and Squatter Areas as Entrepots for Rural-Urban Migrants: Findings from a Medium-sized Philippine City." Paper presented at the 1981 General Conference of the International Union for the Scientific Study of Population, Manila, December 9–16.
————— and —————.
1985 "Mobility and Employment in the Southern Philippines." Final project report to the International Development Research Centre. Cagayan de Oro: Research Institute for Mindanao Culture.
Danao, Efren L.
1985 "The Military Takes the Cake." *Veritas,* vol. 2, p. 13.
DeJong, Gordon F. and James T. Fawcett.
1981 "Motivations for Migration: An Assessment and a Value-Expectancy Research Model." Pp. 13–58 in Gordon F. DeJong and R. W. Gardner (eds.), *Migration Decision Making.* London: Pergamon Press.
————— , and R. W. Gardner, eds.
1981 *Migration Decision Making: Multi-Disciplinary Approaches to Micro-Level Studies in Developed and Developing Countries.* London: Pergamon Press.
————— , Ricardo G. Abad, Fred Arnold, Benjamin V. Carino, James T. Fawcett, and Robert W. Gardner.
1983 "International and Internal Migration Decision Making: A Value-Expectancy Based Analytical Framework of Intentions to Move From a Rural Philippine Province." *International Migration Review,* vol. 17, pp. 470–484.
Dick, H. W. and P. Rimmer.
1980 "Beyond the Formal/Informal Sector Dichotomy: Towards an Integrated Alternative." *Pacific Viewpoint,* vol. 21, pp. 26–41.

Doeppers, Daniel F.
1984   *Manila, 1900–1941: Social Change in a Late Colonial Metropolis.* New
        Haven, Conn.: Yale University Southeast Asia Studies (Monograph Series,
        No. 27).
Dos Santos, Theotonio.
1970   "The Structure of Dependence." *American Economic Review,* vol. 60, pp.
        231–236.
Douglass, Mike.
1983   "The Incorporative Drive: Central Plains Migrants in the Bangkok Me-
        tropolis." *Comparative Urban Research,* vol. 10, pp. 46–67.

————.

1985   "Policies to Strengthen Smaller Cities and Their Relationships With Their
        Rural Hinterlands," NUDS Report, T1.7/C5. Jakarta: Government of In-
        donesia.
Economic and Social Commission for Asia and the Pacific (ESCAP).
1981   *Migration, Urbanization and Development in Indonesia.* New York: United
        Nations.
Elkan, Walter.
1967   "Circular Migration and the Growth of Towns in East Africa." *International
        Labor Review,* vol. 96, pp. 581–589.
Engracia, Luisa and Alejandro Herrin.
1984   "Employment Structure of Female Migrants to the Cities of the Philippines."
        Pp. 293–304 in Gavin W. Jones (ed.), *Women in the Urban and Industrial
        Workforce: Southeast and East Asia.* Canberra: Australian National Uni-
        versity, Development Studies Centre Monograph No. 33.
Fan, Yiu-Kwan and Alan Stretton.
1985   "Circular Migration in Southeast Asia: Some Theoretical Explanations."
        Pp. 338–357 in Guy Standing (ed.), *Labour Circulation and the Labour
        Process.* London: Croom Helm.
Forbes, Dean.
1978   "Urban-Rural Interdependence: The Trishaw Riders in Ujung Pandang." Pp.
        219–236 in Peter J. Rimmer, *et al* (eds.), *Food, Shelter, Transport in
        Southeast Asia and the Pacific.* Canberra: Australian National University.

————.

1981a   "Petty Commodity Production and Underdevelopment: The Case of Peddlars
        and Trishaw Riders in Ujung Pandang, Indonesia." *Progress in Planning,*
        vol. 16, pp. 105–178.

————.

1981b   "Production, Reproduction, and Underdevelopment: Petty Commodity Pro-
        ducers in Ujung Pandang, Indonesia." *Environment and Planning A,* vol.
        13, pp. 841–856.
Frank, Andre Gundar.
1967   *Capitalism and Underdevelopment in Latin America: Historical Studies of
        Chile and Brazil.* New York: Monthly Review Press.
Friedmann, John.
1966   *Regional Development Policy: A Case Study of Venezuela.* Cambridge:
        M.I.T. Press.

—————— .

1973   *Urbanization, Planning, and National Development.* Beverly Hills, Calif.:
        Sage Publications.

—————— .

1985   "Political and Technical Moments in Development: Agropolitan Development
        Revisited," *Environment and Planning D,* vol. 3, pp. 155–167.
—————— , and Flora Sullivan.
1974   "The Absorption of Labor in the Urban Economy: The Case of Developing
        Countries." *Economic Development and Cultural Change,* vol. 22, pp.
        385–413.
—————— , and Mike Douglass.
1978   "Agropolitan Development: Toward a New Strategy for Regional Planning
        in Asia." Pp. 163–192 in Fu-chen Lo and Kamal Salih (eds.), *Growth Pole
        Strategy and Regional Development Policy.* New York: Pergamon Press.
Fuchs, Roland J.
1983   *Population Distribution Policies in Asia and the Pacific: Current Status
        and Future Prospects.* Papers of the East-West Population Institute, No.
        83. Honolulu: East-West Center.
Fuller, Theodore D.
1980   "Satisfaction with Urban Life: The Judgment of Villagers Transplanted to
        Small Urban Centers in Thailand." *Rural Sociology,* vol. 45, pp. 723–730.

—————— .

1981   "Migrant-Native Socioeconomic Differentials in Thailand." *Demography,*
        vol. 18, pp. 55–66.
—————— , Paul Lightfoot, and P. Kamnuansilpa.
1985   "Toward Migration Management: A Field Experiment in Thailand." *Eco-
        nomic Development and Cultural Change,* vol. 33, pp. 601–622.
Gardner, Robert W.
1981   "Macrolevel Influences on the Migration Decision Process." Pp. 59–89 in
        Gordon F. DeJong and Robert W. Gardner (eds.), *Migration Decision
        Making.* New York: Pergamon Press.
Geertz, Clifford.
1963   *Peddlars and Princes: Social Change and Economic Modernization in Two
        Indonesian Towns.* Chicago: University of Chicago Press.
Gerry, Chris.
1977   *Shantytown Production and Shantytown Producers: Some Reflections on
        Macro- and Microlinkages.* New York: Wenner-Gren Foundation.
Gilbert, Alan and Josef Gugler.
1982   *Cities, Poverty, and Development: Urbanization in the Third World.* New
        York: Oxford University Press.
Ginting, M. and R. Daroesman.
1982   "An Economic Survey of North Sumatra." *Bulletin of Indonesian Economic
        Studies,* vol. 18, pp. 52–83.
Goldstein, Sidney.
1978   "Urbanization and Migration in Southeast Asia." *Economic Bulletin for
        Asia and the Pacific,* vol. 29, pp. 100–112.

Goodman, John L.
  1981   "Information, Uncertainty, and the Microeconomic Model of Migration
          Decision Making." Pp. 130–148 in Gordon F. DeJong and Robert W. Gardner
          (eds.), *Migration Decision Making.* New York: Pergamon Press.
Government of Indonesia.
  1985   *National Urban Development Strategy.* Draft Final Report, Jakarta, Sep-
          tember.
Haberkorn, Gerald.
  1981   "The Migration Decision-Making Process: Some Social-Psychological Con-
          siderations." Pp. 252–280 in Gordon F. DeJong and Robert W. Gardner
          (eds.), *Migration Decision Making.* New York: Pergamon Press.
Hackenberg, Beverly and Gerald Barth.
  1984   "Growth of the Bazaar Economy and Its Significance for Women's Em-
          ployment: Trends of the 1970's in Davao City, Philippines." Pp. 259–273
          in Gavin W. Jones (ed.), *Women in the Urban Industrial Workforce: Southeast
          and East Asia.* Canberra: Australian National University, Development
          Studies Centre Monograph No. 33.
Hackenberg, Robert A.
  1980   "New Patterns of Urbanization in Southeast Asia: An Assessment." *Pop-
          ulation and Development Review,* vol. 6, pp. 391–419.

  _____ .

  1982   "Diffuse Urbanization and the Resource Frontier: New Patterns of Philippine
          Urban and Regional Development." Pp. 139–173 in O. P. Mathur (ed.),
          Small Cities and National Development. Nagoya: UNCRD.

  _____ .

  1983   "The Urban Impact of Agropolitan Development: The Changing Regional
          Metropolis in the Southern Philippines." *Comparative Urban Research,* vol.
          10, pp. 69–98.
Hamer, Andrew, A. D. Steer, and D. G. Williams.
  1986   *Indonesia: The Challenge of Urbanization.* Staff Working Paper No. 787.
          Washington, D.C.: World Bank.
Hansen, Niles.
  1979   "A Review and Evaluation of Attempts to Direct Migrants to Smaller and
          Intermediate-Sized Cities." Bangkok: Economic Commission for Asia and
          the Pacific (ESCAP).

  _____ .

  1982   "The Role of Small and Intermediate Cities in National Development
          Processes and Strategies." Pp. 301–325 in O. P. Mathur (ed.), *Small Cities
          and National Development.* Nagoya: United Nations Center for Regional
          Development.
Hariri, Hadi.
  1984   "*Kecamatan* Towns Can Stem the Invasion of Large Cities." *Prisma,* vol.
          32, pp. 50–54.
Hardjono, Joan.
  1977   *Transmigration in Indonesia.* Kuala Lumpur: Oxford University Press.

———— .
1980   "Patterns and Policies in Migration and Resettlement in Indonesia." Paper
        presented at the Meeting on Policy Guidelines and Curriculum Development
        for More Effective Migration and Resettlement Policies, Bangalore, February
        10–16.
Hart, K.
1973   "Informal Income Opportunities and Urban Employment in Ghana." *Journal
        of Modern African Studies,* vol. 11, pp. 61–89.
Hauser, Philip M., Daniel B. Suits, and Naohiro Ogawa (eds.).
1985   *Urbanization and Migration in ASEAN Development.* Tokyo: National
        Institute for Research Advancement.
Hawley, Amos.
1971   *Urban Society: An Ecological Approach.* New York: Ronald Press.
Herrin, Alejandro N.
n.d.   *Population and Development: Introductory Perspective for Planning.* Makati:
        National Economic and Development Authority.
House, William J.
1984   "Nairobi's Informal Sector: Dynamic Entrepreneurs or Surplus Labor?"
        Economic Development and Cultural Change, vol. 32, pp. 277–302.
Hugo, Graeme J.
1977   "Circular Migration." *Bulletin of Indonesian Economic Studies,* vol. 13,
        pp. 57–66.

———— .
1978   *Population Mobility in West Java.* Yogyakarta: Gadjah Mada University
        Press.

———— .
1979   "Indonesia: Patterns of Population Movement to 1971." Pp. 178–191 in
        Robin J. Pryor (ed.), *Migration and Development in South-East Asia: A
        Demographic Perspective.* Kuala Lumpur: Oxford University Press.

———— .
1981   "Road Transport, Population Mobility and Development in Indonesia." Pp.
        355–386 in G. W. Jones and H. V. Richter (eds.), *Population Mobility and
        Development: Southeast Asia and the Pacific.* Canberra: Australian National
        University, Development Studies Centre Monograph No. 27.

———— .
1982   "Circular Migration in Indonesia." *Population and Development Review,*
        vol. 8, pp. 59–83.

———— .
1983   *Population Mobility and Wealth Transfers in Indonesia and Other Third
        World Societies.* Papers of the East-West Population Institute, No. 87.
        Honolulu: East-West Center.

———— .
1985a   "Circulation in West Java, Indonesia." Pp. 75–99 in Mansell Prothero and
        Murray Chapman (eds.), *Circulation in Third World Countries.* London:
        Routledge and Kegan Paul.

———— .
1985b "Structural Change and Labour Mobility in Rural Java." Pp. 46–88 in Guy
       Standing (ed.), *Labour Circulation and the Labour Process.* London: Croom
       Helm.
———— , and I. B. Mantra.
1983   "Population Movement To and From Small and Medium Sized Towns and
       Cities in Indonesia," *Malaysian Journal of Tropical Geography,* vol. 8, pp.
       10–32.
Ingram, G. K., A. Pachon, and J. F. Pineda.
1982   Summary of Results and Policy Implications of the City Study. Urban
       Development Discussion Paper. Washington, D.C.: Water and Urban De-
       velopment Department, World Bank.
International Labor Organization (ILO).
1972   *Employment, Incomes, and Equality: A Strategy for Increasing Productive
       Employment in Kenya.* Geneva: ILO.
Jamias, Eugenia G.
1985   "The Philippine Population Program: An Overview." *Philippine Population
       Journal,* vol. 1, pp. 8–13.
Jellinek, Lea.
1978   "Circular Migration and the Pondok Dwelling System: A Case Study of
       Ice Cream Traders in Jakarta." Pp. 135–154 in Peter J. Rimmer, *et al*
       (eds.), *Food, Shelter and Transportation in Southeast Asia and the Pacific.*
       Canberra: Australian National University.
Johnson, E.A.J.
1970   *The Organization of Space in Developing Countries.* Cambridge: Harvard
       University Press.
Jones, Gavin.
1981   "Labor Force Developments Since 1961." Pp. 218–261 in Anne Booth and
       Peter McCawley (eds.), *The Indonesian Economy During the Soeharto
       Era.* Kuala Lumpur: Oxford University Press.
———— , and H. V. Richter, eds.
1981   *Population Mobility and Development: Southeast Asia and the Pacific.*
       Canberra: Australian National University, Development Studies Centre
       Monograph No. 27.
Kerkvliet, Benedict J.
1980   "Classes and Class Relations in a Philippine Village." *Philippine Sociological
       Review,* vol. 28, pp. 31–50.
Koo, Hagen and Peter C. Smith.
1983   "Migration, the Urban Informal Sector, and Earnings in the Philippines."
       The Sociological Quarterly, vol. 24, pp. 219–232.
La Greca, Anthony J.
1977   "Urbanization: A Worldwide Perspective." Pp. 24–74 in Kent P. Schwirian
       (ed.), *Contemporary Topics in Urban Sociology.* Morristown, N.J.: General
       Learning Press.

Laquian, Aprodicio A.

1971   "Slums and Squatters in South and Southeast Asia." In Leo Jakobson and Ved Prakash (eds.), *Urbanization and National Development.* Beverly Hills: Sage Publications.

———.

1975   "Coping with Internal Migration in the Philippines: Problems and Solutions." Pp. 235–251 in John F. Kantner and Lee McCaffrey (eds.), *Population and Development in Southeast Asia.* Lexington, Mass.: D. C. Heath and Co.

———.

1979   "Review and Evaluation of Accomodationist Policies in Population Redistribution." Paper presented at the UNFPA Workshop on Population Distribution Policies in Development Planning, Bangkok, September 4–13.

Lee, Everett S.

1966   "A Theory of Migration." *Demography,* vol. 3, pp. 49–61.

Lee, Sun-Hee, James T. Fawcett, Robert W. Gardner, and Ricardo G. Abad

1985   "Community, Household, and Individual Influences on Migration: A Test of a Contextual Model in the Philippines." Working papers of the East-West Population Institute, No. 37. Honolulu: East-West Center.

Leinbach, Thomas R.

1983   "Rural Transport and Population Mobility in Indonesia." *The Journal of Developing Areas,* vol. 17, pp. 349–364.

———.

1984   A Study of Intermediate Sized Cities in North Sumatra, Indonesia. Final Report to the National Science Foundation. Lexington: University of Kentucky, Dept. of Geography.

———.

1986a   "Occupational Dynamics and Migration: The Case of Medan, Indonesia," *Southeast Asian Journal of Social Science,* vol. 14, pp. 1–15.

———.

1986b   "Transport Development in Indonesia: Problems, Progress, and Policies Under the New Order." Pp. 190–220 in C. MacAndrews (ed.), *Central Government and Local Development in Indonesia.* Kuala Lumpur: Oxford University Press.

———.

1987   "Economic Growth, Development Planning, and Policy Alternatives in Medan, Indonesia." *Journal of Southeast Asian Studies,* vol. 18, 118–140.

———— and Bambang Suwarno.

1985   "Commuting and Circulation Characteristics in the Intermediate Sized City: The Example of Medan, Indonesia." *Singapore Journal of Tropical Geography,* vol. 6, pp. 35–47.

Lerner, Daniel.

1967   "Comparative Analysis of the Process of Human Migration." Pp. 21–38 in Horace Miner (ed.), *The City in Modern Africa.* New York: Praeger.

Lightfoot, Paul, Theodore Fuller, and Peerasit Kamnuansilpa.
1983   *Circulation and Interpersonal Networks Linking Rural and Urban Areas: The Case of Roi-et, Northeastern Thailand.* Honolulu: Papers of the East-West Population Institute, No. 84.

Linn, Johannes F.
1983   *Cities in the Developing World: Policies for Their Equitable Growth.* New York: Oxford University Press.

Lipton, Michael.
1976   *Why Poor People Stay Poor: Urban Bias in World Development.* Cambridge: Harvard University Press.

_____ .
1980   "Migration from Rural Areas of Poor Countries: The Impact on Rural Productivity and Income Distribution." *World Development*, vol. 8, pp. 1–24.

Lloyd, Peter.
1979   *Slums of Hope? Shanty Towns of the Third World.* New York: St. Martin's Press.

Lo, Fu-chen and Kamal Salih (eds.).
1978   *Growth Pole Strategy and Regional Development Policy.* London: Pergamon Press.

London, Bruce.
1983   "The Political Economy of Urbanization in Asia." *Comparative Urban Research*, vol. 10, pp. 5–20.

Lynch, Frank.
1979   "Perspectives on Filipino Clannishness." Pp. 103–107 in Mary Racelis Hollnsteiner (ed.), *Society, Culture, and the Filipino.* Quezon City: Institute of Philippine Culture, Ateneo de Manila University.

MacAndrews, C.
1978   "Transmigration in Indonesia: Problems and Prospects." *Asian Survey*, vol. 18, pp. 458–472.

"Manpower Crisis Centre."
1983   *Indonesia Times*, April 23, p. 2.

Mantra, I. B.
1980   *Population Movement in Central Java.* Yogyakarta: Gadjah Mada University Press.

_____ .
1981   *Population Movement in Wet Rice Communities: A Case Study of Two Dukuh in Yogyakarta Special Region.* Yogyakarta: Gadjah Mada University Press.

Marcos, Ferdinand E.
1981   "A Choice by Conscience." Address to the General Conference of the International Union for the Scientific Study of Population, Manila, December 10.

Mathur, O. P. (ed.).
1982   *Small Cities and National Development.* Nagoya: United Nations Center for Regional Development.

Maude, A.
1979   "How Circular is Minangkabau Migration?" *The Indonesian Journal of Geography,* vol. 9, pp. 1–12.

McGee, Terence G.
1971   *The Urbanization Process in the Third World: Explorations in Search of a Theory.* London: G. Bell and Sons, Ltd.

_____ .
1973   "Peasants in the Cities: A Paradox, A Paradox, a Most Ingenious Paradox." *Human Organization,* vol. 32, pp. 135–142.

_____ .
1978   "An Invitation to the Ball: Dress Formal or Informal?" In P. Rimmer, D. W. Drakakis-Smith, and T. G. McGee (eds.), *Food, Shelter, and Transport in Southeast Asia and the Pacific.* Canberra: Australian National University.

_____ .
1979   "The Poverty Syndrome: Making Out in the Third World City." Pp. 45–68 in R. Bromley and C. Gerry (eds.), *Casual Work and Poverty in Third World Cities.* Chichester: John Wiley & Sons.

_____ .
1982   *Labor Markets, Urban Systems, and the Urbanization Process In Southeast Asian Countries.* Papers of the East-West Population Institute, No. 81. Honolulu: East-West Center.

_____ and Yue-man Yeung.
1977   *Hawkers in Southeast Asian Cities.* Ottawa: International Development Research Centre.

Meinkoth, Marion R.
1962   "Migration in Thailand with Particular Reference to the Northeast." *Economics and Business Bulletin,* vol. 14, pp. 2–45.

Moser, C.
1978   "Informal Sector or Petty Commodity Production?" *World Development,* vol. 6, pp. 1041–1065.

_____ .
1984   "The Informal Sector Reworked: Viability and Vulnerability in Urban Development." *Regional Development Dialogue,* vol. 5, pp. 135–178.

Naim, M.
1973   Merantau, Minangkabau Voluntary Migration. Unpublished Ph. D. Dissertation. University of Singapore.

National Economic Development Authority (NEDA).
1979   *Philippines: Regional Devlopment Investment Program for Central Visayas (Region VII), Vol. 2. The Main Report.* Cebu City: NEDA.

_____ .
1981   "Interregional Migration in the Philippines: 1970–1975." *Journal of Philippine Statistics,* vol. 32, pp. vii–xv.

_____ .
1982   *Philippine Yearbook 1983.* Manila: NEDA.

_____ .
1984   *Updated Philippine Development, 1984–1987.* Manila: NEDA.

Ocampo, Romeo B.
  1972   Governmental and Non-governmental Programs Influencing Migration in
          the Philippines. Report A–3 of the Intermet Project. Diliman: University
          of the Philippines.
Ogawa, N. and Daniel Suits.
  1985   "An Application of the Harris-Todaro Model to Selected ASEAN Countries."
          Pp. 131–143 in P. M. Hauser, et al (eds.), Urbanization and Migration in
          ASEAN Development. Tokyo: National Institute for Research Advancement.
Osborn, James.
  1974   Area, Development Policy and the Middle City in Malaysia. Chicago:
          University of Chicago, Department of Geography Research Paper No. 153.
Palabrica-Costello, Marilou.
  1980   Differential Migration in a Philippine City. Unpublished Ph.D. Dissertation.
          Department of Sociology, University of Chicago.
Parazo, Chito.
  1983   "RP Looks to Africa, etc., to Export Labor." Bulletin Today, February 23,
          p. 1.
Paydarfar, Ali. A.
  1974   "Differential Lifestyles Between Migrants and Nonmigrants: A Case Study
          of the City of Shirez, Iran." Demography, vol. 11, pp. 509–520.
Pernia, Ernesto M.
  1976   "Trends and Patterns of Philippine Urbanization in the Twentieth Century."
          Pp. 197–226 in Rodolfo A. Bulatao (ed.), Philippine Population Research:
          Papers and Proceedings of an Experts Meeting. Makati: Population Center
          Foundation.

————————.

  1978   "An Empirical Model of Individual and Household Migration Decision-
          Making: Philippines, 1965–1973." Philippine Economic Journal, vol. 17,
          pp. 259–284.

————————.

  1982   "The Performance and Prospects of Small and Intermediate Cities in the
          Philippines." Pp. 125–137 in O. P. Mathur (ed.), Small Cities and National
          Development. Nagoya: UNCRD.
————————. and Cayetano W. Paderanga.
  1980   "Urbanization and Spatial Development in the Philippines: A Survey." Pp.
          30–50 in Survey of Philippine Development Research. Manila: Philippine
          Institute for Development Studies.
————————, Cayetano W. Paderanga, Jr., Victorina P. Hermoso, and Associates.
  1983   The Spatial and Urban Dimensions of Development in the Philippines.
          Manila: Philippine Institute for Development Studies.
Population Reference Bureau (PRB).
  1982   "1982 World's Children Data Sheet." Washington, D.C.: PRB.

————————.

  1983   "1983 World Population Data Sheet." Washington, D.C.: PRB.

————————.

  1985   "1985 World Population Data Sheet." Washington, D.C.: PRB.

Prothero, R. Mansell.
1958   *Migrant Labour from Sokoto Province, Northern Nigeria.* Kaduna, Nigeria: Government Printer.
————— and Murray Chapman (eds.).
1985   *Circulation in Third World Countries.* London: Routledge and Kegan Paul.
Pryor, Robin J.
1977   "The Migrant to the City in South East Asia—Can and Should We Generalise?" *Asian Profile,* vol. 5, pp. 63–89.
————— (ed.).
1979   *Migration and Development in Southeast Asia: A Demographic Perspective.* Kuala Lumpur: Oxford University Press.
Ranis, Gustav.
1974   "Employment, Equity, and Growth: Lessons from the Philippine Employment Mission." *International Labor Review,* vol. 110, pp. 17–27.
Renaud, B. M.
1981   *National Urbanization Policies in Developing Countries.* London: Oxford University Press.
Richardson, Harry.
1982   "Policies for Strengthening Small Cities in Developing Countries." Pp. 327–354 in O. P. Mathur (ed.), *Small Cities and National Development.* Nagoya: United Nations Center for Regional Development.
—————.
1984   "The Role of the Informal Sector in Developing Countries: An Overview." *Regional Development Dialogue,* vol. 5, pp. 3–55.
Rondinelli, Dennis.
1983   *Secondary Cities in Developing Countries: Policies for Diffusing Urbanization.* Beverly Hills: Sage Publications.
Sabot, Richard H. (ed.).
1982   *Migration and the Labor Market in Developing Countries.* Boulder: Westview Press.
Salih, Kamal.
1982   "Urban Dilemmas in Southeast Asia." *Singapore Journal of Tropical Geography,* vol. 3, pp. 147–161.
Santos, Milton.
1979   *The Shared Space: The Two Circuits of the Urban Economy in Underdeveloped Countries.* London: Methuen.
Schatzberg, M. G.
1979   "Islands of Privilege: Small Cities in Africa and the Dynamics of Class Formation." *Urban Anthropology,* vol. 8, pp. 173–190.
Scott, Alison.
1979   "Who Are the Self-Employed?" Pp. 105–129 in Ray Bromley and Chris Gerry (eds.), *Casual Work and Poverty in Third World Cities.* Chichester: John Wiley & Sons.
Sethuraman, S. V.
1976   *Jakarta: Urban Development and Employment.* Geneva: International Labor Organization.

Simmons, Alan B.
1979   "Slowing Metropolitan Growth in Asia: Policies, Programs, and Results."
         Population and Development Review, vol. 5, pp. 87–104.

————.
1981   "Methods for Evaluation of the Impact of Migration on Individuals,
         Households and Communities." Paper presented at meeting of the Technical
         Working Group on Migration and Urbanization, ESCAP, Bangkok, December
         1–5.
———— and Ramiro G. Cardona.
1972   "Rural-Urban Migration: Who Comes? Who Stays? Who Returns? The
         Case of Bogota, Colombia." *International Migration Review*, vol. 6, pp.
         166–181.
Singhanetra-Renard, Anchalee.
1981   "Mobility in North Thailand: A View from Within." Pp. 137–166 in G. W.
         Jones and H. V. Richter (eds.), *Population Mobility and Development:
         Southeast Asia and the Pacific*. Canberra: Australian National University.
Soetjipto, Wirosardjono.
1984   "The Meaning, Limitations, and Problems of the Informal Sector." *Prisma*,
         vol. 32, pp. 78–83.
Speare, Alden.
1974   "Urbanization and Migration in Taiwan." *Economic Development and
         Cultural Change*, vol. 22, pp. 302–319.

————.
1976   "Labor Utilization Among Recent Urban Migrants in Indonesia." Paper
         presented at the CAMS-ODA Seminar on Labor Supply, Makati, June
         21–26.
Standing, Guy.
1982   *Conceptualizing Territorial Mobility in Low Income Countries*. Geneva:
         International Labor Office.
———— (ed.).
1985   *Labour Circulation and the Labour Process*. London: Croom Helm.
Statistics Office.
1981   *Medan Statistical Yearbook 1980*. Medan: Bappeda Kodati.
Sternstein, Larry.
1976   "Migration and Development in Thailand." *Geographical Review*, vol. 66,
         pp. 401–419.
Stretton, Alan.
1979   "Instability of Employment Among Building Industry Labourers in Manila."
         Pp. 267–282 in Ray Bromley and Chris Gerry (eds.), *Casual Work and
         Poverty in Third World Cities*. Chichester: John Wiley & Sons.

————.
1981   "The Building Industry and Urbanization in Third World Countries: A
         Philippine Case Study." *Economic Development and Cultural Change*, vol.
         29, pp. 325–340.
Temple, Gordon.
1975   "Migration to Jakarta." *Bulletin of Indonesian Economic Studies*, vol. 11,
         pp. 76–81.

Thomas, W. I. and Florian Znaniecki.
  1927   *The Polish Peasant in Europe and America.* New York: Dover Publications.
"324,000 Filipinos Overseas."
  1983   *Metro Manila Times,* January 4, p. 3.
Todaro, Michael P.
  1969   "A Model of Labor Migration and Urban Unemployment in LDCs." *American Economic Review,* vol. 59, pp. 138–148.

_____ .
  1985   *Economic Development in the Third World,* 3rd edition. New York: Longman.
_____ and Jerry Stilkind.
  1981   *City Bias and Rural Neglect: The Dilemma of Urban Development.* New York: Population Council.
Treiman, Donald J.
  1977   *Occupational Prestige in Comparative Perspective.* New York: Academic Press.
Udall, Alan T. and Stuart Sinclair.
  1982   "The 'Luxury Unemployment' Hypothesis: A Review of Recent Evidence." *World Development,* vol. 10, pp. 49–62.
Ulack, Richard.
  1975   "The Impact of Industrialization Upon the Population Characteristics of a Medium-Sized City in the Developing World." *The Journal of Developing Areas,* vol. 9, pp. 203–220.

_____ .
  1976   "Migration to the Slum and Squatter Communities of Cagayan de Oro City, the Philippines." *International Migration Review,* vol. 10, pp. 355–376.

_____ .
  1977   "Migration to Mindanao: Population Growth in the Final Stage of a Pioneer Frontier." *Tijdschrift voor Economische en Social Geografie,* vol. 68, pp. 133–144.

_____ .
  1978   "The Role of Urban Squatter Settlements." *Annals,* Association of American Geographers, vol. 68, pp. 535–550.

_____ .
  1986   "Ties to Origin, Remittances, and Mobility: Evidence from Rural and Urban Areas in the Philippines." *The Journal of Developing Areas,* vol. 20, pp. 339–356.
_____ , Michael Costello, and Marilou Palabrica-Costello.
  1985   "Circulation in the Philippines." *Geographical Review,* vol. 75, pp. 439–450.
_____ and Thomas R. Leinbach.
  1985   "Migration and Employment in Urban Southeast Asia: Examples from Indonesia and the Philippines." *National Geographic Research,* vol. 1, pp. 310–331.
Vandermeer, Canute.
  1967   "Population Patterns on the Island of Cebu, the Philippines: 1500 to 1900." *Annals,* Association of American Geographers, vol. 57, pp. 315–337.

Vining, Daniel R.
1985   "The Growth of Core Urban Regions in Developing Countries." *Population and Development Review,* vol. 11, pp. 495–514.
Visaria, Pravin.
1980   "Poverty and Living Standards in Asia." *Population and Development Review,* vol. 6, pp. 189–223.
Visayas Human Development Agency, Inc. (VIHDA)
1983   *The Cebu Labor Situationer: Base to Societal Change.* Cebu City: VIHDA.
Walton, J.
1979   "Accumulation and Comparative Urban Systems: Theory and Some Tentative Contrasts of Latin America and Africa." *Comparative Urban Research,* vol. 5, pp. 5–18.
Weeks, John.
1975   "Policies for Expanding Employment in the Informal Urban Sector of Developing Economies." *International Labor Review,* vol. 3, pp. 1–13.
White, Benjamin.
1976   "Population, Involution and Employment in Rural Java." *Development and Change,* vol. 7, pp. 267–290.

_____ .

1979   "Political Aspects of Income Distribution and Their Measurement: Some Examples from Rural Java." *Development and Change,* vol. 10, pp. 91–114.
Wilson, Godfrey.
1941   "An Essay on the Economics of Detribalization in Northern Rhodesia." *Rhodes-Livingstone Papers.* Livingstone, Northern Rhodesia: Rhodes-Livingstone Institute, 1941–42.
Wolpert, Julian.
1965   "Behavioral Aspects of the Decision to Migrate." *Papers and Proceedings of the Regional Science Association,* vol. 15, pp. 159–169.
World Bank.
1980   *World Development Report 1980.* New York: Oxford University Press.

_____ .

1983   *World Development Report 1983.* New York: Oxford University Press.

_____ .

1984   *World Development Report 1984.* New York: Oxford University Press.
Yap, Lorene Y. L.
1976   "Rural-Urban Migration and Urban Unemployment in Brazil." *Journal of Development Economics,* vol. 3, pp. 227–243.
Young, Mei Ling.
1982   "Circular Mobility and Its Policy Implications." Unpublished paper given at The Third Asian and Pacific Population Conference, Economic Commission for Asia and the Pacific, September 20–29, Colombo, Sri Lanka.
Zelinsky, Wilbur.
1971   "The Hypothesis of the Mobility Transition." *Geographical Review,* vol. 61, pp. 219–249.

Zosa, Imelda A.
    1974   "Migration to Manila and Rizal: Possible Causes and Implications." Paper presented at the Fourth Conference of the Organization of Demographic Associates, Manila.

Index